Experiencing

and the Creation of Meaning

Experiencing

and the

Creation of Meaning

A PHILOSOPHICAL AND PSYCHOLOGICAL
APPROACH TO THE SUBJECTIVE

Eugene T. Gendlin

Northwestern University Press
Evanston, Illinois

Northwestern University Press
www.nupress.northwestern.edu

First published 1962 by The Free Press of Glencoe. Copyright © 1962 by The Free
Press of Glencoe. Northwestern University Press edition published 1997 by arrangement with Eugene Gendlin. All rights reserved.

Printed in the United States of America

10   9   8   7   6   5

ISBN-13: 978-0-8101-1427-2
ISBN-10: 0-8101-1427-5

Library of Congress Cataloging-in-Publication Data

Gendlin, Eugene T., 1926–
    Experiencing and the creation of meaning : a philosophical and psychological
    approach to the subjective / Eugene T. Gendlin.
        p. cm. — (Northwestern University studies in phenomenology and existential
philosophy)
        Originally published: Glencoe : Free Press of Glencoe, c1962. With new pref.
        Includes bibliographical references and index.
        ISBN 0-8101-1427-5 (pbk. : alk. paper)
        1. Meaning (Philosophy) 2. Meaning (Psychology) I. Title. II. Series: Northwestern
    University studies in phenomenology & existential philosophy.
    B840.G37 1997
    121'.68—dc21

                                                                    97-22832
                                                                         CIP

Contents

Preface to the paper edition

Philosophy has moved a long way toward me since this book was first written, almost to the edge where this philosophy begins. The book fits the times much better now. The project on which it embarks is still not widely recognized, but with the current "postmodern" debates, most philosophy and most disciplines are on the brink of it.

The project is to *enter into* how concepts (logical forms, distinctions, rules, algorithms, computers, categories, patterns, ...) relate to experiencing (situations, events, therapy, metaphoric language, practice, human intricacy, ...). We can think with a "....." after every word or sentence. Or we can phrase it: to employ *how experiencing functions in our cognitive and social activities.*

Of course, one cannot stand outside this relation in order to conduct such an examination. The relations to be examined will obtain in the very process of examining. Experiencing will play some of its roles in the process of speaking about—and with—them. This philosophy is therefore constantly reflexive. It can say what it says only as what it talks about also functions in the very saying. And since it tells how the experiential side always exceeds the concepts, this also happens in the concepts right here. The *functional relationships* and *characteristics* set forth in this book are themselves specific ways in which their own formulation can be exceeded. The curiosity about how this might be possible is an appetite I would like to rouse in my reader.

Once we can employ the roles of experiencing to *think with and about* these very roles, we can think with them about anything else as well. The project requires and makes possible *a thinking that employs more than conceptual logic, rules, or distinctions. We become able to think with the intricacy of situations (experience, practice, ...).*

But don't we always employ this already? Logical inferences are never pure. There is always a situation, an implicit experiential context that is *more* than any formed form. What can we add to this? Nothing less than a whole new power of human thinking. If we enter into how this *more* functions, we become able to employ it deliberately, and find that many ways of thought open from it which otherwise did not exist.

But experiencing and concepts (or symbols) are surely not two separated things that have to become "related." Each is always already implicit in the other. There is no "unsymbolized experiencing" any more than there is "pure logic." Even without explicit words or concepts, experiencing is "symbolized" at least by the interactions and situations in which experiencing happens. But if there is always only both, how can we attribute a role to experiencing rather than to the inseparable symbolization? If every moment is both, it has seemed impossible to know what is done by the one rather than the other. But there is a way to discern their different roles: they can be discerned *in the transitions* from one statement or action to another.

The *move* from one step of thought or speech to the next may come by a conceptual inference. Or there may simply be an interruption, a change to something else. One might report events, telling what happened next. We are also culturally habituated to act in certain situations by saying certain common phrases which lead smoothly to other common phrases.

But the next step may also arise through an experiential connection. How we experience the situation may lead us to a next step which makes sense, but could not follow in any of the other ways. This often happens without special notice, but sometimes we pause to refer directly to experiencing. Direct reference is itself a change, and then leads to a further move. There are different kinds of experiential moves. Each exceeds the form that existed at the previous step.

Obviously there is no final formulation of the ways in which moves from experiencing can exceed a formulation. We could distinguish more kinds of further moves or use other respects to distinguish kinds. Our new "basis" is not any one list, but the wider experiential-interactional functioning. Throughout the book I show how we might formulate differently. We can juxtapose other models and approaches with different results, yet we still stand in the ongoing experiencing.

The conceptual variety would be mere relativism if there were nothing else. But when we enter and employ experiencing, even a few distinctions among kinds of moves will open exciting avenues, a whole new arena. When distinctions and concepts are "relative *to*" experiencing, it turns out that they need not be ultimate

Since our project is unavoidable, even a poor first attempt can help, and I think this is a good one. It cannot long remain the only one, so the reader can be ready to improve on what is done here.

The kind of transition I call "direct reference" is itself a kind of symbolizing. It lifts out (creates, finds, synthesizes, differentiates, ...) a "this," which was not a *this* before. When we seem to find what "was" there, we have actually moved further. We do not need a false equation. No equation is possible between implicit and explicit. What matters is the way in which the next step *follows from* (continues, carries forward, makes sense from) what preceded it.

One result is to enable us to enter the implicit context of scientific logic. We must not merely denigrate logic. It has developed enormous sophistication in our time and has brought the wonderful technology that enables many more people to live, and live better than before. But now it is computerizing our decisions and redesigning the animals with careless genetic engineering "for the market." It threatens to redesign our bodies as well. As we become able to think in the implicit experiential context of science, we can develop ways to bring more than the market to bear on scientific and social policies.

On the other side there has also been a great development in human experiencing, with therapeutic and interpersonal processes. Where people used to be silent, now they have a developed vocabulary with which to explore and express their experiential and relational intricacies. The old community in which people related mostly in roles has broken down, and new kinds of community in which we can relate from our intricacy are only just beginning to develop, from coming freshly into language (for example, "focusing partnerships," "changes groups," and many kinds of support groups). How to think with all this is an exciting and still very open question.

Both developments require examining the relation between experiencing and concepts. That is the project which this book opens.

Today most philosophers find only discouragement in the recognition that all statements and logical inferences are conditioned by someone's situation, by the biases of culture and social class, usually summed up as "history and language." Wittgenstein, Dilthey, and Heidegger have powerfully shown that our subjective experiences are not just inner reactions; they are our interactions in life and situations. They are immediate interactional meanings. This brings a vast change. It eliminates the old model of the five senses and interpretation.

Wittgenstein has convincingly shown that the sense we make with language is not controlled by concepts, logical forms, distinctions, rules, or generalizations. But if universal and "objective" concepts are not possible, it can seem as if there is nothing for philosophy to do.

There is no pure logic, no neutral conceptual inference alone, but the import of this has been misunderstood. It is true that conclusions do not follow just from clean rational progressions, objectively and neutrally by logic *alone*. Not only are there all sorts of "biases," but nothing can be fitted into logic without first being cut into the little unit factors which can fit into logical slots. If one slightly changes even one such unit, the logical inferences are utterly undone. The use of logic is always enmeshed in the wider context from which units must first be made. Adding one more little bit from there can lead the cleanest logic into contradictions. So it is not mysterious why logic and conceptual inference can always be disorganized and ruptured. Logical arguments now seem useless in philosophy. It has been understood that everything depends on what one fills into the logic, and this cannot be decided by logic.

This recognition leads many philosophers into an error. Because logical conceptual inference is never pure, these philosophers deny and ignore *the evident power of what is (wrongly called) "pure" logical inference.* But we can come to understand what sort of a process "pure" logical inference really is, and why it has its great power. We can enter and examine the implicit experiential functions involved in pursuing the logical implications *as if alone.* At other times, perhaps moments later, we also need to explicate the implicit context, rather than only holding it as if apart. Very different implicit experiential roles make that possible as well. Logic and experiencing are both involved both times, but in quite different ways.

How can one dismiss logic, just when it is changing everything around us? In the current debates, only one group seems to appreciate the powers of logic, while the other is alone in knowing the limits. These two groups hardly speak to each other. *We can hope to develop a society-wide understanding of the power of logical deduction, as well as ways in which we can employ the wider process of human sense-making. They have distinguishable powers.* We need to become able to think how they function in each other.

Rather than being mired in one hopeless mix of broken concepts and biasing experiences, we can open a new arena: we can enter and speak with (and thereby about) some of the roles played by ongoing experiencing.

From where does this philosophy stem? It moves on from Dilthey, Husserl, Sartre, Merleau-Ponty, (and indirectly Heidegger),[1] and also McKeon, Peirce, and Dewey, as well as Plato, Aristotle, Leibnitz, Kant, and Hegel. My recognition of certain difficulties is very European, but my emphasis on situations, practice, action, feedback, transitions, and progressions is very North American.

A new philosophy can begin with the recognition that we can assume neither that the world is ordered as a logical or conceptual system, nor that it is arbitrary as if "anything goes." There was always a conflicting variety of "ultimate" definitions of truth and goodness. The great error today is to assume that something is lost by this recognition. Instead, we discover that we can think with the greater precision and intricacy that is characteristic of situations, experience, practice, action. This is *more orderly and precise* than the pretended, overarching definitions.

Rather than a second choice or compromise, *it becomes our preference to speak and think with the way words can exceed their conceptual structure* even while employing that structure. In use they always elicit effects that are more precise and demanding than could follow just from the structure.

There are ways to employ this experienced "excess" deliberately in a stronger and more critical thinking. We need not lose the conceptual implications if we also think with the experiencing. In this way we always have *more than logic* in play, not less.

We are introducing a great change in the relation between

concepts and experiencing. We are changing the notions of perception, interpretation, and mediation. We deny not only the ultimate validity of any set of general, cultural, historical, conceptual, or linguistic assumptions, but also the postmodern assumption that all order, meaning, and rationality in situations is totally derivative from historical determinants. It is true that we are never without them, but life and situations always make much more intricate sense than could follow from just the historical determinants. They do not function like logical premises, as if all further happenings will be subsumed under them. They are not "the" conditions that make experience possible. History and culture only elaborate an animal body that lives interactionally directly in situations and continues to perform vital and noticeable functions in speech and thought.

Applying any concept elicits an experiential feedback. We can let our next step of thought come from this experiential feedback, rather than only from the concept. We can think with both conceptual and experiential steps, a "zigzag" which employs both powers. It can make new sense and lead us to modify our concepts, rather than being confined in them or ending in mere contradictions. Experiential thinking moves beyond postmodern "rupture" and contradiction.

The introduction and chapter I lead to the project of examining the roles which experiential meaning plays in cognition. This is only a modest statement of the problem as is proper before embarking. A number of strands both in philosophy and in the social sciences lead to this problem and project.

Chapter II shows that experiential meaning plays vital roles in cognition.

Chapter III presents some "functional relationships" between experiencing and cognition, especially "metaphor," "comprehension" (when one speaks from what is now called a "felt sense"), "relevance," and "circumlocution."

The "theory" of metaphor (really the relationship of the logical and experiential functions in metaphor) is currently still working its way through the climate of thought and research.[2] Currently the metaphoric creation of new likenesses, the "emergent qualities," has been recognized, but it is not yet understood that every word has a newly precise emergent meaning in its situation.

Is it creation? Might it not be a synthesizing, a differentiating, a making, or a finding? We know that no one of these conflicting cognitive systems has priority over the others, and they do not have priority over the way the metaphoric process functions: it gives an immediate result which we only later explain by interpolating similarities and differences. (See my "Crossing and Dipping" and "What Happens When Wittgenstein Asks 'What Happens When . . . ?'")

Chapter IV-A presents *the reversal of the usual philosophical order.* Rather than giving some cognitive system priority and reading it into experience, our philosophy recognizes the priority of making experiential sense (as in metaphors or in speaking from a felt sense). Once that has occurred, we can explain it by interpolating cognitive units in retrospect (but this is a further experiential process which brings new further implications).

The reversal makes a new and more radical empiricism possible. The current rejection of empiricism in favor of the view that we "construct" nature stems from the recognition that different hypotheses bring different findings. This creates the illusion that empirical findings depend just on the hypotheses (and on the biases, political pressures, and choices among questions and approaches). The desire for a single map or system must be given up (why would we want nature to be so poor?), but not truth. Our scientific assertions change all the time, but what this book calls "metaphor" and "comprehension" leads to a kind of truth that does not require statements which remain the same.

Empirical findings do not depend just on the choice of the

hypotheses. Experiencing (event, nature, practice, situation) does respond differently to different hypotheses, procedures, and ways of unitizing, but always with more intricacy than could have been derived from what we had in our approach to it. Contrary to the current view, nature is not arbitrary or invented. It is more orderly than a cognitive system. It is a "responsive order" which gives various, but always more exact, results than could have been constructed or deduced. It leads to an empiricism that is not naive.

Chapter IV-B lays out ten "characteristics" which have been called "a logic of experiencing" (of some of its roles in cognition). These characteristics show how differently experiencing and logic function together, compared to logic "alone." Here are some examples:

Experiencing is "non-numerical" and "multischematic," but never just anything-you-please. On the contrary, it is a more precise order not limited to one set of patterns and units.

When we think with experiencing as well as logic, a sub-subdetail can come to redetermine the widest categories. A theory may lead to an experiential detail, but from the detail much can follow which cannot follow from the theory.

Between two things many new experiences can be created. Therefore, any concept or relationship can be applied (found, created) between any two things. (But even wild playful metaphors have to make sense where they occur.)

Unlike the usual model of limited degrees of freedom, *the more* requirements one imposes, *the more* new possibilities are opened. When any two meanings cross experientially, the result is not their lowest common denominator, but new experiences which could not have followed logically from either. In retrospect, we commonly but wrongly say that they "were" implicit, but the relation which does obtain can be characterized and employed.

Chapter V moves in line with these characteristics. It shows that one can go on from any point not only from what is being said, but also from the process of saying it. The chapter is self-instancing. It moves many times from the process side of what it says.

The chapter also shows *the IOFI principle* ("instance of itself"). Any human meaning is always "such" a meaning, but not in one category or under one universal. Rather, from any "particular" supposedly subsumed under a category we can generate countless new universals. These are ways in which any "this" experiencing is *an instance of such* experiencing. Each universal (each respect in which we say it is "such") can be taken as an experiential "particular" from which new universals can be generated. Thinking is much more powerful when it can move along IOFI lines.

Chapter VI shows how one can take all texts and propositions experientially even if they were not so intended, and how one can think on from any text or proposition both experientially and logically.

Chapter VII shifts the usual representational puzzle in the social sciences to a new approach in terms of different *manners of process*. It is shown how the content of experience is generated by the process of experiencing. The kind of content one will find depends upon what manner of process is happening.

The process variables for research proposed here have led to the *Experiencing Scale* and a continuing sequence of research studies,[3] as well as the "focusing" procedure used in many fields to teach direct reference to one's (at first unclear) bodily sense of any concern, project, or juncture of a discussion.[4] The kind of thinking that was developed in this book has had applications in various fields, including physics[5] and the teaching of writing.[6] There have been many developments.

A professor of architecture in Austria says, "The style today is called 'individual,' because each architect takes little bits from old buildings and puts them together in a new arrangement. But I teach the students to use focusing. With focusing I take a building I love, for instance my grandmother's old house in the mountains, and I let the felt sense of it come to me. [This is the felt meaning, the bodily 'comprehension,' the .....] *From the felt sense* I design a whole new modern building which uses nothing that looks like my grandmother's house."

Neither in life nor in philosophy are we limited to rearranging the existing, already-formed things and concepts. We can engage the experiential meanings. We can deliberately employ and expand the vital roles which they perform.[7]

Philosophy can reopen the old assumptions and conceptual models if we think with our more intricate experiencing as well as with logic. We can think everything more truly if we think it philosophically, that is, with attention to how we think it, and with the critical understanding that no concept, rule, or distinction ever equals experiencing. Our more intricate experiencing may carry it forward, but is not thereby replaced. It is always freshly there again, and open to being carried forward in new ways, never arbitrarily, but always in quite special and precise ways.

Notes

1. For my relation to Heidegger, see my "Phenomenology as Non-Logical Steps," *Analecta Husserliana* 26: *American Phenomenology: Origins and Developments*, ed. E. F. Kaelin and C. O. Schrag (Dordrecht: Kluwer, 1989), 404–10. See also my "Analysis," in M. Heidegger, *What Is a Thing?* (Chicago: Regnery, 1968); "Befindlichkeit," *Review of Existential Psychology and Psychiatry* 16, nos. 1–3 (1978–79): 43–71; and "Dwelling," *The Horizons of*

Continental Philosophy, ed. H. Silverman et al. (Dordrecht: Kluwer, 1988), 149–50.

2. See my reply to Mark Johnson in *Language Beyond Postmodernism: Saying and Thinking in Gendlin's Philosophy,* ed. D. M. Levin (Evanston: Northwestern University Press, 1997). See also H. J. Schneider, "Die Leibbezogenheit des Sprechens: Zu den Ansätzen von Mark Johnson and Eugene T. Gendlin," *Synthesis Philosophica* (Zagreb, 1995).

3. See "What Comes After Traditional Psychotherapy Research?" *American Psychologist* 41, no. 2 (1986): 131–36. See also *Focusing Folio* 16 (research issue), nos. 1–2 (1997).

4. See *Focusing,* 2d ed. (New York: Bantam Books, 1981), and *Focusing Partnerships* (New York: Focusing Publications, Focusing Institute, 1996). See also *Focusing-Oriented Psychotherapy* (New York: Guilford, 1996), especially chapter 21 on values and experiential differentiation, and "A Philosophical Critique of the Concept of Narcissism," *Pathologies of the Modern Self,* ed. D. M. Levin (New York: New York University Press, 1987), 251–304. In German, see *Körperbezogenes Philosophieren* 5 (Würzburg: Focusing Bibliothek DAF, 1994).

5. See E. T. Gendlin and J. Lemke, "A Critique of Relativity and Localization," *Mathematical Modeling* 4 (1983): 61–72.

6. See P. Elbow and P. Belanoff, *A Community of Writers* (New York: Random House, 1989), and S. Perl, "A Writer's Way of Knowing: Guidelines for Composing," *Writing and the Domain Beyond the Cognitive,* ed. A. Brand and R. Graves (Portsmouth: Boynton-Cook Press, 1994).

7. See "Process Ethics and the Political Question," *Analecta Husserliana* 20, ed. A.-T. Tymieniecka (Dordrecht: Reidel, 1986); reprinted in *Focusing Folio* 5, no. 2 (1986): 68–87.

Also see the following:

"Thinking Beyond Patterns: Body, Language, and Situations," *The Presence of Feeling in Thought,* ed. B. den Ouden and M. Moen (New York: Peter Lang, 1992), 25–151; "The Primacy of the Body, Not the Primacy of Perception," *Man and World* 25, nos. 3–4 (1992); "Meaning Prior to the Separation of the Five Senses," *Current Advances in Semantic Theory,* ed. M. Stamenov (Amsterdam and Philadelphia: J. Benjamins Publishing Co., 1992); "Die Umfassende Rolle des Körpergefühls im Denken und Sprechen," *Deutsche Zeitschrift für Philosophie* 41, no. 4 (1993): 693–706; "Crossing and Dipping: Some Terms for Approaching the Interface between Natural Understanding and Logical Formation," *Minds and Machines* 5, no. 4 (1995) [Spanish translation in *La Aportación de Eugene T. Gendlin,* ed. C. Alemany (Madrid: Brouwer, 1997)]; *A Process Model,* in eight parts, available from the Internet at http://www.focusing.org (1996); "How Philosophy Cannot Appeal to Experience, and How It Can," *Language Beyond Postmodernism: Saying and Thinking in Gendlin's Philosophy,* ed. D. M. Levin (Evanston: Northwestern University Press, 1997); "What Happens When Wittgenstein Asks 'What Happens When . . . ?'" In press; "The Responsive Order: A New Empiricism," *Man and World.* In press; F. Depestelle, "A Primary Bibliography of Eugene Gendlin," *Tijdschrift voor Psychotherapie* 1 (1996).

Preface

This philosophical treatise (Chapters I–VI) is preceded by an introduction and followed by a final chapter (VII) that concern the behavioral sciences. The purpose is to show the relevance the philosophic discussion has, and the differences it can make, in the employment of concepts and method in science. Other sciences, history, social problems, religion, aesthetics, or many specific philosophical issues might equally well have been chosen to provide illustrations; I chose the behavioral sciences (chiefly psychology and psychotherapy) as my main source of examples because here I have firsthand experience of practice and research and because the current conceptual problems in the behavioral sciences are especially in need of the philosophic task that this book attempts.

When I speak of the main part of this book as philosophical and the introduction and final chapter as concerning behavioral science, I am distinguishing two types of discussion: the "philosophical" type considers the nature of concepts as such, their criteria, method of employment, and their formation; the "scientific" discussion concerns the subject-matter area (in this instance, behavior). To some extent, one must always carry on both types of discussion. One's analysis of the nature of different concepts must be illustrated in terms of their practical employment and in terms of the differences arising from their use. On the other hand, the employment of concepts must often be viewed in the light of the question: what part of what we assert is intended to characterize what we study, and what part does not necessarily pertain to what we study but rather arises from the concepts themselves that we employ in our studying?

Thus the two types of discussion must always be in close relationship to each other, yet they are distinct. The philosophical discussion, which concerns concepts as such, requires the illustrations and the testing ground that can be provided only by the concepts' actual employment. Conversely, the scientific employment of concepts often involves problems concerning the concepts.

Since philosophic issues so often concern the ultimate nature of different kinds of concepts, one must view such issues in reference to the work done by the concepts and the differences made by them—for concepts and logical schemes are tools with which we are enabled to see and interpret experience. Once we have employed these tools, what we have discovered with them need not be identified with the tools themselves. What a certain concept or scheme enables us to see—once we see it—can be seen even when we temporarily lay the concept down. If you discuss something that seems true to you, and you happen to use in your discussion some concepts whose assumptions someone questions, you need not therefore discard what you are trying to discuss. Instead, you can employ different concepts. If these change what you meant to say, then you must examine the difference. However, if you do not refer to that which experientially you wish to say, then there is no knowing what difference the different concepts make. Similarly, with philosophic issues, we must look not *only* at the interplay of philosophic principles, definitions, and demonstrations, but *also* at the differences they make and at the meanings they allow us to form. And these differences are seen, most importantly, in science.

But the fitting of concepts to human experience and observation in the behavioral sciences requires concepts and methods very different from those that are current. Just as special non-Newtonian concepts have had to be fashioned for physics, so also in the behavioral sciences new concepts and a new method are now widely being called for. To formulate these new kinds of concepts and a method for their employment we must investigate the primary relationships between experience (as we have and feel it) and symbolization.

The method that then arises retains logical positivism, yet it can *also* systematically employ concepts along a new dimension that includes and very much extends the phenomena with which the existentialists are concerned and makes our symbolization of these phenomena much more articulate.

Logical positivism and existentialism can be advanced, not by changing either, but by adding a missing systematic piece between them. This piece has, of course, a broader significance than just their need for it: it is the relationship between symbolizing and preconceptual experiencing. In this relationship meaning is formed, and hence we must inquire into the function of experience and of symbols in the formation of meaning.

Philosophy always attempts to bridge this gap between intellect and experience. It has always been clear that our concepts *refer to* experience and it has always been clear that concepts are *formed from* (or on the occasion of) experience. Yet, from Plato to Russell, while the tools of the intellect are elaborated, strategems must connect these tools to the experiential functioning in which they are formed. Whether the result is Plato's "kinship" between the ideas and the soul, Hume's natural relations, or Kant's insistence that the understanding has invariant categories, whether it is Hegel's identification of the laws of spirit and reality or whether it is Dewey's insistence that biological processes already manifest his rules of inquiry—some logical scheme has been substituted for the prelogical functions of experience and symbols in which meanings are formed. We must examine the functions of experience and of symbols in relation to each other. On these functions we must found our analysis of meaning. That is the primary task of this book.

The philosophic reader can begin with Chapter I and end with Chapter VI. He can leave the Introduction and Chapter VII for a later time when he will want to see the philosophy in a specific context.

The reader who is chiefly concerned with the behavioral sciences or psychotherapy can begin with the Introduction and move from it to Chapter VII via the brief statements preceding each chapter. Thereafter he may wish to see the treatment of the problems that are implied but not dealt with in the Introduction and in Chapter VII.

I have written the Introduction as a swift and perilous descent from the philosophic level on which it begins, through discussions of behavioral science and the one science of psychology, down to the specific area of psychotherapy. At such a pace, of course, one can only sketch the work now barely begun: the work of applying the basic frame of reference to science, to psychology, to existential concerns, to positivistic methods, to human data of science as having special characteristics that can be formulated in a basic theory, to new conceptual models of ongoing change in psychotherapy and research. These sketches attempt to contribute. But if, after the Introduction, the reader is all the more aware of the problems that only the philosophy can deal with, then the Introduction has succeeded.

I am grateful to my teachers, Richard McKeon and his associates, who taught me philosophy, Carl R. Rogers who over a period of ten years has given me much more than I can say, and Warner A. Wick and Charles Morris who not only taught me but also helped, encouraged, and contributed to this book; I am grateful to Kenneth A. Telford whose ability, exercising its influence through days and nights of discussion, organized much of what I think, to Aage Steen Ekendahl for constantly lively discussion and insight, to Hellene Sarett for vital, welcome, and knowing companionship, to Fred M. Zimring for collaboration in Chapter VII and for years of collaboration in the whole venture of a theory of experiencing in psychology and psychotherapy, to Edwin N. Barker for collaboration in the Introduction and in its battles, to Ariadne Beck, Allen Bergin, Leif Braaten, John N. Butler, Desmond Cartwright, Rosalind Dymond Cartwright, Joe Hart, Jan Majde, Michael Porges, John Shlien, Donald Sundland, T. M. Tomlinson, and a number of others for many helpful discussions, to many others who will notice the results of their help, and most especially to my parents and to my wife.

Experiencing

and the Creation of Meaning

Introduction

1. THINGS, LOGIC, AND EXPERIENCING

Besides the logical dimension and the operational dimension of knowledge, there is also a directly felt, experiential dimension. *Meaning* is not only *about things* and it is not only a certain *logical* structure, but it also involves *felt* experiencing. Any concept, thing, or behavior is meaningful only as some noise, thing, or event interacts with felt experiencing. Meanings are formed and had through an interaction between experiencing and symbols or things.

In the past, meaning has been analyzed very largely in terms of things (objective reference, sense perception) and in terms of logical structure. Of course, meanings were viewed as concerning experience, but "experience" was usually construed as a logical scheme that organizes sense perceptions or as a logical construct that intervenes to relate and predict observations of behavior.

Today, however, we can no longer construe "experience" so narrowly. Besides logical schemes and sense perception we have come to recognize that there is also a powerful *felt* dimension of experience that is prelogical, and that functions importantly in what we think, what we perceive, and how we behave.

The task at hand is to examine the relationships between this felt dimension of experience and the logical and objective orders. How can logical symbolizations and operational definitions be related to felt experiencing? Or, to reverse the question: what are the functions of felt experiencing in our conceptual operations and in our observable behavior?

1

One group of modern thinkers (Bergson, Sartre) have especially pointed out this concrete affective side of experience and its central importance in human life. They have also pointed out how difficult is the application of logic and concepts to experience as actually lived and felt. They have said that only "intuition" or actual living can grasp it adequately, while concepts and definitions can distort and deaden it. The attempt to define, they say, can turn living experience into abstractions or into dead objects of study. Thus, despite its crucial importance, felt experience has been conceptualized only vaguely, and only as it occurs at a few crucial junctures of life (for example, "encounter," "commitment"), rather than as the ever present and ever powerful factor it is.

These views in modern thought lead to the problem of effectively studying directly felt experience, of employing its meanings in science and life, of making thought concerning it possible for more than a few initiates—in short, the problem of *relating* concepts to felt experience without distorting or deadening it.

The other side of modern thought (pragmatism, logical positivism) has emphasized the logical and empirical requirements of science and meaning. Precise logical definitions and empirical testing are necessary to advance science, and only on the basis of these can we continue to work for the unbiased type of truth that makes men free and permits any man, if his findings can be objectively defined and tested, to question or disprove accepted tenets.

However, to remain only within current concepts and methods of science and logic imposes severe limitations. This side of modern thought leads to the problem of *extending* science to human behavior—without distorting or diluting logical precision and objective empirical criteria.

These two sides of modern thought really define the basic task as it is posed today. For we cannot really be content to lose either side or to leave both as they are. Current scientific methods need to be not only analyzed as they are now, but extended. Nor can we indefinitely leave the ever present concrete sense of "experience" in a vague no-man's land. It functions importantly in human behavior. The study of human behavior can be guided and aided if we can learn what kind of concept *can* relate to felt experience and how concepts of this kind can, in turn, relate to objective concepts and measurements.

In order to embark upon this task, we shall have to be clear that we require more than a logical scheme of "experience." We must be concerned not only with what is already logical, but with experience before it is logically ordered. We must be concerned with experience as it functions in the *formation* of meaning and logical orders. We must investigate prelogical, "preconceptual" experience as it *functions together with* logical symbols, but not substitute one for the other. Our remaining entirely on the logical level cannot reveal how experience functions together with logic. Thus we cannot consider experience to be a logically schematic construct, no matter how complex. At best we can have a scheme of how experience and logic can relate. Even then, experience must be referred to directly—it must be thought of as that partly unformed stream of feeling that we have every moment. I shall call it "experiencing," using that term for the flow of feeling, concretely, to which you can every moment attend inwardly, if you wish.

Experiencing plays basic roles in behavior and in the formation of meaning. If logical schemes are not considered in relation to these roles of experiencing, then logical schemes are empty.

We have many schemes, each exclusive and basic. We are jaded sophisticates when it comes to systems and schemes. Relativism, positivism, and pragmatism have told us that all schemes are largely the same, or that they are all largely meaningless, or that they can often be judged equivalent. We have come to know that one can equate or throw away schemes without even studying them.

The relativity of schemes mirrors the broader relativity of cultural forms. Today, in the West, society no longer gives the individual any one scheme or set of forms with which to interpret experience. The individual is aware of many different, contradictory, and unrelated forms and schemes. Thus he has come to confront life and experiencing directly.

It is therefore characteristic of our time that the basic question changes from one concerning only theories and schemes to one concerning the relation between all symbolizations in general on the one hand and experiencing on the other. We have called into question all manner of schemes: our one-time characteristic and established art forms, philosophical schemes, religious codes, social patterns, moral values, rituals, and so on.

Spengler, Toynbee, and many others raise the question: is this relativity a sign of social disintegration? They see a general historical pattern applicable today: in times of social disintegration the long-established schemes become "relative," and the individual is given the (often desperate, yet maximally human) opportunity to interpret life and experiencing directly. The historical crossroads of such a time is: either the reimposition of certain set values and schemes, or a task never before attempted: to learn how, in a rational way, to relate concepts to direct experiencing; to investigate the way in which symbolizing affects and is affected by felt experiencing; to devise a social and scientific vocabulary that can interact with experiencing, so that communication about it becomes possible, so that schemes can be considered in relation to experiential meanings, and so that an objective science can be related to and guided by experiencing.

Social and scientific entry upon the dimension of experiencing will require *both* experiencing and logical symbolization. Meaning is *formed* in the interaction of experiencing and something that functions symbolically. Feeling without symbolization is blind; symbolization without feeling is empty.

The problem of the interaction between felt experiencing and symbolization is crucial today both in philosophy and in the behavioral sciences. We are acutely aware of the effect of feeling upon intellect. Our time has uncovered a host of ways in which intellect is affected by preconceptual experiencing: culture, economics, biological drives, psychological needs, early upbringing, class interest, sex, taste, purpose, and so on. A great deal of what philosophy used to consider upon purely rational grounds must now be considered in relation to preconceptual experiencing. In all these areas the rational, logically constructed view of "experience" has given way. As a result, philosophy has grown thinner and thinner. Politics was lost to sociology. Ethics went to psychology. Metaphysics was dropped out. Epistemology became logic only. The intellect was reduced to the few formulae with which linguistic syntax is built. Philosophy has had to flee all these areas, lest it become a mere "rationalization" of a more powerful kind of "experience" than it can understand.

But the roles of felt experiencing in all our conceptual operations are not illegitimate "biases." They are natural and proper functions. These functions can be studied, and then it is seen that the functions of experiencing in cognition are much broader, more varied, and more essential than has been realized.

We cannot even know what a concept "means" or use it meaningfully without the "feel" of its meaning. No amount of symbols, definitions, and the like can be used in the place of the *felt* meaning. If we do not have the felt meaning of the concept, we haven't got the concept at all—only a verbal noise. Nor can we *think* without *felt* meaning (Chapter II). Only a very few considerations can be held in mind in a verbalized form, yet thinking involves the simultaneous role of many considerations. We "think" them all in a felt way. "Let me see, now, there is this, and this, and that," we may say to ourselves, meaning a whole complexity by the word "this" and by the word "that." We know what we mean by "this" and "that" because we directly feel the meaning. This felt experiencing, not verbalizations, makes up all but a small part of what we think. Concepts are not meanings at all, except in relation to experiencing.

Until now we have largely taken concepts at their logical face value. We must reckon with the fact that in actual thinking a concept is not at all only what it logically seems. Thought as it exists in humans (in contrast to a page of symbolic logic) involves *many* meanings, and these are felt and can give rise to many *further* concepts and changes in concepts. Concrete (verbal and other) behavior involves connections, relationships, and orders, which are very much more than and different from those of logic. To express them in terms of logic only is to "rationalize," that is, to ignore the experiential factors that really relate to (and interact with) the use of logical symbols. A concept in actual thought is not only the logical pattern and implications that it has at a given moment. It also involves a felt experiencing of meaning, which can lead—in the next moment—to radically different concepts, new differentiations of meaning, contradictions in logic yet "predictable" as human behaviors.

But surely, if the role of concrete experiencing vis-à-vis concepts is so ubiquitous, then we must investigate not only the logical intellect but also the ways in which it functions together with experiencing. If the scope of pure logic and intellect alone has become so narrow, that is an indication for a wider inquiry into the nature of logical symbolization *in its relationship to* experiencing. Such an inquiry attempts to restore power to intellect by providing a systematic method for the interaction between logical symbolization and experiencing.

Analyzing and systematizing the interaction between experiencing and logic does not affect the relationship between logic and empirical testing. We do not propose to alter the nature of objective scientific terms. That is to say, we do not propose to alter the relationship between logically precise statements and operational empirical testing. We propose to add a body of theory consisting of concepts of a different type —concepts that can refer to experiencing, and that can grasp the way in which experiencing functions. We propose to distinguish this different order of concepts from logical and objective concepts, and to provide systematic methods for moving back and forth between the two orders.[1]

1. To include concepts that can provide a relationship to *concrete* felt experiencing will be a considerable struggle. The struggle will be analogous to that undertaken by the empiricists of the seventeenth century when they insisted that *concrete* empirical testing must be included in the scientific endeavor. (Of course, this is only an analogy: they included *concrete* external operations, while we mean to retain the fruits of their struggle and to add another quite different relationship between science and something *concrete*.) Before Galileo there was only one order of concepts in science: the logical order. Galileo added concepts that referred to the results of concrete external operations, a second order of concepts: the empirical test result observed. It was difficult, at that time, to explain why this second order of concepts was needed. After all (his opponents said), everything that can be talked about is already included in our science. If Galileo wants to know what will happen when one drops two cannon balls, we can figure that out too. But Galileo meant to use the actual concrete dropping of the balls, not only the logically deduced concept thereof. Yet such concrete operations did not seem, at that time, to have any possible relation to science.

The two cannon balls Galileo dropped were two *concrete* objects. Science, it was said, deals with the "universal," not the concrete. One cannot import the concrete into science, for (so it was said) science consists of "universals," statements, propositions, laws. It is clear, however, that Galileo's empirical testing did not import the concrete particular itself "into" science. Rather, the empiricists added to logical science a *relationship* to concrete operations. This relationship could be made

Heretofore, either it was assumed that meaning lies in felt experiencing—and logic distorts it, or it was assumed that meaning lies in logic and feeling is a chaotic morass to be avoided. It is not so. Meaning is formed in the interaction of experiencing and something that functions as a symbol. This fact has been viewed as a troublesome chaos instead of as the basic source of order in human behavior. For, when symbolized meanings occur in interaction with experiencing, they change. And when one employs symbols to attend to a felt meaning, it changes. The effort is vain merely to "observe" feeling and then say what it means. We need to understand and systematically employ what happens in an interaction between symbols (selective attention is already a "symbolic" process) and experiencing. So long as we only exclaim: "But everything changes!" we view as merely troublesome the human functioning in which meaning and order are formed.

When we investigate this functioning (of experiencing and symbols) we find, first, that there are several very different kinds of such functional relationships between experiencing and symbols (Chapters III, IV). We find, secondly, that we can employ them (Chapters V, VI, VII).

The "meanings" of experiencing as such are "preconcep-

---

systematic (the systematic criteria of empirical testing). As a result of this relationship one could now have two—carefully distinguished—kinds of concepts: the logical deduction on the one hand, and the statement of the observed consequence of a concrete operation on the other hand. In this way even a conclusion that came from a tight logical deduction could be thrown into question by the observation of operational consequences—and this could occur even if the statement of the observation was logically contradictory to, and as yet unreconciled with, the logical deduction. Thus the two orders of concepts could be put into systematic and fruitful interaction with each other without their being confused.

Now the above description is analogous (*only* analogous) to the present task. Presently, we must leave the logical and the empirical testing orders intact, but must add still another, third, dimension: concepts that can refer to experiencing. We must, again, provide systematic methods to allow logical and objective concepts to profitably relate to the quite different experientially referring concepts.

tual." We can investigate the orderly changes occurring when the "preconceptual" interacts with symbols (words, objects, behaviors, persons), and we can employ that interaction.

Philosophy requires another Copernican Revolution to recognize felt experiencing as a center of consideration in its own right, not merely as revolving around the requirements of logical constructions. A genuinely radical empiricism cannot simply construct experience as a logical patterning tailored to the convenience of this or that analysis of what valid propositions require. We must have concepts in direct reference to experiencing. We must inquire into the ways in which logical order can relate to concretely felt experience.

If we succeed in an analysis of the formation of meaning in the interaction of experiencing and symbols, we can then approach philosophic and theoretical problems in new ways. Such a philosophy could aspire to being not merely another scheme, but a philosophy of the relation between any schemes and experiencing. Nor would this be only a static philosophy *about* the formation of meaning, but it could *employ* schemes and experiencing to form meanings as a discourse progressed (Chapters V, VI). Philosophical, ethical, political, and generally theoretical issues are entirely different when approached through this frame of reference and method. The behavioral sciences also require a conceptual apparatus that can be a medium between experiencing on the one hand, and logical and objective concepts on the other.

If the basic philosophical task of this book is achieved, there follow for the behavioral sciences some results of which this chapter will now give examples. The apparatus will serve for the effective isolation of observable variables, for the formation of fruitful predictive hypotheses, and for the connection of hypotheses to better selected and defined operational conditions. It will also serve to permit us to *employ* logical constructs, yet move from them back to the experiencing they represent and forward again with systematic transformation that permits the formulation of equally applicable but differently formulated logical constructs. It will also serve to formulate some conditions and limitations that must be considered whenever any sort of logical ordering is imposed upon experiencing or upon the observed phenomena it determines. For logical order must be used by science, yet logical order relates to experiential phenomena only in certain ways, and not in others.

If we take account of the basic modes in which logical order can interact with experiencing, the basic modes in which experiencing functions together with symbols and objects, this leads to a rudimentary theory of human phenomena, a basic "personality theory" if you wish. Its basic terms are not logical definitions of contents out of which personality is supposed to be constructed. Rather, the basic terms concern the function of experiencing. We can then define specific terms and employ them in theory concerning, for example, psychotherapy and personality (see also Chapter VII). We can use such theory to lead to definitions of objective variables and operational research.

The remaining section of this introduction will now sketch these directions for behavioral science, personality, and psychotherapy theory and research. These directions, however, depend upon the accomplishment of the basic philosophical task to which the main chapters (I–VI) are devoted.

2. A DESCRIPTION OF EXPERIENCING

What, then, is this "concrete" or "preconceptual" experiencing? We cannot talk about it without the use of symbols. Even to pay attention to it is a symbolic process. Yet there are many *different* ways in which symbols and concrete experiencing can function together. And we require experiencing to move from one to another of these ways of using symbols. Thought as we actually have it always requires experiencing; thought is really a functional relationship between symbols and experiencing.

In my first rough descriptions of experiencing, I will chiefly employ a use of symbols which I term "direct reference." I will ask you to let my symbols refer directly to your experiencing.

I use the word "experienc*ing*" to denote *concrete* experience, because the phenomenon I refer to is the *raw*, present, ongoing *functioning* (in us) of what is usually called experience. Let me describe it:

It is something so simple, so easily available to every person, that at first its very simplicity makes it hard to point to. Another term for it is "felt meaning," or "feeling." However, "feeling" is a word usually used for specific contents—for this or that feeling, emotion, or tone, for feeling good, or bad, or blue, or pretty fair. But regardless of the many changes in *what* we feel that is to say, really, *how* we feel—there always is the concretely present flow of feeling. At any moment we can individually and privately direct our attention inward, and when we do that, there it is. Of course, we have this or that specific idea, wish, emotion, perception, word, or thought, but we *always* have concrete feeling, an inward sensing whose nature is broader. It is a concrete mass in the sense that it is "there" for us. It is not at all vague in its being there. It may be vague only in that we may not know what it is. We can put only a few aspects of it into words. The mass itself is always something there, no matter what we say "it is." Our definitions, our knowing "what it is," are symbols that specify aspects of it, "parts" of it, as we say. Whether we name it, divide it, or not, there it is.

Let me give a few very simple examples, just to point your attention toward experiencing. In each example I will be using symbols that will specify some specific aspect of experiencing. Yet I would like you not so much to think of the specific aspect I refer to as to notice where you are inwardly looking.

First, feel your body. Your body can, of course, be looked at from the outside, but I am asking you to feel it from the inside. There you are. There, as simply put as possible, is your experiencing of this moment, now. But we need not remain with that global feel of your body. Let us "divide" it a bit, although no hard and fast division into parts is really possible. Let us create a few aspects of it. We do this with symbols. The symbols will be my sentences, below:

Perhaps you feel some tension, or perhaps you feel ease. These words ("tension," "ease") give certain qualities and specify certain aspects of your present experiencing. Let us fashion another, different sort of aspect: how does your chest feel when you inhale?

Nor need we remain with entirely present descriptions. You will have an equally present felt meaning (aspect of experiencing), in the sense that you will have the felt meaning now, if I ask you: how do you generally feel before a meal when you haven't eaten for a long time? (You feel hunger—using the word to refer to your inward sense of it.) Or recall the way you feel after you have filled your stomach, the heavy satiation. Boredom, that strained impatient deadness which hurts in quite an alive way, often is another aspect you can specify in experiencing.

But I am sure you are beginning to notice that I am each time asking you to attend inwardly to some aspect of feeling. All the thousands of different kinds of feeling and feeling tones, felt meanings, and so on are aspects of feeling, of "inner sense," a location, a referent of your inward attention. This inward referent (always this or that concrete aspect you attend to) is what I term "experiencing."

Notice, it is always there for you. It may not always be clearly definable. In fact, when you pay attention you can notice that it is really never just any given definable quality or tone or content. It can always be further differentiated and further aspects of it can be specified. A concrete aspect of experiencing accompanies every description, every meaningful thing you say. Above and beyond the symbols there is always also the feeling referent itself. Always it is concretely and definitely there, present for you, an inward sensing.

Let us move from these very simple examples to more complex ones. Consider a sentence: "What is the law of supply and demand?" In what way do you have *your* meaning of the sentence? Of course, the sentence is objective, spoken or written. But for *you,* how do you have its meaning—what it is to you? You have it in your experiencing. Let us say you have read the sentence. Does it have meaning for you or not? If it is in a language you know and makes sense, then you have an experiential sense of its meaning. Where do you find such an experiential sense of meaning? Again, it is in the same location, with the same inward reference of attention to the ever present feeling mass, that you find meaning. The sentence, of course, consists of the verbal noises (or auditory images of noises). But their meaning? It is *felt* by you. If you must now say what this sentence means (using your own words), you must refer your attention to this *felt* meaning— that is to say to your experiencing. You must refer to that aspect of your experiencing which constitutes the meaning of the sentence for you. We could say that it is a "part" of your inward body sense, for it is located within this bodily, felt, inward sense. However, it is obviously a quite specific aspect of your total body feeling that your attention specifies. We say you are "concentrating" on it. Concentrating on *your* meaning, your attention is focused inwardly on this aspect of your felt experiencing.

A situation in which you are and behave appropriately usually does not require your telling yourself in words what it is all about. For example, you walk across the room and sit down. You may not need words, at least not the thousands and thousands of words that would be necessary to verbalize everything the situation means to you—everything it must mean to you if you are to walk across the room correctly and sit down in a chair. You do not need to have all these many, many meanings explicit and separated. The felt experiencing of the moment interacts with *things* and *events,* and enables you to respond properly. Your response most often springs from the inwardly felt experiencing without *verbal* symbolization.

Notice that, depending upon what you need, you can focus on a very general, broad aspect of experiencing, such as feeling joyful or tense, or you may focus on a very, very specific and finely determined aspect, such as, "What is the law of supply and demand?" Either way, you refer to an experiential felt sense, and either way you have something concrete and definitely present to you, though its meaning may be vague.

Perhaps now you know where I wish to point your attention when I say "experiencing." Perhaps you can appreciate the ubiquity, the constant presence to you, to me, and to anyone, of this concrete feeling datum: experiencing.

Now, if it is the case that we are really dealing with *experiencing* whenever we feel something, whenever we mean something, whenever we live in a situation, whenever we think, then experiencing is obviously so ubiquitous and so basic that we must take it to be a very fundamental phenomenon.

Experiencing is an aspect of human living that is constant, like body life, metabolism, sensory input. In this constancy it differs from the intermittent aspects of life, such as looking, moving the legs, thinking, speaking, and sleeping, for we do the latter only sometimes. Thus experiencing underlies every moment's special occurrences of living. In a theoretical way we could consider it as the inward receptivity of a living body, although we must take care not to forget that one can "specify" highly detailed aspects of it, each of which can be referred to very specifically by our attention, and each of which can be employed to give rise to very many specific meanings. Experiencing is a constant, ever present, underlying phenomenon of inwardly sentient living, and therefore there is an experiential side of anything, no matter how specifically detailed and finely specified, no matter whether it is a concept, an observed act, an inwardly felt behavior, or a sense of a situation.

We can be very modest, or very grandiose, about experiencing. In a modest way we can say: experiencing is simply feeling, as it concretely exists for us inwardly, and as it accompanies every lived aspect of what we are and mean and perceive. Or we can be grandiose about it and say that for the sake of (this or that aspect of) experiencing mankind do all they do in a lifespan. Within experiencing lie the mysteries of all that we are. For the sake of our experiential sense of what we observe, we react as we do. From out of it we create what we create. And, because of its puzzles, and for the desperation of some of its puzzles, we overthrow good sense, obviousness, and reality, if need be. The speaker who has temporarily lost his inward datum of what he is about to say, cannot continue to speak. He is lost, pauses, searches to "remember"—that is, he searches with his attention inward to find again that concrete and definite *feeling* of what he wants to say, so that his words may pour out again. If he cannot find it, he is lost. Similarly, if our direct touch with our own personally important experiencing becomes too clouded, narrowed, or lost, we go to any length to regain it; we go to a friend, to a therapist, or to the desert. For nothing is as debilitating as a confused or distant functioning of experiencing. And the chief malaise of our society is perhaps that it allows so little pause and gives so little specifying response and interpersonal communion to our experiencing, so that we must much of the time pretend that we are only what we seem externally, and that our meanings are only the objective references and the logical meanings of our words.

I want to emphasize one vital characteristic of experiencing: any datum of experiencing—any aspect of it, no matter how finely specified—can be symbolized and interpreted *further and further,* so that it can guide us to many, many more symbolizations. We can endlessly "differentiate" it further. We can synthesize endless numbers of meanings in it.

Given a sentence or situation, an observation or behavior, a person or a moment's speech by a person, or anything, we can focus on our experiencing of it, and we can say what it means in a sentence, in a paragraph, or in a book. It does not have only one meaning but, depending upon the symbols we apply, the behaviors and events that occur, it can be differentiated and symbolized in the formation of very many meanings.

3. THE DEMANDS OF EXISTENTIALISM AND OF LOGICAL POSITIVISM CAN BE INCLUDED

Today, in the behavioral sciences, there are very many calls for a new development in scientific method. First let me describe the two extremes of the current controversy in the science of psychology.

At one extreme are the orthodox in scientific psychology who wish to investigate only what can be investigated with current scientific concepts and methods. Often they hold that genuine science must exclude the clinical area. They consider it a threat to science to attempt investigations that (as they see it) *cannot* be scientifically based, fearing that the vagueness and unmanageable morass of subjectivity will overtake and destroy the hard-won integrity of scientific methods.

At the other extreme are the so-called "existentially oriented." These are supposed to hold views opposite to the scientific orthodoxy, but in reality they often agree on one fundamental point: that scientific investigation of humanly important areas should not even be attempted, and that it will not be possible. However, their fear is different. Rather than fearing that the integrity of science will be lost in the attempt, they fear that the integrity of human experience will be lost.

Thus both extremes of the controversy often agree that to fashion defined concepts about human experience is impossible, and the attempt dangerous. Nor can we scoff at these fears. Today we may take for granted that science must be based on empirical tests and that these tests must be so well defined, and the steps so explicit, that they can be repeated publicly anywhere and as often as necessary. But such an outlook of empirical integrity is rare in history, extremely difficult to sell to a whole society, and even in our own day accepted only by some societies. We would not want this social acceptance of empirical integrity lost in emotionalism, and yet, recent and current history shows that misfortune to be anything but impossible.

Similarly, there is much validity also in the fear that an attempted science of man could destroy the integrity of human experience. People have always fallen into the trap of interpreting their experience only through stereotyped concepts whereby the actual stream of experience is largely missed. Just recall, for example, the battle the impressionist painters fought to convince people that snow does not always *look* white. Or recall the many American tourists who interpret their experience in Paris as exactly what the guidebook and other Americans have told them. Already today, even without a science of psychology, very many people feel constrained to interpret themselves as the concepts and contents given us by Freud or by the Sunday-magazine test-yourself psychology. Young people take vocational tests to find out what their interests are—as if a test could substitute for a direct differentiation of their own actual experiencing of interest! And if experiencing and its directly felt significances even now struggle against the imposition of these constructs, we must indeed fear that attempts at scientific concepts could rigidify, stereotype, and destroy the integrity of experiencing.

The two fears can be somewhat allayed, if it is clear that we must seek altogether new *types* of concepts—without destroying the precision and methods of traditional types of concepts, and without substituting concepts for experiencing.

a. The values of the existential therapists (their emphasis on problems of importance, their wealth of implicit hypotheses, their richness of observations) deserve to lead to much more than the current "protest" movement. This book provides for the "existentially oriented" a type of concept, a method, and a theory upon which existential concerns and subject matters may move toward greater clarity, usefulness, and a much wider scope:

(1) Experiencing is involved in *every* instance of behavior and thought. Thus it is not necessary to limit oneself to just a few dramatic life situations or dimensions of life. One need not concern oneself only with the crucial junctures of "existence," "commitment," "encounter," and so on. Every situation, behavior, and concept, every therapeutic statement and response, every meaning we have and every responsive event that occurs—involves and shapes ("symbolizes") experiencing.

(2) We can refer directly to experiencing—and we can devise a type of concept that can be employed *along with* systematic direct reference.

Because experiencing can be referred to directly, as well as with concepts, therefore we need no longer fear the distortive power of conceptualization. Rather than assuming that concepts must substitute for experiencing (and then deploring what a poor substitute they necessarily are), we can employ concepts *and* a direct reference to experiencing. Several different systematic ways of doing so are possible and must be formulated.

Since experiencing functions in every instance of thought, we can take any concept in any theory or discourse, and we can refer directly to the experiencing that is involved in having that concept at that given point in the theory or discourse. We can refer directly to the experiencing—and we can do so without in any way obscuring the logically defined concept. We can let the defined concept stand—yet also refer directly to experiencing as it was involved in having that concept. By so doing, we can move on to further and different symbolizations —and these again, while logically defined, need not prevent us from referring directly to the experiencing.

We cannot discard the logical precision of concepts and science and the objectivity of empirical criteria. The "existentially oriented" err when they believe that they must discard all language so that the aliveness of experiential meanings can be protected. For language is not simply the rigid boxes they so fear. There is no necessity that language kill experiencing. We shall devise a method so that language can help us refer to our experiencing, help us create and specify aspects of it, help us convey these sharply or roughly. We can use any word in an experiential sense. We need not limit ourselves only to the word's logical and objective definition. Of course, an experiential use of words is different from a logical and objective use. It is necessary to distinguish between the experiential and the logical use of language else we lose the precision of words when used logically and objectively. But we need not lose this, nor need we be limited by it. We can have both. Any word, concept, thought, event, behavior, can be viewed in reference to experiencing (the aspect of experiencing that it specifies). This possibility will allow us to interpose a medium between the rigidly defined concepts and the unstructured experiencing. We can fashion a method for using such a medium so that neither precision nor experiencing will be distorted. For any concept, behavior, or event, in any context, we may introduce some symbols that *refer* to the aspect of experiencing that—in that context—constitutes our experienced meaning of the word, behavior, or event. Only a systematic way of employing symbols *in direct reference to experiencing* can actualize the potentialities of the current "existential protest."

b. On the other side, an inclusion and employment of experiencing can guide us to select and create effective scientific variables, operational definitions with which *important* predictions can be made successfully. A new inquiry or step of investigation requires defining new variables. It is perfectly all right to term this portion of the scientific labor "prescientific." It is not at all permissible to omit this portion of the labor from the total endeavor of science. The role of theory is different from that of testable propositions. Theory has the role of *leading to* testable propositions. If we can employ some theoretical terms (carefully labeled as such) to refer to experiencing, and if we can devise a systematic apparatus of such terms, and ways of relating this apparatus to objectively precise terms, we can use such terms to help us newly define observational variables. These variables, once isolated and defined, can then go to make up testable propositions, and the orthodox scientific method can take it from there. However, the requirement that one be "scientific" *before* one has devised variables is deadly. It means we can never *extend* science. It means that to get to our aim we must already be there (like the boy who says he got out of the well by running home to get a ladder). We must devise systematic modes of reference to and conceptualization of experiencing. Then we can use these to extend logical objective science at every step at which new operational variables are sought.

4. PRECONCEPTUAL EXPERIENCING IS THE BASIC FACTOR TO WHICH ARE DUE THE MANY CURRENT CALLS FOR A NEW METHODOLOGY IN THE BEHAVIORAL SCIENCES

Having spoken with the two extreme groups in the behavioral sciences (the existential and logical positivist groups) let us now turn to the larger middle group. The majority, in the behavioral sciences, senses order in human behavior and experience, yet it also senses that this is a special type of order. From this large middle group many "calls for a new methodology" have recently been issued, not only in psychology, but also in anthropology, sociology, economics, and other sciences that concern human behavior.

In our discussion of these "calls" for a new methodology, we will again emphasize the new *type* of concepts we wish to introduce: concepts that can directly refer to experiencing, and that can permit the employment of the several relationships that obtain between conceptual order and preconceptual experiencing.

To existentialists we said that the new type of concepts and method could broaden their scope and provide a systematic method for their concerns. To logical positivists we said that the new type of concepts and method would extend logical and empirical definitions of variables. We must now say that the new type of concepts and methods will deal with that with which the middle group is concerned, that is to say with the difficulties and the peculiar nature of the observable phenomena regarding which they are calling for a new methodology.

To provide new *types* of concepts is a rather radical departure. More usually, the call for new methods concerns a specific science (for instance, anthropology, psychology) or specific matters studied in one science (for instance, cultural values, psychotherapy). *But we soon see that the difficulties in these several sciences are inherent in the nature of experiencing,* and with it we must deal if we are to have better concepts and science concerning observable human phenomena.

For example, in each of these sciences the investigation of human behavior is said to be unfruitful or difficult for the following reasons:

1. the phenomena are always *changing;*
2. it is so difficult to *generalize usefully,* and
3. soon some *newly created* product or behavior occurs that does not fit;
4. behavior is so *complex* and finely determined;
5. a whole host of factors always *interpenetrate* so that each affects and limits the use of any of them;
6. no vocabulary of words or variables can even approach the *sensitivity* of a penetrating human observer;
7. it seems as if human phenomena are *individual* and unique and require the methods of *literature and the humanities;*
8. anything that bears the stamp of human experience can be endlessly *interpreted* and differentiated through more human experience;
9. the really *significant* areas of human life, love, and death are omitted by science;
10. explanation always *reduces* what it explains to a few units;
11. scientific statements themselves change culture and society so that *science changes what it studies;*
12. only *participant observers* can investigate and observe

much of what must be studied, yet this provides neither a genuine participant nor an unbiased observer;

13. there are no defined *observable variables* and since one can isolate and define infinite numbers of variables in any observation, one cannot hit upon those which would be useful in formulating significant predictive hypotheses.

This informal list of difficulties in the sciences does not give the basic factor. That factor is experiencing.

Experiencing it is, that:

1. is changing;
2. is not equivalent to generalizations;
3. soon allows the creation of a new aspect that does not fit;
4. is complexly and finely determined;
5. is such that whatever factors one isolates, they mutually interpenetrate and limit what we can say with any one of them;
6. requires and provides the sensitivity of a human observer, and gives the phenomena the nature they have, which requires such sensitivity;
7. is currently better dealt with in literature and the humanities than in science;
8. is capable of endless further interpretations and ways of symbolizing;
9. provides the significance not only of certain interesting areas of life, love, and death, but of everything else;
10. cannot be reduced to the units of any explanatory system;
11. is creatively changed by the application of symbols and inquiry;
12. is not the same in a participant observer as in an unbiased observer or in a spontaneous participant;
13. actually gives us whatever hunches we get to select

those behavioral variables which we think worth defining for use in predictive hypotheses.

The difficulties of science in this informal list are due to the basic character of experiencing— the "preconceptual" type of order it has, and the ways it relates to the logical orders we attempt to impose in scientific inquiry.

This "preconceptual" character of experiencing has not been appreciated; consequently the application of logical and scientific order to organize observations of man has lagged.

Science must use logically defined concepts that mean the same whenever they occur. These logically defined concepts have what I call "logical order." Without them we cannot have science. However, we require propositions that can be tested successfully by applying to the actual order of observed events. Only when the order of concepts and propositions bears some relation to the actual order of events (and when variables are isolated and defined in accordance with the order of events) can predictions be verified. Thus we must take account of the kinds of relations that logical order can have to the preconceptual. That is the task of this book. In this way we can fashion concepts and methods for the type of order that the preconceptual can attain in interaction with logic.

To describe the "preconceptual" in its functional relation to logical order is to formulate a theory (Chapters III, IV, and VII).

5. THE PRECONCEPTUAL CHARACTER OF EXPERIENCING

I will begin my description of the "preconceptual" type of order by talking about the human body, and the type of order it has.

1. The human body is, of course, not merely an order or

an abstract pattern. It is a *concrete* mass in process. With one act of pointing at it, we can point at a concrete "this" which includes all the many complex organizations in the body (all its biologic and symbolically conditioned patterning). In fact, only by such a pointing at it, concretely, can we encompass all of its orders at once.

2. Furthermore, the living body is not an order of material parts, but it also includes "unfinished" or "potential" patterns for certain preordered interactions with objects in the environment. These objects may or may not be present, yet the body order includes the patterns of interaction that *could* obtain if they *were* present.

Much of the organization of the digestive, respiratory, reproductive, and nervous systems can be understood only with reference to objects in the environment that have an orderly role to play in these body systems. We say that not only is the body order "structural," it is also "functional" in that it includes the orderly patterning of many functions that will not actually occur till certain objects present themselves.

3. It is *impossible to isolate units in the body, except* if a specific and limited point of view is taken. From a given point of view certain systems or organs or cellular processes can be studied as units, but even a slight shift in point of view will require different modes of isolating units.

In some respects the body is one interpenetrating system in which every aspect of order involves every other aspect. In other regards, one can divide, but only with respect to some one limited point of view, which one will have to forego for other respects.

4. The many different kinds of orderly units we may isolate are related to each other in ways that logical patterns cannot represent. The ordering of all these aspects is *more than logical*. Here I quote the biologist Weiss:

Now in order to get the conditions for this given process to occur in a localized part of the cell you must have, according to some of the older biologists, a physical framework of some kind, a microskeleton separating the cell into little chemical laboratories with different chemical properties. This we now know is not true. . . .

What is it then? Well, obviously, you have numerous such processes going on, all very subtle and fussy in their requirements. Let's take just two of them. If these two processes go on in what we call an organized cell, side by side, the conditions of their operation must be mutually compatible. . . .

Thus you can set up systems, as we have tried to do, which are mutually supporting each other, one creating the conditions under which the other one can go on. You can figure this out for two reactions, but you cannot possibly do this for more than two. You are up against conceptual problems, very much like the three-body problem in physics, if you have three such interdependent reactions.

Now I think organization consists essentially of just this interdependency of component reactions, rather than of any fixed framework.[2]

The example from Weiss illustrates that although a logical scheme may fit a given relationship between two orderly aspects, yet the simultaneity of many orders soon exhausts what can be represented by a logical scheme.

The actual order is supralogical. It is more than a given logic can represent, although a given logic can fit some given aspect or relation.

The type of order I have been describing is the type I term "preconceptual." I have described the living body (according to one view) because it permitted me to present this type of order.

If there were an inward body sensitivity (if we could feel the body from the inside) then one would expect it to have the same type of order as the body has. And, indeed, it appears

2. Paul A. Weiss in "Concepts of Biology," A Conference, ed. R. W. Gerard, *Behavioral Science*, Vol. 3, No. 2 (April 1958).

to have that type of order. I think it a useful theoretical position to hold that experiencing is an inward sensitivity of the living body. However, from a philosophic point of view I do not make this assumption, since we do not need to make it. We do not need to say, for example, that any aspect of experiencing is always multiply meaningful *because* it is an aspect of the body and its organization. It is enough to note that we find it the case that any aspect of experiencing is always multiply meaningful. And so I will simply say that upon examination we find the order of experiencing to be similar to the body order, the "preconceptual" type of order I have been and will be describing.

Thus I want to use the four points of my description of the body order as a poetic image to prepare the ground for the analogous four points in the following description of the "preconceptual" order of experiencing:

1. Experiencing is *concrete*. It is the felt apperceptive mass to which we can inwardly point. It is a "this" or a "this way I feel." It is not to be equated with logical definitions and schemes, for these are abstract only. They *represent* something but are not *in themselves* something. On the other hand, experiencing (any aspect of it) is a physically felt "this," such as hunger or pain. We can give our attention to it. It is what we inwardly "are," "mean," or "feel" at a given moment. Very little of what we are, mean, or feel is ever in the form of explicit verbal symbols or visual images. Even the most intellectual ideas and arguments as well as situations and behaviors involve a felt apperceptive mass. We can hold in mind only a few verbal symbols at one time. Their meanings and their connections in our arguments exist for us only as felt. Only by inwardly "pointing" at such a *concrete* felt datum can we encompass at once all the meanings and orders we are using simultaneously.

2. Any aspect of experiencing has very complex "unfin-

ished" orders. Whatever way it may already be symbolized, it also provides the possibility for very many other symbolizations to occur. Many events, behaviors, or verbal symbols may complete it ("finish" it). We can apply one set of symbols after another, and successively differentiate. In part it depends upon the point of view we take, the respects in which we are concerned, the questions we ask, the scheme we apply, the behaviors that occur, just what meaning will be symbolized, but each of these produces only exactly just that meaning which occurs. No matter how finely we have already symbolized and differentiated it, the meanings in any aspect of experiencing are potentially so many that we cannot exhaust them. Just which meanings we will conceptualize depends partly upon the symbols we apply. Without symbols the felt meaning is incomplete, not really a meaning, just an *orderly* relationship to symbols—*when* symbols occur. ("Symbols" here can be words, things, situations, events, behaviors, interpersonal interactions, and so on.) These "incomplete" or "unfinished" or "preconceptual" meanings do not already exist as such, yet in some sense they exist (in a "preconceptual" sense) since we cannot get any and all meanings by applying symbols; on the contrary, each set of symbols gives us a different meaning—and not whatever meaning we wish but only just this meaning, which results from the application of this set of symbols to *this* aspect of experiencing.

The preconceptual is not constituted of actual defined existent contents or meanings. These are *not* interpenetrating units, forms, meanings, orders that—if we could only represent them all—could be equated with a moment or aspect of experiencing. All these meanings "exist" in a sense, but it is not the sense of marbles in a bag. These "implicit" meanings are not complete and formed (under cover, as it were). When they become "explicit," they become different from what they were, when they are "implicit." They were "preconceptual" aspects of this protean type of order, and only as they interact with symbols do they become completely formed. Thus upon the symbols that will interact with experiencing depends just what aspect of it will (then be said to) have been there. This "implicit" preconceptual complexity awaits future symbols.

3. Any aspect of experiencing can be further differentiated and divided into two, seven, or any number of subunits. Whatever way of dividing it there will be, it will be with respect to the scheme or point of view we employ or the behaviors and responses that occur. There are *no given discrete units* in experiencing (or any aspect of it) except as units are further specified and created. By the application of some scheme there will be units. With respect to another scheme, different units arise.

4. The interrelation of all these possible meanings is so complex as to exceed any one logical scheme. A logical scheme can be applied to this or that aspect or relation, thereby symbolizing it, but the "preconceptual" order cannot be logically represented. It is *supralogical*, or, if you wish, *prelogical*, capable of functioning in the creation and application of very many different logical schemes.

How can this protean preconceptual type of order be conceptually investigated? What kind of concepts can fit it?

6. CONTENT CONCEPTS ARE INEFFECTIVE TO ORGANIZE OBSERVATIONS

First of all, what kind of concepts are not suited to the preconceptual? I call them "Newtonian" or "content" concepts. Physics has succeeded in fashioning concepts other than Newtonian; the sciences of man can do likewise. The Newtonian concepts picture static, defined "things" that exist in a space-time container. The container is neutral; it does nothing to the things. The things are defined by their traits. They are what they are, or confusion results. (For example, confusion results when it is found that motion in the container affects the definition of things, that the container itself affects the things, that from different points of view, the things are different, and so on.)

The Newtonian concept, for example in psychology, views the human individual as constituted of "things"—defined contents. Personality is a structure of such contents, between which dynamic theories posit force relationships. Experience and awareness are neutral containers; the contents are said to be "in" the individual or "in" his experience. The "unconscious" is another neutral container. Whether they are "in" awareness or "in" the unconscious, the contents are viewed as already defined, fully formed, and unaffected in their nature by "coming into" awareness. But experiencing is preconceptual, not constituted of just certain given defined contents. It is a process, an activity, a functioning, not a bag of static things. Thus, for example, it is too limiting to study the supposedly static contents of the unconscious, and their supposed force-field relationships.

Some examples will show the great difference it makes to alter personality theory and the theory of the unconscious in this way.

For example: personality theory leads to such statements as "you are a hostile person." It purports to tell a content of what "you are," your personality. [3] Now, for one thing, it

3. In more precise language, current theories would formulate this statement as follows: Behavior becomes predictable when observations of behavior are organized by means of constructs of personality-content categories, such as "hostile."

If the conclusion of the present discussion is correct, it follows that behavior might be more effectively predicted by use of constructs of experiental process and its differentiation. Although the method here proposed would employ such constructs in direct reference to experiencing, they have the status of theoretical constructs and would be evaluated in terms of the success of the variables and predictive operational hypotheses they lead to.

is doubtful that there is such a thing as "you" apart from the flow of experiencing, which most truly is what you every moment are. For that is what you are inside, to yourself. But, in the fashion of current theory there are supposed to be "contents" "in" you, such as "hostility." Let us say you apply it to a given moment in a given context: you have been trying very hard to get along with someone you care about, and just afterwards you drop the ashtray on the rug. Your hostility made you do it (so it is said). You are not even aware of the hostility (so much the worse for you). It is a well-defined content, "hostility," there "in" your unconscious. It determines your behavior, makes you drop ashtrays on rugs.

Now, if you wish, you can directly refer to the experiencing you have at that moment, and you can perhaps differentiate it (with the aid of the symbol "hostility" or some other words) as some aspect of tension, of trying hard, of jitteryness, of that which (you would now say) made you drop the ashtray. You didn't especially notice this at the time, but now that you are applying these symbols and now that your attention is focused in this way, you differentiate (or synthesize, or create, or discover—put it any way you wish) an aspect of your experiencing which you call "this" or "this way I felt." If you are stubborn you can say, "This wasn't hostility, it was jitteryness." But you need not limit yourself to either concept, you can directly refer to your experiencing—to this aspect of it. Then you will find that it contains very much more, potentially, if you will continue to apply symbols (or events, or behaviors, attention, or whatever).

If you refer directly to it, and not just to the logical meaning of "jittery" or "hostile," you will find much more in this aspect of concretely felt experiencing. Perhaps you will now say that you felt apprehensive, lest that other person become impatient with you. His high position made you afraid. His secure ease also made you afraid, for he could afford to lose you but you had to be glad to receive his time and attention. You would not blame him for your lowly position, of course, but you never do like being put into such a position. Of course, now that we discuss it, who likes to associate with someone on the basis of needing something from him which he may or may not want to give, and that—as you, of course, knew all the while—was how it stood. What is more, we have all been in situations of this kind as children, and so you might feel some loss of adulthood when you must plead, appeal, or please. So it may well be that, as you attend directly to this aspect of experiencing, you find—as you use symbols along with your reference—that all these many meanings can truly be said of how you felt, and were aware of feeling, although not in such words and detail. It is now clear that one may truly say that you were angry or hostile, but only if one wishes to oversimplify so grossly. There is no such simple and pre-defined content as "hostile." Instead, you will always find a subtle, richly complex maze of many many meanings, perceptions, interpretations, past, present, and future concerns. To use content terms usefully, one must let them refer to the experiencing itself, and one must be willing to apply this and other symbols to differentiate it. You can do so with any aspect of any moment's experiencing.

In the light of the above, what becomes of the current terms of personality theory, and the contents with which behavioral scientists have been attempting to study behavioral phenomena? *Content categories would seem to be ineffectual, if the phenomena are more basically ordered by a process in which contents are at most momentary, and can be endlessly differentiated by the symbols and events that occur.*

We will require "process" categories that attempt to distinguish, not contents, but different modes or dimensions of process.

Our concepts will have to follow a "process" model, rather

than a Newtonian "content" model. We will have to devise categories for a felt, preconceptual process that we can only momentarily divide into contents. As an example, I may speak of *a boy* who happens to be running, or I may speak of *a running*, which happens to be a boy. Thus, a "running" is a process. In this way I can conceptualize it so as to include all the changes of the boy's limbs and the changes in his position in space. I need not say: "Where is he?" "As soon as he is located, he runs to another place." "How hard he is to pin down!" I can say: "How fast is this running? How effortful is it? How does it differ from a walking, a sitting, or a lying? What *kind of* processes are these as distinguished from a sleeping, an attending, an interacting?" Thus the process model leads me to different questions—questions about characteristics of ongoing change, rather than questions that assume static contents, and so are not applicable to the ongoing changes.

But even process types of concepts will not suffice, unless we allow at least some of them to refer directly to experiencing. (We can distinguish those that do from those that are not intended to, and thus keep our propositions in orderly definition.) For we cannot expect even a process logic to be fully adequate to experiencing. We must let the concepts *refer to* experiencing, for they cannot fully *represent* it. Just as the biologist allows his concepts to refer to actual concrete cells (so that he can then tests his concepts against concrete phenomena) so also we must let our concepts refer to the experiencing in the human agent. In that way we can make transitions between different theories that are not logically consistent with each other (a method for this is given in Chapter VI); we can let concepts help us, but dissolve them again when we wish to get at new aspects of concrete phenomena. For we know that the concrete phenomena can support many logical definitions but not the limiting choice of any one. The phenomena simply cannot be expected to be found orderly in the simplistic sense of one logical system. We must use our logics and concepts as directly referring to experiencing so that our process theory can grasp this preconceptual way experiencing behaves and determines observable events. Then it will lead us to isolate more "powerful" observable variables more efficiently than at present. The propositions we make with these can be called "science," can be tested, and can then stand alone.

What I have been saying will be illustrated by the following examples from a particular area in the behavioral sciences (psychotherapy).

7. ILLUSTRATIONS IN THE AREA OF PSYCHOTHERAPY

What I will say about psychotherapy has practical value. However, I wish my examples to illustrate the theoretical and research uses of concepts that refer to experiencing.

A moment's experiencing contains implicitly so many meanings that no amount of words can exhaust it. To react in one familiar situation involves the use of so many learnings, so many past experiences and events that a whole warehouse could not store the books that would have to be written to symbolize them in writing. A live human at one moment is all these insofar as they function and make a difference, now. Therefore, personality change can occur. For the sheer logical content of what is said is only just what is said. The effect (if any) of saying it in psychotherapy occurs via the experiencing of what is said. That includes not merely this or that meaning, but broadly the whole life of the person as it occurs in this present. Thus all areas of the personality are involved (and can change) in any one moment's experiencing even though verbally just some small meaning is thought or spoken.

Thus, by telling you an incident about my boss at work I

can be experiencing (and grappling directly with my experiencing of) my self in relation to others in all circumstances, as well as my many experiences of my early family upbringing insofar as that is a part of me and functions in the preconceptual experiencing of the present. For past experience does not function in the present as the discrete events that have happened in the past. These are past. What is present is the experiencing of now, and the past events have made it what it is. All the past and all the complex aspects of myself today can be involved in the experiencing of my telling the incident. They can be here now to be worked with. On the other hand, the logic and concepts of what I say are only about a trivial incident. We must take what I say as indicating and referring to my present experiencing, not to these limited conceptual contents.

The client in psychotherapy (really also anyone who wonders about himself and his own behavior) can find answers to his self-addressed questions only in his experiencing—only by referring directly to it, specifying aspects of it, and using sym bols together with it. The attempt, made by some clients, therapists, and individuals generally, to *replace* the experiencing by use of explanations will neither really explain nor change anything.

If you have trouble getting to work, for example, it is futile to ask yourself, "Am I just lazy?" "Do I have a wish to fail?" "Am I turning my basic hostility inward, on myself?" "Am I just avoiding responsibilities?" Such questions, spoken as it were in mid-air, are ineffective and, when experiencing is directly referred to, and differentiated, one always finds that the terms in these questions are much too gross and general to have any real bearing on anyone.

Only by referring directly to his experiencing can the individual even find (and later interpret) in himself that which— in our example—makes it difficult for him to get to work.

Directly, in his experiencing, he can refer to that "draggy feeling" with which he "wrestles" when he tries to work. As he attends directly to it, he may find (differentiate) an apprehension of failure, a conviction that he will fail. Then he may find, further, that, no—it isn't that he will fail at his work. Rather, he feels a deep conviction that it is surely impossible to do what he really wants to do in his work. More exactly (as he differentiates further) he depends on his work to make him feel the sort of person he wishes he were. But, as it happens, he is sure this work, no matter how well done, won't give him that needed sense of himself. It is this "heavy sureness" (so it seems at this moment, now) that he has to "drag" to work, and that makes it so hard. In fact, he doesn't even let himself "interact directly" with his work (he now finds, as he differentiates further). The "heavy conviction" he has been referring to really gets "between" him and his work. How different would a fresh spontaneous process of work feel! He can just "taste it" (as we say). But, no. He must keep himself at it, in this "heavy" and ineffective mode.

Now, it is clear that here the individual is using words meaningfully, but what are these words all about? They don't really make the sort of logical or objective sense that we seek in science. Rather, the individual is referring concretely to the process of experiencing within him momentarily. He is using words to point to inward referents. These he points to with phrases such as "heavy sureness"—phrases which have only a puzzling logical or objective meaning.

We need to order and study this kind of "verbal behavior," if we want to eventually predict about behavioral variables before, during, and after this kind of "verbal behavior," and if we want to relate it to other behavioral variables and predict their changes. We can expect to succeed in such predictions and such isolating of variables only if we will take into account the preconceptual, differentiable process of experiencing.

Not the verbal *content,* but the *kind of process* occurring, will determine whether we should predict therapeutic changes in later behavior. The extent to and mode in which the individual refers to his experiencing, the mode in which he relates the symbols he speaks to it and brings it into interaction with the other person—these variables of process will determine whether he is *merely* using words, or whether his words are part of a deeper process. What his words are *about* will not tell us this. If we conceive of his personality as constituted of contents (which his words are logically *about*) we cannot even formulate questions to get at what personality change is occurring.

Similarly, the therapist's behavior can be studied. We may predict certain changes in the client when the therapist's behaviors and speeches intend to refer to the client's experiencing. We predict different changes, or none, if the therapist merely leads from what is *said* through logical or explanatory connections to some other things that, again, are only *said.*

The therapist can consider the client's statements as indicative of some present aspect of experiencing (for there always is such a present experiencing). If he so considers statements, the therapist will not care quite so much about the logical meaning, consistency, and truth of what is said. He will be able to consider many different statements by the client as bringing him a sense of the present experiencing that the client now has. The therapist can then fashion his own responses to help refer to that experiencing, to maximize it, bring it into interaction. To do this, it does not matter whether the initial statements were "true" or "false," adequate representations or mere hints, concerning the present experiencing.

The therapist will also be aware that if he uses his own (perhaps more open and more easily symbolizable) experiencing, he can fashion many more symbols for his own version of the client's experiencing than the client momentarily is able to do. In this way the therapist can provide the client with a more open, more direct manner of process than he has until now been capable of having. The client's experiencing is altered in its manner of process right there, in the moment. All the explanations of why the client is as he is cannot be as effective as the very change in the manner of his process itself.

We know, but currently find it hard to investigate or explain, why the client's change and improvement depend so largely upon the interpersonal relationship with the therapist. This is what really changes him, for alone he can think about the same things, yet he remains as he is. We can account for this only if we notice (as we easily can in our own experience and in observations) how different is the experiencing of an individual in a relationship with another, than it is when he is alone, and also, how there are differences in his manner of experiencing in different relationships. I may say and think the same given content under these different circumstances, but my experiencing along with this content will be widely different. My sense of you, the listener, affects my experiencing as I speak, and your response partly determines my experiencing a moment later. What occurs to me, and how I live as we speak and interact, is vitally affected by every word and motion you make, and by every facial expression and attitude you show.

It is not merely a matter of what *I think* you feel about me. Much more, I am affected even without stopping to notice it by every response you give me. *I* experience *your* responses. I may come away thinking that, in my opinion, you can feel little liking for me, yet my whole experiential life in the time I spent with you will have been affected not by this opinion of mine, but by our moment-to-moment behaviors which you helped make, which were part of my experiencing as I spoke, thought, felt, and was. Thus it is not the case that I tell you about me, and then we figure out how I should change, and then somehow I do it. Rather, I am changing as I talk and think and feel, for your responses are every moment part of my experiencing, and partly affect, produce, symbolize, and interact with it. And only by this experiencing process (and the difference you make in its character) do I change. What I figure out will not change me, for even if I know why I am as I am, this only proves how necessarily I am a product of what happened to me. It cannot tell me how to become actually different. It can only tell me why I am not different. All our personality theories and their contents really explain only why one is as one is and cannot change. Yet I do change, and I change as I interact with you. For contents exist only as aspects of process. I am already different, because my experiencing is occurring with you, and it is different and new as your behaviors vitally affect what it is in me. And so, as I tell you how I always am, already I am living a process of being otherwise.

Without experiencing we have no theoretical account of therapeutic personality change, or even its possibility.

One of the most frequent errors of therapists is to expend their efforts in "digging" into the client to find the reasons why he is and must be as he is—rather than providing in the moment the kind of concrete experiencing process that will constitute his having changed.

Now, if we can so describe the sort of therapeutic situation and the functions of experiencing that make for personality change, then clearly we can hope to look for and define the behavioral differences by which we notice it, and the behavioral differences in client and therapist speech and action that bring it about. But these will be differences in manner of *process,* not content. They will be behavioral differences selected by considering *how experiencing functions,* and the resulting differences in the manner of behavior, interaction, and so forth. They will not be the repressed or aware personality contents with which in the past we have been attempting to organize human phenomena.

In the above description I have been illustrating five assertions:

1. We must employ the conceptual model of "direct reference" to experiencing, if we want to understand how the symbols and behaviors of therapy interact with experiencing. This can lead us to define some behavioral variables. Let us define, as one behavioral variable, the use of language in what I term a "nonsocial" way (example: "heavy sureness"). We are currently using this behavioral index in a research instrument (the EXP scale).[4] This is one index among others in one scale among others in which several independent judges

4. What is more, it is usually this type of highly specific and experiential variable (based on a distinction in experiencing) that alone can define the much more specific, operational variables that are always used, even when the concepts of a hypothesis appear to be quite general. For in all the experiments on "anxiety," "conformity," "authoritarianism," "intelligence," "defensiveness," "intrapunitiveness," "hostility," "reinforcement," "conflict," "transference," the actual phenomena of the human research subjects are—as operationally produced—very much more specific than these generalized concepts. Hence we will be able to conceptually state what we operationally do only if we fashion much more specific concepts—first as experiencing distinctions, and then as theoretical concepts fitting the actual operational procedures employed. For example, the 250 or so different operations that have, at one time or another, been employed as operational "indices" of the term "anxiety" in some theoretical hypothesis cannot well be interrelated and correlated unless more specific terms are developed and theory can organize these more specific terms, so that different operational indices follow from different theoretical distinctions. Similarly, different psychotherapists or different individuals may say the same thing in terms of these general concepts we now use, but only experiential distinctions can lead to a verbal and operational vocabulary in terms of which we can investigate what they do, or observe. In this way, any investigator is well advised to put himself into the place of his subjects and to make the experiential distinctions that will enable him to conceptualize just what specifically he hypothesizes is going on in them in terms of their experiencing, from which step he can then make a conceptual distinction in the general concept that can go along with the specific operational definition and that defines a more specific and effective research variable.

apply observation categories to tape recordings of psycho-therapy. Chapter VII discusses more research examples.

2. Conceptually, only those meanings which are defined and thought or spoken are "present" at a given moment. On the other hand, "pre-conceptually"—in the felt experiencing —very many presently functioning meanings, past events, and learnings are "present." Broad personality change can there-fore occur through experiencing.

3. *What* the individual experiences (the "content") varies as he differentiates further and further—and as he uses sym-bols in interaction with his experiencing—and as the ther-apist's responses and behaviors interact with the client's expe-riencing. It is therefore not likely to be very useful to attempt to define "the" contents of the client's experiencing. Just as it seems we know what "the" real meaning is, it changes—and, since this is psychotherapy, we *want* change. Let us not, then, study personality change in terms of categories that imply stasis. Or, if we must employ such categories, let us be aware of the actual preconceptual nature of experiencing and the momentary and limited applicability of content categories.

4. *How* the client's experiencing functions in his behavior will be a good theoretical basis for predicting whether real change is occurring or not. Definitions of various dimensions of the manner of process can lead to behavioral definitions upon which we would predict later indices of change. These purely behavioral hypotheses will not require "theoretical" terms, such as "experiencing," but in order to first look for and then to define them we require concepts that can refer to experiencing and to the several ways in which it can function in interaction with verbal symbols, behaviors, and interper-sonal responses (Chapters III, IV, VII).

5. Symbols do not always "*represent*" the "implicit" mean-ing of experiencing. Sometimes they merely *refer* directly. Sometimes they *creatively form* a new manner of experiencing

with new meanings. Similarly, behaviors and personal responses can have these several modes of interaction with experiencing.

Both for theory and for the search for behavioral variables
we require the concepts of these *several* types of interactions
with experiencing.

For example, in my description of the therapist responses
that change the manner of the ongoing experiencing of the
client I meant to illustrate the need for the conceptual model
in which symbols or things create new experiencing as they
symbolize (I chiefly employed this mode in my descriptions
of psychotherapy). Any interaction of experiencing and "symbols" must be considered in each of these modes. In Chapter
III I will define these different modes and their overlapping.
At this time I want only to emphasize that the different kinds
of symbolization are functional relationships between symbols
and experiencing, and that "symbol" includes words, things,
behaviors, responses—anything that has with experiencing
one of the roles I will functionally define. Therefore, the different kinds of "symbolization" I will define can be *theoretical
models* for the study of observable phenomena.

In this introduction I have often used words interchangeably,
where clearly the words are really different and it is implied
that we will show when and why they may be equivalent. (For
example, I have used as equivalent terms "form" meaning,
"create" meaning, "find," "finish," "synthesize," "specify," "differentiate," "symbolize further.") Also I have said that the
implicit meanings of experiencing are shaped, altered, and
finished by interaction with symbols, yet I have referred to the
experiencing involved in any already symbolized meaning or
concepts as "it," and I have said that "it" functions in the
symbolizing of further meanings. I have called experiencing
by the names "apperceptive mass," "data," "flow," "process,"
"feeling." I have used the concept of *time* freely, in such sen-

tences as, "As he differentiates further he will *then* say that the earlier feeling *was* really such and so." These and many other signs throughout this introductory chapter point to the fact that even the few applications outlined here require the treatment of the basic problem with which the book deals. The main chapters will deal with these and many other problems in the context of the basic philosophic task.

Some readers will want to be concerned only with this introduction and Chapter VII. For these readers each chapter is preceded by a very brief statement, so that they may know the role of each chapter in the main work. One may read this book by going from Introduction to VII via these brief introductions. Chapter VII is again written for the nonphilosophical reader. The main work is a philosophical one.

CHAPTER I *The Problem of*

Experienced Meaning

Brief   The actual philosophic treatise begins here, since
Statement   the introduction was a general survey.

The basic problem is now formulated: "How does felt meaning function in cognition?"

The problem is further illuminated by a series of other important psychological and philosophical problems that really reduce to this basic problem.

The ground is further prepared by distinguishing the basic problem from two other philosophic problems that will *not* be involved in the treatise: the causation or origin of experience, and the validity of cognition. Thus the treatise will not affect any position one might take regarding the biologic or other origin of experience, and the empirical or other criteria of truth.

The problem having been defined and isolated, we are then ready to treat it.

[A]
Statement of the Problem

Meaning is experienced. It is not only a certain relationship between verbal symbols, between symbols and things, or between symbols and perceptions. If meaning were only

44

these "formal" and "objective" relationships, our speaking would be like the speech of a phonograph record. A phonograph record may "obey" all the rules of logic, syntax, and of the objects about which it speaks, yet it has no experience of the meanings it speaks. When we humans speak, think, or read, we *experience* meaning.

Therefore, there are at least two dimensions of meaning: (1) the relations of symbols to each other and to objects, and (2) our experience of the meaning.

We are most aware of this second, experienced dimension of meaning in those cases where the symbols do *not* adequately symbolize the meaning we experience. In those cases we go on talking around what we mean—we may wave our hands, point our fingers, tell long stories of events, give examples, invent metaphors, pause to grope for words. In such cases we are intensely aware that we are *experiencing* a meaning. Another way to phrase it is that we *feel* the meaning. We notice that the symbols that usually contain our meanings seem inadequate to this present felt meaning. We notice that meaning is not only a matter of things and symbols and their relationships; it is also something felt or experienced.

The present essay deals with meaning as experienced. The terms "felt meaning" or "experienced meaning" will be employed. The reader is asked to allow these terms to name the experienced dimension of meaning, as he experiences it. Other ways of phrasing, which might help clarify what "felt meaning" is, might be: "our experience of a meaning," "our having of a meaning," "our phenomenological apprehension of meaningfulness," "the meaningfulness *to us* of a symbol or thing or experience," the "feel of a meaning."

At the outset, we encounter a problem in investigating experienced meaning. Meaning occurs for us when something experienced assumes a symbolic character. We employ words as symbols. We can also employ acts or images or some inner act of holding something in awareness, labeling it "this." Whatever we do when we have a meaning, some act of symbolizing is involved. (Note that "symbolizing" is used here in a much wider sense than usual.) However, an inquiry into felt meaning must be able to refer to and examine felt meaning as such—not only its symbolizations. Yet, felt meaning occurs only as one dimension of a totality that also includes symbolization and symbols. It would seem that we can talk or think only in terms of symbols. Yet we wish to inquire into the experienced dimension of meaning, not the symbols. If symbolization is involved in every case of meaning, and if inquiry itself can proceed only in terms of symbols, how can we hope to inquire into the experienced dimension of meaning as such?

An inquiry into experienced meaning can overcome this problem because experienced meaning *functions* in cognition. Experienced meaning will be investigated as functioning in the context of symbolic cognition.

The experienced dimension of meaning (felt meaning) functions importantly in all knowledge. Here is a short list of some examples of the roles played by felt meaning in knowledge. (a) Dewey[1] says the "feel" of meaning "guides our inferential movements." (b) Merleau-Ponty[2] points out that a *sens emotionnel* guides us in speech, when we know what we are about to say, but the particular words come only as we open our mouth to let them out. (c) In articulating any experience or observation the felt meaning is had first. (d) Articulations and symbolizations *proceed from* it. (e) Also, parts can often be explicitly stated, whereas the whole gestalt

1. John Dewey, *Experience and Nature* (La Salle, Ill.: Open Court Publishing Co., 1925), p. 299.
2. See Appendix.

of something can be had only as a felt meaning. (f) Relationships of different aspects of a question emerge for us through our putting their felt meanings together. We feel, or sense, relationships that only afterwards receive adequate symbolizations from us. Hypotheses, as Dewey points out, simply "spring before the mind," as we feel and sense problems. They come as first symbolizations of possibly relevant *felt* meanings. Later we shall attempt a more adequate and systematic inquiry into the many functions of felt meaning. Some of its functions were cited here only to show that felt meaning functions vitally in the having and the forming of cognition.

The problem of this essay, then, is: *how does felt meaning function in cognition?*

As we have already noted, if this problem is capable of a solution, then felt meaning must be capable of being examined as such (rather than only its symbols). If felt meaning can be *examined* as such, then it is already presupposed that it can function in cognition as such. The examples just cited of its functioning in cognition, as well as other more systematically presented examples to follow, will establish THAT felt meaning as such functions in cognition (Chapter II). When that is satisfactorily shown, we shall be able to turn to the problem of this essay: how does it function? We shall expect both a general account of how this functioning in cognition occurs, how it is possible, and an inquiry into its particular kinds of functions.

We will now briefly list a few problems of philosophy, psychology, and other fields for which the problem of the function of felt meaning is a vital question. We will not solve, or even adequately state these problems, but will, in a few paragraphs, allow these problems to illuminate the one problem of this essay. In this way we will define the problem more closely and also show some of its importance.

[B]

A Few Problems That Lead to the Problem of Experienced Meaning

Our problem is: how does felt meaning function in cognition? This problem is vitally involved in the following problems, here stated in barest outline:

1. METHOD IN PSYCHOLOGY

Carl Rogers says:

> There is a rather widespread feeling in our group that the logical positivism in which we were professionally reared is not necessarily the final philosophical word in an area in which the phenomenon of subjectivity plays such a vital and central part. Is there some view, possibly developing out of an existentialist orientation, which might preserve the values of logical positivism and the scientific advances which it has helped to foster, and yet find more room for the existing subjective person who is at the heart and base even of our system of science?
>
> But what is most urgently needed of all is a method whereby we might give operational definition to the construct *experience* in our theory, so that discrepancies between self-concept and experience, awareness and experience, etc. might be measured. This would permit the testing of some of the most crucial hypotheses of the theoretical system.[3]

A very large and crucial part of psychology concerns what is experienced, yet present scientific method does not refer directly to something experienced. Wherever experiences are referred to, the present scientific method substitutes theoretical constructs and external observations. A widely held methodological view in psychology even asserts that there is no internal

3. Carl R. Rogers, "A Theory of Therapy, Personality, and Interpersonal Relationships as Developed in Client-centered Framework," in S. Koch, ed., *Psychology: A Study of a Science,* Vol. 3 (New York: McGraw-Hill Book Company, 1959).

experience (the "empty organism" view of some forms of behaviorism).

Thus, while in psychotheraphy and related fields the whole subject matter concerns persons who grapple with and try to articulate intensely felt experiences, the science that studies this subject matter often insists that only external observations may be employed as empirical referents. There is widespread dissatisfaction with the present method's inadequacy in dealing with subjectivity, but subjectivity itself is not yet being employed as a reference of scientific concepts.

Conversely, there is also widespread dissatisfaction with the incapacity of research results to apply in modifying practice.[4]

These two dissatisfactions show that the scientific method that dominates contemporary psychology does not adequately tap subjectivity. It can not investigate nor apply its concepts to subjectivity, or to the practice that involves it.

More specifically, the issue is whether subjective experience may be referred to directly by scientific concepts, or whether

4. Carl Rogers (seminar, 1956) says that in psychology, science moves from clinical experience to hypotheses and theory, but that there is no reverse movement from tested research results to application in practice. He attributes this lack to the artificiality that attaches to anyone's behavior when he attempts to put into practice behaviors that research has shown to be effective. His assertion is of interest to the problems of this treatise. Since research results and theories are stated in terms of theoretical constructs and external observations (and omit subjective experiencing), naturally such results and theories offer no guide for their application except in terms of externally described behavior. In practice, however, imitations of external behavior can turn out to be quite different, depending upon subjectively held attitudes. If behavior could be described finely enough to measure the presumed externally observable differences made by different subjective attitudes, even then no guide would be offered the practitioner, since he would have to acquire the subjective attitudes and experiencing, before he could master these behavioral refinements. The conditions of this acquisition are quite different from any mere learning of behavioral technique. Finally, even research dealing with such externally observable fine distinctions in behavior requires distinctions in subjective experiencing, in order to ask the right questions and formulate hypotheses regarding the externally observable differences. Therefore, application of research findings to practice requires terms that refer to subjectivity.

only externally observed behaviors may be so referred to. For example, verbal sounds, behaviors on tests, perceptions of dots of light, are externally observable behaviors. On the other hand, many terms coined by Freud, such as "anxiety," "hostility," "oceanic feeling," "castration fear," referred initially to experienced feelings. The current scientific method reduces these to "theoretical constructs" plus "observable behaviors"; for example: "anxiety" was first defined by Freud as that sort of fear for which no object to be feared is known. This is a phenomenological articulation of a feeling. In the current methodology it becomes a theoretical construct (repressed material is close to consciousness) plus observable markings such as measurable physiological stress or blockage of some test performance.

The present essay does not oppose any empirical scientific procedures now extant, such as the finding of observable markings for constructs, or experiences. However, as currently used, the scientific method does away with the initial experiential referent; for example, "anxiety" is currently used as a theoretical construct and has no reference to the experience of the feeling. The present essay raises the possibility of direct reference by scientific concepts to the initial experiential referent. It does not eliminate the need for other kinds of reference.

When psychotherapists discuss their cases, they constantly refer to their own and their clients' experienced feelings. When these same people discuss research or theory, they speak as if they had never discussed their cases and as if nothing experienced could be referred to scientifically. Hence their discussions of cases are extremely rich and instructive while their theory and research is incapable of referring to much of the subject matter.

Physical science has for its subject matter physical objects and processes, that is, the objects of external observation.

Hence, for physical science, the terms that refer to *external* observation are terms that refer *directly* to the subject matter. However, terms that refer to external observation can refer only *indirectly* to subjective personal experience. Hence the issue is: can there be scientific terms that refer *directly* to the subjectivity that is the subject matter of much of psychology?

This is the problem of this essay—how does felt meaning function in cognition?—now phrased in the context of scientific method in psychology.

2. PROBLEMS IN PSYCHOLOGY

Many problems in psychology raise our problem in particular contexts. Here we will briefly cite three current examples.

a. Content of psychotherapy. It is a current issue just what type of *content* is optimal for psychotherapy: should the client focus on his past and childhood traumata, or should he focus on his present problems? Should he focus on his conflicts with his parents; on his relationship with the psychotherapist; or on his power-seeking desires; or on his sexual conflicts; or on his life purposes and needs for meaning? Different schools of psychotherapy can be recognized in these different emphases on what the optimal content of psychotherapy ought to be. It is also recognized that all these different schools of psychotherapy report roughly the same degree of success and that in all of them experienced therapists have better results than inexperienced ones.[5] Hence, the assertion is often made that in some as yet unknown way the same process occurs in all of them. How can one refer to this "same" process?

It is fairly clear, as soon as one is allowed to refer to sub-

5. Fred E. Fiedler, "A Comparative Investigation of Early Therapeutic Relationships Created by Experts and Non-experts of the Psychoanalytic, Non-directive, and Adlerian Schools" (unpublished Ph.D. dissertation, University of Chicago, 1949).

jective experience itself, that there is in all therapy a working with inner experiencing. It is a process of inner grappling. Most clients experience it as something akin to an ongoing physiological changing.

It is not clear as yet what an adequate science would conclude about this process. However, this process cannot be referred to at all except by scientific terms that refer directly to experiencing. The following is an example of the *kind* of assertion that refers directly to something experienced: the different contents (past, present, sex, power, meaning, relationships, and so on) may be considered to be different sorts of symbolizations of felt experiencing. This assertion would explain the common observation that some clients talk about any of these contents *along with* an inner experiencing of a profound changing process and a profound grappling with felt experience, whereas other clients who also talk about all these contents do so *without* such a grappling process. Any of these forms of symbolization can be used along with an ongoing changing in subjective experiencing, or they may be mere symbolic contents without such a changing. The point here is not the possible validity of this assertion, but rather that such an assertion cannot even be stated as a hypothesis unless felt experiencing can be referred to and studied. This again is the problem of this essay.

b. Subception. It is well established that selection and distortion mechanisms function to determine what a person will perceive. At present, this is called "subception" and implies that the organism differentiates, perceives, and then suppresses cognitive meanings that it finds conflict-raising. This involves assigning cognition to noncognitive levels of awareness and perception. Rogers writes:

Subception. This construct was formulated by McCleary and Lazarus. It signifies discrimination without awareness. . . . It is this capacity which in our theory permits the individual to discriminate an experience as threatening, without symbolization in awareness of this threat.[6]

Subception raises the problem of unaware cognition preceding and duplicating aware cognition. Highly differentiated cognitions on an unaware level seem to select what may then (again) be perceived on an aware level. If this is so, then there is a duplication of differentiation and perception. It would seem that before one perceives and differentiates (that is, cognizes), one's observations are censored and selected by a little man in the machinery who also cognizes, and does so first, and often with more intellectual refinement than the con-

6. Subception is vital in most theories of psychotherapy. Here are some other psychologists' formulations of this problem. Otto Fenichel: "There are defensive attitudes against painful perceptions." "There is forgetting or . . . misinterpreting of outer events to achieve wish fulfillment. None of these neurotic falsifications of reality can be distinguished exactly from repression."—*The Psychoanalytic Theory of Neurosis* (New York: W. W. Norton & Co., 1945), p. 30.

Harry Stack Sullivan, *The Interpersonal Theory of Psychiatry* (Norton, 1953), writes as follows. "The self system from its nature . . . tends to escape influence by experience which is incongruous with its current organization." "Thus we almost never grasp the character of . . . situations which provoke anxiety" (p. 190). Here it is not yet clear whether Sullivan also assumes symbolic cognition prior to conscious cognition, or whether the distortions of perception are simply incongruity. However, Sullivan also says: "I am afraid that for practical purposes all human behavior purely and unquestionably manifests the organization of experience into what are in effect signs, whether signals or symbols . . . I am concerned exclusively with covert and overt symbolic activity— that is, with activity influenced by the organization into signs of previous experience in terms of satisfaction, or in terms of avoiding or minimizing anxiety." Here Sullivan disagrees with Rogers by asserting that symbolic activity has a much wider scope than awareness. (Rogers equates the extent of awareness and symbolization.) It is quite clear now that since *all* human behavior is symbolic for Sullivan, the selection by the self-system is a symbolic process.

In all these views, then, it is vitally important that meaningful, seemingly cognitive perceptions occur on an *inexplicit,* covert level of experience. How is there a function of meaning of this kind in perception and interpretation? It is again the function of felt or experienced meaning in (and determinative of) a cognitive process.

scious person possesses. If one is not forced to this assumption, then cognition cannot be a matter of awareness only.

Cognition must be viewed as including processes of which we are unaware (or partly aware) that play a natural role in it. Feeling and other organismic processes must function in cognition at a stage before conscious conceptual symbolization ever takes place. What is the relationship between experiencing as an organismic and felt process, and conscious conceptual symbols? (This again is a version of our problem.)

c. Articulation of experience. Freud's theory posits as crucial the "making conscious of the unconscious." Rogers focuses on the "congruence" that he sees as optimally obtaining between feeling, thought, and expression. These and other theories attribute to feeling or experience a cognitive significance that can be represented in thought. Furthermore, all these theories pose the problem of just what is really meant by the "adequate," or "correct," or "congruent" representation, in thought, of experience or feeling. What potential cognitive status does experience or feeling have, such that thoughts and expressions may represent it adequately or inadequately? What constitutes adequacy?

Some views, such as Freud's and Rogers', conceive of this relationship of congruence as an equation. Experience, thought, and expression are viewed as having the same kind of meaning; therefore an equation is possible. Others, for example Sullivan, conceive of the relationship between experiencing and its meaning as an energy transformation (theoretical construct: "dynamism"). In this view adequate relations between experienced needs and thought (or expression in interpersonal relations) are a certain type of energy transformation. However, Sullivan retains alongside this view the more traditional Freudian view of nonconscious symbolic meanings, explained for him by dynamisms.

It is evident that all these views imply our problem: the sense in which experience or feeling has meaning apart from conceptualization and expression, such that the latter two could possibly be adequate to it.[7] Again, this is a context in which our problem appears: what is the function of felt meaning in cognition?

3. EXPERIENCE AS A SOURCE OF MEANING

Experience as a source of meaning is involved in a great many theoretical problem areas. Some of the problems just discussed involve it. Other examples are the philosophic discussions concerning how assertions are "based on" experience or "warranted by" experience. Wherever experience is meaningful and this meaning is to be articulated, there arises the problem: how is experienced meaning related to articulated meaning such that the latter can be said to be the articulation of the former?

4. THE DEPENDENCE OF INTELLECT

The last two centuries have seen a great diminution of the status of the intellect. It has come to be viewed as dependent on many nonintellectual factors. Even in the Middle Ages when faith vied with intellect for supremacy, intellect retained its classical relationship with the intelligibility of reality (through God's archetypes or through the logos of substances). Recently intellect has become dependent. Positivistic science views intellect as an extension of animal conditioning. Historical science views it as largely determined in its selections and prime concepts by the historical epoch. Sociology shows it to be a product and mirror of societal needs and peculiarities. Marxism asserts it to be a superstructure of class interests. Romanticists, as well as Bergson and many others, view it as distorting and ossifying a reality that is more truly lived or

7. We can restate this problem as follows: what relationship or relationships exist between a felt meaning and a symbolic formulation? We shall investigate the function of felt meaning in cognition precisely by investigating such relationships, and we shall find them various.

felt. Freud shows that it unwittingly mirrors psychologically repressed material. McKeon shows its prime principles, rules, and methods to have varieties the choice of which is not based on substantive considerations of the subject matter.

Alongside this development, philosophy has become increasingly interested in human functions that are not strictly rational. Not that these (art, myth, religion, language) were not always philosophical topics, for they always have been. But, they have become prime foci from which principles are derived that rule even reason or at least stand equal to reason.

A pitfall of this development lies in the submergence of such primacy as is natural to the intellect. Only the intellect studies these its own competitors. Only the intellect makes the potentiality of the meaningfulness of these other realms actually meaningful. A poisoning of the wells lies at the bottom of many of the views described above. The dilemma, however, that all these views present is this: there really is some relationship and some dependency of intellect on these areas of human experience, yet all articulated meaning also depends on intellect's own nature and validity. What then, precisely, is the relationship between intellect and the felt aspects of experience? What are the proper dependency relationships of intellect? Precisely in which ways are felt experiences influential upon intellect? In short, how does felt meaning function in cognition?

[C]
Certain Related Issues That Are Not Involved in the Present Task

We can now delimit our problem. To do so we will show that certain questions are clearly different from our problem and need not be involved in our inquiry. Our problem will be much more clearly defined when we have shown that the issues of the validity and causation of cognition are not involved in it.

The present investigation will take no stand on any issues concerning the validity of cognition. There are many philosophic accounts of principles of cognition that determine validity. Some are empirical, some a priori. Some of these principles of validity are called by names that recall data of our awareness, such as "experience," "custom," "consciousness," "concept formation," "intuition," "observation," and "human nature." However, an account of the validity of cognition cannot help but offer principles *for* the validity of all valid cognition. First and foremost, then, such principles refer to validity. Valid cognition defines all such principles, since principles can be worth something only if they are principles *for* (and therefore defined by) that of which they are principles.

Hence, even though some of these principles are called "experience" (and other terms recalling what we experience), they are never actually *intended* to refer to what we experience. Instead, they state what experience *must* be, *if* cognition can be valid. They must not be interpreted as statements about experience. Rather, they are statements about all valid cognition. Anything that we actually do experience, on the other hand, is already the product of operations that are determined by these basic principles of all valid cognition. Anything we actually experience must be seen in this way, *if* cognition about it is to be *valid*. Hence, from the viewpoint of the validity of all cognition and the principles of this validity, anything that we actually experience must be considered as already subject to these principles (even if these principles bear names like "experience").

For example, Kant means by "unity of apperception" not

our own sense of our own "I," but rather a philosophical principle of the unity of contents of consciousness, which is necessary (in his analysis) for all cognition. On the other hand, for him our own sense of our own "I" is merely one of the many contents unified by the principle, "unity of apperception."[8]

Nor is this situation in philosophy in any way deplorable. A principle has to be defined by (and considered as) what it does to that of which it is a principle. If, then, the validity of knowledge is the context in which such terms are principles, they are defined by, and as, necessary rules of valid cognition, and are not meant to refer to our own experience of ourselves, as we are aware of it. It is necessary to affirm this especially of "empirical" principles, since these sound like references to our own experience. However, as principles *of* all valid cognition they are not—in this respect—different from nonempirical principles. The difference lies in that empirical principles are theoretical constructs about experience, while nonempirical principles are theoretical constructs about God, mind, archetypes, or other things. Both kinds of principles, however, are controlled by what they do, that is, by how they function as principles *of* the validity of all knowledge.

The present essay does not concern the validity of cognition.

8. Kant sharply separates the "empirical" and "transcendental" senses of experience. The transcendental sense of "experience" is already presupposed in what we individually experience and is therefore not dependent on it. Dewey, after a discussion of the existential "feel" or meaning, also says in effect: let's leave this "existential" aspect of thought and get on with our theory of knowledge which has to do with "objective reference . . . and existing organic structure which enforce correct participation by the organism in the course of events."—*Experience and Nature,* p. 347. To confuse the two discussions (validity aspect and existential aspect of thought) would be an error, as he says. But one need not "mistake the island (of consciousness) for a solid complete continent," (*ibid.*) in order to study the island *as such.* Dewey studies it as such in these few pages. One need not assert that it determines its own cause or its own validity. On the other hand, one need not treat the island as if nothing on it or about it could be seen, except from the viewpoint of the continent. Although the island cannot govern validity, neither can validity govern what *must* be found on the island. What really is found is itself also an independent starting point.

It cannot, therefore, accept principles of the validity of cognition as referring to experienced meaning, nor, conversely, can it say anything about when and how cognition is valid. If it attempted to do the latter, it would indeed employ mere products of the rules of valid cognition and set up, with these products, new rules of validity. But if it did the former, and accepted epistemological principles as terms that refer to our own awareness, it would assert that we experience just what we must experience if cognition is to be valid. This we may not assert, if we are to investigate how cognition is related to what we actually do experience. If there are requirements for what we *must* experience, if cognition is valid, then this essay must let those requirements stand. On the other hand we must look at what we actually *do* experience (and how that functions in cognition). The rules of cognition itself (even where they set up what must be experienced) are already adequately dealt with in every good philosophy.

If what we have to say about the functions of felt meaning in cognition were to necessitate that we choose one account of validity in cognition over another, we would, of course, have to take careful note of that. However, such will not be the case. We may often have to discourse about cognition in the terms of one account or another, but alternative accounts, when set next to each other, will swiftly reveal that anything we legitimately have to say regarding the present problem is equally capable of being said in other good accounts of the validity of cognition. If this were not so, we would be saying something about the rules of validity, which we shall not be entitled to do.

2. THE CAUSATION OF COGNITION

There are many accounts of the presence of cognitive and potentially cognitive elements in our experience. For example, there are biological and environmental factors that condition actions, habits, symbols, and hence the meaningfulness of experience. Then again, there are intelligible forms in things. Then again, reason is a capacity to grasp forms, which in turn come to us from various possible sources. Finally, there are spontaneous faculties within man through which meaning may arise in experiences.

If we look *directly* at the meaningfulness of experience as we find it in our awareness, we are, of course, not entitled to assert anything about the origin of this meaningfulness. Whatever its origin, we are looking at it when it is already extant. We may speak of its origin in order to clarify something about it, but whatever account of its origin we choose, we must make sure that we don't rule out the possibility that other accounts would serve equally well. Otherwise we will be asserting something of its origin, which we are not entitled to do. Conversely, we shall not accept as our starting point anything about cognition (or felt, experienced meaning) that ought to be true of it because of its alleged origin, unless we can find it directly in our analysis of it, regardless of this alleged origin.

Dewey calls consciousness an "island" and warns against mistaking this island for the whole continent. We shall keep in mind that our island stops on one side at the waters of its origin and on the other side at the waters of its validity or objectivity. We shall inquire into a relationship that lies on the island, namely the relationship of felt meaning and cognition.

3. EXAMPLE AND DISCUSSION OF THE SEPARATION OF THE PRESENT PROBLEM FROM THESE PROBLEMS

In Dewey's theory of knowledge, concept formation involves felt meaning performing a function that he terms "suggestion,"[9] that is to say, the "arising" of suggested solutions to

9. John Dewey, *How We Think* (New York: D. C. Heath and Co., 1933), Chaps. 6, 7, and 11.

present problems. Dewey offers a complex epistemology in which such suggestions appear as the raw material to be refined and converted into hypotheses and then controlled and tested for logical consistency and objective confirmation. Of suggestion itself, Dewey shows that it is caused by a personal and cultural past—caused, as is all experience, by environmental interaction. Not much is said about how suggestion *itself* operates or emerges.

This study will principally consider felt significance itself. Suggestion, then, for example, may still occupy its place in the process Dewey describes, regardless of what this study will say about the nature of suggestion itself. This illustrates that the separation of the problems is possible.

Our problem has thus been specified within limits that exclude both causation and validation of thought. These limits include only the experienced (felt) meaning itself, prior to and emerging into formulation, not the criteria external to that formulation, vital though these are to formulation in other respects.

In the present study, the functions of felt or experienced meaning will be investigated. It must be an investigation of "experience" in the sense of direct datum of awareness, since *experienced* meaning is the subject of this treatise. Moreover, psychology newly demands the actually experienced as the referent of theory. As long as psychology was a causal, explanatory science, it was merely one of many sciences *presupposing* principles of knowledge. Experience as explained by such psychology does indeed presuppose categories of valid knowledge applied to observation. However, as soon as psychology approaches the experienced directly—as an existential event, not only as a product of theoretical constructs— then psychological theories (which are all ultimately about experience) dare not presuppose a notion of experience without independent reference to what can be experienced. That would be philosophized psychology.[10] The parallel evil, a psychologized philosophy, would arise were we to give primacy to a direct exposition of experience in order to prejudice the theory of knowledge—as if deriving theory of knowledge from such a direct exposition.[11] It is necessary to avoid both these errors. A proper treatment of the problem must investigate the functions of *experienced meaning* in *cognition* without either one prejudicing the other.

Before going on to Chapter II the reader may wish to see the Appendix, in which some contributions of Husserl, Sartre, Merleau-Ponty, and Richards are cited. These also help to define the problem of the present work.

10. For example, when the data of experience are forced to fit a theory of experience that assumes that terms such as "whole," "part," or "integrate" are especially applicable to it.

11. As when it is claimed that something experienced shows that "whole," "part," or "integrate" are the basic categories of all formulation.

CHAPTER II *Demonstration That Felt*

Meaning Functions in Cognition

Brief   The role of felt meaning (experiencing) is *described*
Statement as it functions in thought, observation, action, speech,
and other contexts. Special roles of felt meaning
(which cannot be accounted for by an analysis of symbols alone) are then described in problem solving,
remembering and articulating, and psychotherapy.

The descriptions of this chapter are not yet systematic. Their purpose is only to fully locate the roles
of felt meaning in the reader's own experiencing, and to
demonstrate that felt meaning does have essential roles
in cognition (see also Appendix), that we can *directly*
observe these, and that we cannot deal with them by an
analysis of symbols alone because felt meaning performs
functions that symbols alone cannot perform.

Chapter II can be viewed as several descriptive demonstrations that felt meaning can be directly referred to
as it functions in relation to symbols, but *as something
other than symbols*. This demonstratum is essential to
the philosophic treatment that follows, for we can inquire into *how* felt meaning functions only with direct
reference to it, as well as to symbols.

Introduction

This chapter demonstrates *that* felt meaning does function in
cognition. Later we will deal with *how* felt meaning functions.

63

We are most aware of the dimension of felt meaning when our symbols fail to symbolize adequately what we mean. At such times, felt meaning appears clearly different and richer or more specific than the meaning inherent in the available symbols.

The problem of the inadequacy of symbols to express a felt meaning covers many philosophical problem areas: seeking for relevant words; articulating experience; whole as over against parts; practical wisdom applicable to particulars as against theoretical science; degrees of explication; focus of attention in contrast to its fringe; connotative in contrast to denotative meaning; emotive in contrast to cognitive meaning; implicit and explicit meaning; conditions of the whole discourse system related to specifiable meanings within it; earlier products of inquiry functioning in newly formulated problems; and so on. In all these, felt meaning plays a role and cannot be articulated adequately in symbols.

The instances just cited are merely haphazard examples of many problem areas that have been treated in philosophy often and thoroughly. It may seem that some system will be required to arrange and relate these problems, and that felt meaning functions differently in each.

Each of these examples is an instance where philosophical analysis stumbles over some function of felt meaning necessary to account for some cognitive operation. However, there is no need to discuss felt meaning as it happens to appear at the point where some philosophical analysis stumbles. We don't wish to prejudice this inquiry by adopting one of these different types of philosophic analysis and its terms and principles. Nor can we arbitrate among them. Therefore our haphazard list of philosophical problems need not be systematized; rather, we may consider these to be examples illustrating felt meaning in two ways: (1) they are examples of the ever-present role of felt meaning; (2) felt meaning stands out because some specific aspect of cognition cannot be accounted for without the function of felt meaning. Our demonstration that felt meaning functions in cognition will be divided according to these two foci:

1. Felt meaning functions as an ever-present experienced parallel of all concepts, observations, actions—whatever is meaningful to us. The experienced dimension of meaning is present, both when we conceptualize our experience and when we do not.
2. Some specific cognitive operations depend upon specific functions of felt meaning.

Our demonstration that felt meaning does function in cognition thus will fall into two parts: first, we shall show that the felt dimension of meaning always is present; then we shall show that it performs various specific and crucial functions in some kinds of cognition.

[A]
Demonstration *That* Felt Meaning Occurs in *All* Cases of Human Cognition

1. THOUGHT

Often it is said that any moment's focus of attention also involves meanings that lie beyond the immediate focus. Another traditional way of stating this is that only part of a presently held meaning is symbolized explicitly. A meaning always includes some inexplicit aspects that are not symbolized just then.

This "fringe" of attention or explication is a fringe only at some given moment. At the next, it might be brought into focus and made explicit. The importance of this inexplicit "fringe" lies in the fact that it occurs in every instance of thought. Let us demonstrate this.

To think a sentence or a thought, we must employ symbols. These symbols (verbal or other) make our meaning explicit. However, the separate meaning of each symbol by itself remains inexplicit at this point. For example, we think, "Democracy is government by the people." The symbol "government" helps make our meaning explicit. What "government" itself means is a necessary part of the symbolization, yet it isn't itself explicit to us. If we ask *then* what is the meaning of "government," we may think, "Oh yes, government is distribution of power vested in administrative persons." Again, we will employ many symbols, the meaning of which we certainly *have* (or experience, or feel), else these symbols could not help us make the meaning of the term explicit. Yet, what each of these meanings is will be implicit at this point. Our attention will be focused on the symbols' role in helping explicate "government." Their own meaning will be considered a "fringe."

This paradigm of "fringe" and "focus" doesn't quite clarify the relationship between explicit and implicit aspects of the meanings. If we focus on the meaning of some term *x,* then the meanings of the defining terms, *a, b, c* certainly are within our center of attention, inasmuch as these meanings *constitute* the meaning of the term *x.* Their meaning is implicit, yet just these meanings make up the explication of the term *x.* The so-called "fringe" must be in the "focus" in order to perform the function of defining. What is called fringe meaning is really felt meaning. It is very much within the focus of attention, although implicit. We have here an example of a universal function of felt meaning. We have shown that some felt meanings are needed to *explicate* a meaning. Such felt meanings are not meanings that are not in focus or not being explicated, but precisely the opposite. It is when we explicate a meaning and focus on it that this meaning is felt or experienced while it is being explicated. A meaning is explicated in terms of symbols whose meanings are felt or experienced. It is this feeling or experiencing that constitutes the "having" of an explicated meaning.

We have been demonstrating that the thought of a meaning necessarily includes the "feel" of this meaning, that is, felt meaning. This has been shown to apply not only to "fringes" of what is being thought, but to the very meaning on which we are focusing. It has been shown to apply not only to unsymbolized or presymbolized meanings, but also to the very meaning for which symbols are presently being thought. Our conclusion is that when we think a meaning, both symbols and felt meanings are necessary.

Another way of phrasing this conclusion, perhaps more in accord with modern habits, is to say that symbols are "associated" with felt meanings, and that these associated felt meanings constitute our experience of meaning.

If the reader is not convinced that this conclusion holds, he can demonstrate it to himself at any time. Let him simply ask himself what he means by any word or symbol. He will find himself *feeling* the sense of this meaning. He may explicate it and expand it, but he will never have it except as a felt sense. This felt sense might not be associated with appropriate symbols, or it may be associated in his awareness with symbols that explicate it. To some extent he can have the meaning with or without the proper symbols. He cannot have the meaning without the sensed feel of it.

2. OBSERVATION

Like thought, observation involves felt meanings. Something observed is always observed as *meaningful.*

Most meanings functioning in observation are felt meanings: we may think, "This is a chair," but usually we take in what we observe without such explication. We experience or feel the meanings of what we observe. We know that we recognize what we see or hear, or we feel that it is strange in some respect. We orient ourselves in situations and make appropriate responses, all on the basis of the felt meanings of observation.

The reader may demonstrate this to himself by looking at his present surroundings and asking himself what in his present experiencing constitutes his observation of it. He will find a complex of familiar felt meanings that to him mean knowledge of the observed surroundings. If he wanted to, he could think explicitly of his chair, the walls, the drapes, and so on, but he needn't do this. He knows what they are as he observes them.

Occasionally we do think out explicitly some part of what we observe. In that case, too, felt meanings must play a role. What we have said of thought in the preceding section applies to this more infrequent aspect of observation. Meaningful, explicit thought regarding some part of an observation involves our feeling the meanings that the symbols explicate.

We conclude that felt meanings constitute the meanings of observation that we don't make explicit, and that they play a necessary role also in the observations we do explicate.

3. ACTION

Considered as something observed from the outside, an action is like any other observation.

From the phenomenological viewpoint of the agent, an action has felt meaning even before he can observe it externally.

As we do something, we may pay attention to the "feel" of this action from the inside. If our action takes place in the light or makes noise, we can observe it externally, as well as attend to the "feel" of it. When the action doesn't have the intended results, we are especially aware of the "feel" of it. For example, when driving a car, if we step on the brake pedal, but find a moment later that we have stepped on the gas instead, then the externally observed action and the result are not "appropriate" to the "feel" of the intended action. In what way do we know this "feel"? What we have already discussed applies here. We may have thought explicitly, "I will now step on the brake," or we may not have thought anything. In either case, we have some "feel." Later, this "feel" might be articulated: "I was about to step on the brake," or "I am stepping on the brake," or "I meant to step on the brake but I missed it."

Generally we act with such a "feel" of the action to guide us. Actions only rarely have explicit symbols. Whether or not explicit symbols are present, there is a "feel" of the action. To demonstrate the role of felt meaning in an action another way: suppose we are learning to dance. We may see a dance step performed, we may know and be able to describe it in all sorts of symbols, but we lack the "feel" of the action until we learn to dance. The "feel" of an action is not the same as feelings about the situation. "I wanted to stop because the light was red," is not the feel of the action of stopping. It is a felt meaning, but not the felt sense of the acting, a feeling of movement that usually is symbolized kinesthetically, at least at first.

We can demonstrate to ourselves that our actions have felt meanings, by focusing our attention on our felt experience as we perform an action. We may find ourselves looking back or forward to this feel of our actions. It is usually there ready to be observed.

4. SPEECH

In speech, as in all action, there is both external observation and the felt sense of what is intended. The "feel" of what we intend to say is especially noticeable when we hear ourselves just having said something that doesn't quite mean what we intend. What we intend to say is not explicit until we say it. There is usually a smooth transition from intended implicit felt meaning to explicit speech. Whether or not felt meanings are noticed, they are present in normal speech, as in thought and action.

If we observe ourselves speaking, we will find that what we are about to say and what we have said is meaningful to us in a felt sense.

5. ART, RELIGION, EMOTION, PERSONS

Most of life's actions, observations, and situations occur without verbal symbols. Whether there are verbal symbols or not, felt meaning is present whenever any of these have meaning to a person.

There are certain realms of life where meanings are symbolized in terms other than words, and these are therefore most likely to call our attention to this dimension of felt meaning. Felt meaning is not necessarily so different in these cases, but since verbal symbols are absent, the felt meanings are more noticeable.

Works of art symbolize their meaning in terms of colors, shapes, sounds, volumes, motions. Because we are not so aware of a system of symbols in these media, we are ready to assert the fact that we have a *felt* sense of works of art. Let us ask ourselves what we experience in viewing some painting or statue. Whatever we may be inclined to answer in words, first we will find ourselves observing internally our felt sense of the impact on us of the work of art. It will be symbolized (at least at first) only by the actual object of art.

Religious services, strong emotions, our acquaintance with persons—these also are cases where meaning certainly is ex-

perienced, but because our verbal symbols usually are inadequate, we are aware strongly of felt meaning. At least
some of this meaning usually can be explicated in terms of
verbal symbols. Whether so explicated or not, felt meaning is
experienced in these cases, and we may easily demonstrate
its presence to ourselves.

Many different contexts of felt meaning have been mentioned. Our purpose in this section has been to show, not differences among the functions of felt meaning, but that felt
meaning accompanies all meaningful experience and constitutes our experienced sense of meaningfulness.

[B]
Demonstration *That* Felt Meaning Performs Specific Functions
Necessary in Cognition, Other than the Experienced or As-
sociated Parallel Side of Cognition

The preceding section showed that felt meaning functions
as the experienced side of all thought, observation, action, and
the like. In this section we shall attempt to show that some
kinds of cognition depend on specific functions of felt meaning. In these specific functions felt meaning cannot be considered merely as an experienced parallel side of cognition.

1. PROBLEM SOLVING

What is our experience of the process of thinking about a
problem? Dewey says that "suggestions" arise, which are
rough hypotheses, possible solutions. They pop into the mind
when one thinks about the problem.

The inference occurs via or through the suggestion that is aroused
by what is seen and remembered. Now while the suggestion pops
into mind, just what suggestion occurs, depends first upon the

experience of the person. This is in turn dependent on the general state of culture of the time . . . upon the person's own preferences, desires, interests, or even his immediate state of passion. The inevitableness of suggestion, the lively force with which it springs before the mind . . . indicates the necessity of controlling the suggestion which is made on the basis of an inference that is to be believed.[1]

We note here that Dewey indicates the process by which suggestions "pop into the mind" or "spring into the mind," but he does not analyze the experience of that process itself. He is concerned with the causation of the suggestion (experience, culture, passion, and so on) and with its control for valid inference. Nothing in his analysis need be contradicted by our use of it to call attention to our experience of arising of suggestions.

Dewey reminds us that, when confronted with a problematic situation, one "reflects" on it. It is a "dubious and perplexing situation." It involves "tension." As far as these descriptions go, they do describe the experiencing of attempting to solve a problem. Let us add more detail:

We observe (and hence interpret) the problem. We think "about it." In some way there are present to us a great many meaningful experiences that relate to the present problem. We are not aware explicitly of all of these, not even as felt meanings. On the other hand, we do sense more meaning than we have symbolized. We sense relationships among the aspects of the problem itself, although the symbolized version only states separate aspects. We "mull over" these aspects together. We sense relationships of these aspects to other experiences, some of them more explicit, some less so. We employ symbols, but invariably the processes of meaning that occur exceed the meanings that are symbolized. Inference

1. John Dewey, *How We Think* (Boston: D. C. Heath and Co., 1933), Chap. 6.

"involves a leap beyond what is given and already established," says Dewey. When finally the "suggestion" occurs and a possible solution is symbolized, what has occurred in between? At times nothing that was in awareness, at other times a great deal. Indeed, except where really nothing aware has occurred, we can always note felt meanings occurring vitally in the process of attempting to reflect on a problem. Even where nothing extraneous is brought to awareness, the problem itself, the problematic aspects of it, are "mulled" or "sensed," even as Dewey says, as a "tension." This "tension" may involve dissatisfaction, but it also embodies the meanings forming the problem. This is not to be confused with dislike for the situation. For example, we might wish a problem to remain unsolved, yet we would appreciate it as a problem only to the extent that we sensed, felt, experienced the meanings that together do not resolve, that together are a problem. In a conscious attempt to solve a problem, we focus our attention on an enlivened feeling of these meanings. We present them to our attention repeatedly. As in all thought, the symbols at a given moment are few compared to the number of inexplicit meanings held in awareness.

We need only observe our own experience when we try to solve a problem. If we see a problem, we must have surveyed something complex enough to present a problem to us. During the very first moments while we attack the problem, we must have in mind a great many more meanings than we symbolize explicitly in words. Even one sentence about some aspect of a problem, if we repeated it to ourselves, would obstruct our thought about how "that" relates to something else. Problem solving does not occur until we can name the meaning of the one sentence "that" and, holding "that" in mind, are able to turn to other aspects of the problem to see how they relate to "that." This relating of aspects is one function of felt meaning in problem solving. It is a function of the felt meaning, not merely of the term "that." Of course the term "that" does not symbolize the meaning adequately. The felt meaning is quite indispensable in this process of cognition. Felt meaning performs here a more specific function than was described in our earlier discussion. There, felt meaning was our experience of the meaning of all symbols.

In the present instance, we have a symbol: "that," which doesn't symbolize by rendering the meaning in symbols, but which only serves as a grip on the felt meanings performing essential functions in the process of solving a problem.

Jacques Hadamard[2] gives examples of mathematicians who employ dots or circles in much the fashion that our previous example employed the word "that." He concludes: "What may be the use of such a strange and cloudy imagery?" "I need it in order to have a simultaneous view of all elements of the argument, to hold them together, in short, to achieve that synthesis which we spoke of. . . ." Here again, felt meanings function to make problem solving possible, while the symbols (dots) are mere grips, referring to felt meaning.

Although Hadamard appears to make synthesis his prime principle, we shall refrain from doing so. Viewing many aspects at once and as a whole is only one vital function of felt meanings. Another, for example, is remembering relevant past experience. Indeed, often such memories appear of their own accord. However, if we set ourselves to seek them, what do we do? We focus on our felt sense of some aspect of our problem and we try to intensify it. We enliven our feeling of it. We go over it time and again. We "mull it," savor it, define it further and further. We pick up every new felt sense that appears and explicate it.

Sometimes we suddenly have three or four ideas at once, too many to explicate. Hastily we review them: there is "that"

2. Jacques Hadamard, *The Psychology of Invention in the Mathematical Field* (New York: Dover Publications, 1945), pp. 76–77.

and "that" and "that" and "that." We assign them spots, or movements of the arm, or places in space, or some other sort of momentary handles. Then we take them up in turn. We aren't sure that we will retain them, until we have them symbolized properly. Here is a use of Hadamard's "spots" that holds in mind different and even unrelated meanings. It appears that Hadamard's spots help us to hold felt meanings in awareness, whether for synthesis or simply for memory.

These instances are sufficient to demonstrate that the experienced process of problem solving involves specific functions of felt meaning. It is not only the ever-present experienced side of all symbolic meaning, but felt meaning also functions vitally without symbols in the process of obtaining adequate symbols of new ideas.

2. REMEMBERING OR ARTICULATING

The case of something forgotten we seek to remember is a further example. Fenichel states: "The forgetting of a name makes us feel . . . the psychic unconscious . . . subjectively. One knows that one knows the name and still one does not know it." [3]

This knowing is sufficient to indicate that we do know the name. It will help us reject the incorrect possibilities that occur to us. It will allow us to know,[4] when we do remember,

3. Otto Fenichel, *The Psychoanalytic Theory of Neurosis* (New York: W. W. Norton & Co., 1945), p. 148.

4. As has been stated in Chapter I, this study is not concerned with issues of validity. However, since phenomenologically given experience is so often said to be infallible or self-evident, we need to point out here that this study claims no inherent validity or self-evidence for a felt meaning.

Without crossing the bounds of our study, we may demonstrate the lack of infallibility by citing some simple descriptions of error in our interpretations of our feelings: it is an accepted fact in psychology and in common observation that often we have feelings the meaning of which we do not know. We reflect. Sometimes then we find, "Oh yes, I know what's troubling me; I'm tense because tonight I have that particular that we have the name that was previously "on the tip of our tongue."

Here we note a felt meaning that functions (a) to indicate something potentially known, (b) to indicate incorrect and correct formulations of it, (c) in the process of recall, because to recall something, we concentrate our attention on the "feel" of it.

These functions of felt meaning are needed not only in

---

unpleasant thing to do. Gee, I didn't realize how much I don't want to do it!" Other times we try repeatedly but we can't move beyond some vague, undifferentiated stress of feeling. Most often we don't even try, we just go along without ever finding out just what we felt. This is so because we feel continually and only bring to light what is really important to us. At still other times, we find out just what our feeling is, and then much later we find out that what we found then, now seems to have been wrong. This can occur in two different ways.

(1) We may find that we were wrong because we didn't discriminate finely enough, as for example: "Oh, it isn't that I find this thing tonight so unpleasant; in fact, I'm looking forward to it. It's just that it involves the possibility of having to argue with Mr. *X*. and *that's* what I find so unpleasant." It is evident here that we were on the right track before. Also, it is clear that this differentiation process often can continue on and on. "Oh, it isn't arguing with Mr. *X* that I find so unpleasant, it's that I really love to argue with him and I'm afraid he'll find out about it and ridicule me for it."

(2) The other kind of being wrong about what we found out is the instance where we are simply altogether wrong, as for example: "Oh, it has nothing to do with tonight. It's really such and such, and I was just really not thinking about that."

Now, we know we can be wrong in both these ways, because we often find ourselves wrong in these ways. In a given case at a given moment, we usually can't tell whether we are right or wrong.

There is even the possibility of arguing that we are always right, merely that we change. We think we feel now the same feeling and interpret it more truly, but every moment's feeling is different and right for itself. Since these are purely hypothetical views, one must accept the difficulties of both positions and surrender the comforts of both positions: no validity can be derived from the notion that every moment's feeling is different (except the specious one that I think I feel what I think I feel). On the other hand, no certainty exists that the feeling I *re*interpret now is really the same as I had before and misinterpreted, since perhaps it has changed.

Since we are not concerned with validity, we cite these descriptions of misinterpretation of what we feel, only to indicate that no infallibility is claimed.

recall, but also in many other instances. Not only memories, but also original experiences are first conceptualized with the aid of similar functions of felt meaning. Later, it will be our task to inquire into *how* it functions. For the moment it must be clear *that* it does so. A felt meaning may function as described in (a), (b), and (c) above, in every case in which something as yet unsymbolized is to be symbolized. Take, for example, our impression of a person we just met: we have not as yet thought explicitly what our impression is. When we attempt to do so, the felt meanings in our awareness function, just as in recalling a name, to tell us that we do have an impression, that it is not so and so, that these and these words do not describe it adequately, and we concentrate further on the feel of the felt meaning to obtain more adequate explication of it.

There are very many instances in cognition where something experienced is to be articulated. In all such instances felt meanings perform special functions on which the formulation of symbols depends.

Psychotherapy is a special area in which the articulation of experience constantly occurs. The individual in psychotherapy struggles with many experiences that he has never symbolized before and for which he knows no symbols. It is therefore a special area, which we will discuss next. However, no area of experience, no matter how conventional and familiar, can be articulated without felt meaning's functioning as just outlined.

3. PSYCHOTHERAPY

This description is meant to serve as further evidence that felt meaning plays a crucial role in the understanding and articulation of experience and observation.

Also, this role of felt meaning implies something about a

science of the therapeutic process: science depends on data offered by practice, *not only on data of theoretically inspired observation*. The role played by felt experience in the practice must be included as data in the science of therapeutic practice. A whole mass of data becomes available, if concepts may refer directly to felt experiences.

The following describes experiencing in the psychotherapeutic process in client-centered therapy. However, the description is shaped so that it might very well fit any type of psychotherapy, despite differences among the different methods. Client-centered therapy seems to be exclusively an exploration of the client's felt experience in his own terms, whereas other methods offer diagnostic concepts from the therapist's theoretical frame of reference. However, on closer examination it is found that other schools of therapy place equal emphasis on the client's own direct discovery of the feelings and experiences within him that the diagnosis in general previsions. In Freud's words, the diagnosis is a conceptual scaffolding which, as in the case of a building to be built, is taken down as needless when the real building comes into existence. The diagnosis can be made in a day from interview and projective test material. The client's own discovery and grappling with the feelings and experiences within him takes a long time and consists of feelings, not of concepts —consists of his experienced particulars, not of conceptual generalizations. Hence, all forms of therapy consist of a person's efforts to experience more deeply and to come to grips with and symbolize his own felt experience for himself.

The client. Whatever the client may say, at a given moment, the psychotherapist listens both to the spoken content and to the feeling the client expresses in saying it. For example, the client may use five or six sentences to describe a certain troubling situation. The therapist may respond: "You're afraid"; or, "You're puzzled why you should behave that way"; or, "This makes you resent him" or something of the sort. In doing this, the therapist is indicating that he understands the verbal content ("this" and also that he *understands the client's feeling* about "this." In most social situations we focus on the verbal, cognitive content, paying little attention to our feelings unless they are especially sharp. Usually we expect others to do the same. Feelings are usually considered irrelevant, obstructive to the task at hand, impolite. In the therapy situation, the focus is therefore uniquely different from most social situations, since the focus is on the feelings.

Of course this initial description is much too simple. In the first place, understanding is not always so easy. Often the counselor will have to await several clarifications and corrections before he will understand and be able to respond in a way that shows that he does. Often the context—what the client *has been* saying—will be necessary to understand him *now*. Sometimes it is not clear how what he now says relates to the context. Sometimes the therapist can see several ways in which what was said might be meant; at other times he may see no way to understand it, so that he will simply have to say "I don't follow you." All these things occur in understanding the intellectual, verbal content, and in most cases that is necessary before the feeling accompanying it is understandable.

Nor is the feeling always clear. Sometimes it is a unique feeling, so that giving it a general name doesn't seem to make it understandable. At other times, the individual relaxes, as if relieved of a tremendous strain, when the feeling is named. You can see him simply relax all his limbs and exhale a long, "I *sure* am."

Often it is necessary for one of the two people to invent some new way of speaking, in order to name some feeling. Sometimes not only a name, but a poetic image is needed.

Either person may invent it. We are describing two possibilities here: referring and conceptualizing, using these two words to stand for the following: client and therapist often go along for quite a while talking about "this" or "how this feels" or "this all-tied-up feeling," where the words *name or refer to a feeling* that is presumably felt by both persons, but is not yet characterized or symbolized. On the other hand, either person often invents a way of characterizing or *conceptualizing the feeling* so that the client feels, "Yes, that's just it." For example, a feeling may be described by some poetic image invented on the spot, such as: "You're comfortable as long as you have fences to divide different areas, and to let you know where you are. But the open prairie scares you."

It is an important theoretical question why it makes so much difference to a person to conceptualize a feeling in words that really seem to convey it. However, in describing the experience of such conceptualizing, there is simply no question that it does make the feeling more intense, more clear, more real, and more capable of being handled. The client feels as if he now knows where, in him, it is to be found. He feels as if he had grappled with it and now owns it, instead of being dogged by something partly unknown. We could multiply descriptions of the difference it makes. Among other differences, accurate conceptualization tends to allow the client to continue exploring the feeling and other feelings connected with it, so that he soon finds himself again confronted by something vague yet important and once again proceeds to symbolize that. In this way *a flow or a process develops*. The exploration of feeling develops on its own power, even though the client may have come in feeling that he had nothing to say. Or, if he has come with a very full, prepared agenda of intellectual or situational content, he soon drops this agenda.

One reason for the development of this flow of feelings is that a person nearly always has some feeling—for example, being stuck, being embarrassed at not knowing what to say or do next, being uncomfortable about expressing something, feeling unwilling to go into something. Some feelings are expressed along with intellectual content, others by silence or gesture or voice quality. They are not "conscious" most of the time, but they are not unconscious either. They have a kind of *subliminal* status such that any attention devoted to them makes them conscious. The client himself often is surprised by what he finds he has just expressed. (Of course the client may give the counselor cues to other feelings that are very much unconscious, but the counselor is concerned with what the client feels *now*, not with repressed or merely probable feelings in general, such as being afraid of x, if x is not now being thought about, or fear of castration, or some other feeling that may be potentially in the person but is not now part of that of which he is aware, or almost aware.) The counselor follows the *intended* expression of the client, but he takes the client in more broadly than the client puts himself forth. Responding to a feeling is not a matter of seeing through someone. If the feeling the counselor senses is in no way related to the client's present expression, the counselor's stating it would merely follow the counselor's interest and interrupt the development of the client's own process of moving from feeling to feeling. On the other hand, the counselor finds much more in the client's present expressing than the client usually expects. But the counselor only responds to what he thinks is really there now. The counselor is, of course, willingly corrected, since he is not concerned with what is true about the client in general but only with what is part of experiencing right here and now. The client is the only one who can say what is and what is not part of his present experiencing.

The word "feeling" is used, in this sort of description, to stand for a number of different occurrences. (a) It stands for the *felt meaning* of a situation or of a whole series of contents. For example, when the counselor responds to a long series of descriptions with, "You wonder how anybody can be that way," and the client assents, it is clear to both persons that the counselor really has understood all that was said, else he could not have grasped correctly the felt meaning of the whole communication. Trainees in nondirective therapy often begin by repeating much of what the client says. No one feels "understood" by repetition. One is prone to repeat yet again, as if just the fact that the counselor repeated the words showed that he doesn't understand. On the other hand, the client is satisfied that the counselor understands, if the counselor indicates that he has grasped *the felt interpretation* of the whole of what was said, even if that is indicated in only one or two words.

(b) "Feeling" also stands for an emotion. (This division is purely descriptive, can overlap, and is not intended to be in any way a best sort of division.) Sometimes a client will experience a feeling (in this sense) and will not know what it is, or in some other way will be puzzled about it. After his feeling this emotion repeatedly and expressing it in different ways it may suddenly "open up" and be full of characteristics both general and particular, concerning something, and have all sorts of connections.

Both (a) and (b) above are descriptions of occurrences in which feelings are found to have or to be meanings. In (a) we described how *the meaning of what is being said is most often a feeling.* In (b) we described how *a feeling, no matter how vague it may be initially,* is capable of becoming sharper and at the same time of being found to be *full of meaning.*

These processes occur quite independently of what the client plans to talk about. He discusses some specific topic, or he may seem to skip from topic to topic as his feelings make connections different from those implicit in the situations. It is the client's present, momentary experiencing that is being symbolized. Of course, he often talks about the past, about external situations, or about himself in general. However, he is immersed in his immediate experiencing in this moment (perhaps concerning the past). From out of these present, immediate feelings he attempts to form the symbols of his communication. The counselor also attempts to express and help symbolize what the client feels and is *now*.

The therapist. We now describe the experiencing of the therapist as he participates in the client's becoming aware of his feelings.

The therapist listens and tries to understand. Then (by habit, but at first deliberately) he attempts to feel for himself sharply the "feel" of what the client is communicating. It may be the "feel" of what is being said, or it may be the "feel" of the whole experience of having the particular person with specific facial and tonal expressions saying what he now says. The therapist usually focuses in his own experiencing on *the "feel" of this present expression* of the client. At appropriate times, when the client has finished talking for the moment, the therapist will respond *from out of* this "feel" that has been forming while the client spoke.

By "*from out of*," we mean that while listening, the therapist does not usually have time to divide his attention enough to ask himself just how he would express or symbolize this feeling. Hence, he does this out loud, spontaneously, when he responds. The very same relationship usually exists between what we intend to say while speaking and what we do say. What we say arises for us *from out of* the as yet not articulate meaning we *feel* and are about to express.

This relationship between the verbally symbolized meaning and the feeling "from out of" which the meaning arises is crucial. We can observe this relationship from moment to moment in our experiencing; we speak and act from out of felt meanings. The therapist similarly is *guided* in his choice of words by *the feeling* which he has obtained in listening to what the client has expressed.

Sometimes the therapist cannot express the feeling. Then he probably responds, but expresses that he senses something he can't describe yet, or perhaps makes some reference to "this feeling that. . . ."

While listening, a therapist usually has a feeling that constitutes for him what he has gathered as the real *meaning to the client* of what the client has expressed. Of course, sometimes the therapist doesn't gather any such feeling. He doesn't understand what the client is communicating, or he hears only the words and does not sense how what is being said feels to the client.

At still other times the therapist believes that he has understood, yet it turns out that he really didn't understand. Usually, in such a case, the client will express himself again, and the therapist then will have both the feeling he had a moment ago, from which what he thought he understood had followed, and the feeling he has just got, which is different in some way, and from which something different follows. Thus, even misunderstanding and being corrected is an instance of this same relationship of a meaning following "from out of" a feeling.

To describe this experience further, let me describe how my own past experience functions in my understanding a client. Most of the time my own past experiences do not occur to me while I'm counseling. It is true that we understand people and things on the basis of our own past experience. But that is an explanation. When I counsel I do not usually think of my experiences. I follow and understand the client's. Once in a while I find myself thinking that his wife is like mine, or different, or that in some situation I felt as he now does; but these are stray thoughts when they occur, and are quickly gone again. My understanding of the client does not consist of memories. My understanding, and my words that express the understanding, rise out of a feeling. As I look at that feeling more closely, I find that what I understand "follows from out of" my felt sense of all that came before. For example, the individual is now describing his marriage. He describes various behaviors of his wife and himself and then says "and that gets me mad" (or perhaps I say it because his voice expressed it). Now, my "understanding" this feeling means that it seems to me to follow from my feel of the descriptions that came before it. If he had said, "She makes dinner for me every night," I would not have understood. (How can you get mad at that?) But if he had said, "She insists on making dinner *every* night," I would begin to feel some expectancy of being about to understand. I don't, as yet, of course, but he will go on expressing why. Meanwhile, I have a feeling of this emphasized "every." A multitude of things he might say would be understandable as following from the feeling that I now have. It is a vague feeling; I cannot predict from it what he will say. Furthermore, when he does continue, he will probably not feel anything I could have invented from the feeling I had. Rather, what he will continue to express will modify and define the feeling I had. For example, I may feel (though I don't have time to think all this explicitly) that something is rigid or monotonous about this "every." I may, half unaware, expect him to approach a feeling of that sort, and expect to find that the anger expressed in his voice was due to that. It may be that my own wife or myself are troublesome to me because of rigidity and that is why I half expect him to feel the same way. But at the next moment he may go on to say that "she's so damned perfect" and, even though this was not what I expected at all,

I can see how it follows from the preceding, and it somewhat clarifies my feeling of his anger. Again, and nearly always, I have a somewhat incomplete feeling from which further expressions will seem understandable, and which will be further and further modified.

Now, my own past experience can be said to make it possible for me to understand all these different relationships between feelings. But, if my own past experience itself stays in my mind, then it interferes, rather than helping understanding. For example, if, in the above, my own feeling about rigidity were really to occupy my present feeling, what the client said couldn't follow from it. I would know from his words that he didn't feel as I do, but I could not follow him in feeling.

In these observations I have tried to show that understanding and interpreting are processes chiefly consisting of felt meanings related to, and following, each other, and that explicit symbolization of them depends on these felt relationships.

It is often possible, especially if objective situations are involved, to understand that something follows, without having more of a feeling of it than the mere thinking it demands. ("The mere thinking it" is based on some felt meaning.) However, optimally, understanding the person depends on feeling this understanding in a broader way, collecting into one feeling mass the understandings of many expressions, allowing the mood and interaction of the person to be felt, as well as his verbal meanings. The broader this feeling mass is, the more understanding can arise, that is, the more of his expressions will be felt as capable of following "from out of" this feeling mass (with some modification of it at every step, of course).

For example, he may say, "She's so damned perfect," and the *present* voice quality, and perhaps some speeding up of his speech when I am about to say something, may give me a feeling that somehow *I* am being held off. Perhaps he is angry at me. Perhaps he feels that I want him to stay together with his wife and he isn't sure I'm willing to understand his not wanting to. Perhaps this or that, but I don't have time to think of all these possibilities. The peculiar total feeling of this moment is with me and is being modified, but from this broader total feeling many different things the client might say next would be understandable. For example, suppose he next says, "I know it's all my fault"—I shall then be ready to follow him in a search into his own faults, but I shall carry with me the feelings I just sensed, of resentment and of my possibly being included in it, and of anger at the seeming perfection of others, and—in the total of this feeling—many more nuances. Probably I will now respond in some way that reflects both his consideration of his own fault and something that has to do with understanding this from the total present feeling. Perhaps, given many more nuances of the actual situation, I will feel and therefore express: "You take some of the blame, but it makes you mad to think that it's all your fault." Although here, in my description, that doesn't seem to follow at all from the preceding, or to be in it, yet it or something like it would feel to me to be expressed in it, and would rise from out of the total feeling. Most often it would be at least *in the right direction* of the client's feeling and would enable him to express explicitly the feeling that in this moment underlay some of what he said. Most often this is a conversation, and only occasionally do I have the sense that I am not sure whether he feels something like what I sense he feels or whether it may be quite different. That is to say, only rarely am I guessing, and then I probably say so. Most often I feel as if I know what he feels. All the last modifications plus the next have been in line with, and have gone to make up, this feeling. His corrections and additions not only modify it but confirm some of it. The same is true in his view of me. He knows I understand, and, whatever feelings of surprise or liking or anger he may have about my understanding him, and however he might not be convinced that I do, yet each response of mine conveys to him the degree to which I do. And, since I respond to what he has just expressed, and not to something I divine or guess, it is not mysterious. Only the breadth of this understanding and the inclusion and focus on feeling is really very different from ordinary conversation.

In the second half of my description (the part about the therapist) I wanted to emphasize the role felt meaning plays in my understanding. The feeling that plays this role is essentially *vague* enough so that a vast number of possible things might be understandable *from it,* and so that it could be modified in this vast number of ways, but, at the same time, the feeling is definite enough and *confirmed* enough to be distinctly felt and to constitute a sense of definite knowing. These two sides (vague and definite) can be seen in the observation that I never know for sure what the other person will express next, but that when he does express something, it most often follows understandably from this feeling, no matter how surprising it might be in other respects.

Also, this description leads to the observation that feelings in this role are concretely experienced bases for understandings and are quite distinct from verbal and conceptual formulations that more or less adequately express this or that aspect of such a feeling. Often, for example, the client will listen to what he or I have just said, try to feel that, and compare it directly with the present feeling he was attempting to express. Then he may say: "Yes, that's just it; I've really said it there. I didn't know, while I was saying it, how true that is." Or, he may say: "Well, yes, but that's not quite it. I don't know why, but it's different." What he and I are really dealing with, throughout, are felt meanings, and the verbal symbols are relative and dependent on these.

In this chapter we have attempted to demonstrate *that* felt meaning functions in cognition, both as an ever-present experienced dimension of all meaning, and as specifically necessary functions on which many kinds of cognition depend.

Let us now turn to the question: *how* does felt meaning function in cognition?

How Felt

Meaning Functions

Brief
Statement

Chapter III formulates seven radically different modes in which felt meaning functions together with symbols. In each mode many different symbolizations are possible. The modes are not simply different symbolizations, but entirely different ways in which symbols and felt meaning may function together. They are seven different definitions of the role of "symbols" as well as seven roles of felt meaning.

Since "symbols" in this treatise includes anything that may have *the role of* a symbol (including things, persons, behaviors, and whatever), the reader is asked to keep in mind that the seven kinds of relationships between symbols and experiencing are really seven fundamental conceptual models in terms of which human phenomena can be considered by theory.

These different modes of relationship between experiencing and any events are not the result of *already logical* relationships. Rather, they are the modes by which meaning and logical order are first created. Thus, they are fundamental to all meaning, logic, and order in human phenomena.

These different modes do not reduce to each other and cannot be "reconciled" with each other. (That is to say, one can reconcile them by applying one to the other, but one may just as well apply the second

90

to the first. That shows that they remain and are fundamental.)

[A]
Parallel Functional Relationships of Felt Meaning in Cognition

a. Illustrations. Section A of this chapter considers those
functional relationships between felt meaning and symbols
which are called "parallel." These occur in cases where felt
meaning and symbols are in a parallel, one-to-one relationship. Later, we shall deal with another group of functional
relationships that are "nonparallel."

Of the "parallel" functional relationships, the first to be
considered is "direct reference." Let us cite some illustrations
of direct reference in order to communicate directly what is
meant by the term.

Consider the sentence: "Democracy is government by the
people." Now, note your experiencing in reading the words.
Probably you have taken the words in, felt that you know
some of their meaning. Probably, you did not pause to make
the meaning of democracy explicit to yourself in words.
Rather, the merely felt, implicit meaningfulness you experienced was sufficient for you to understand what was said
about democracy.

If you now try to define the term, you can observe what
you do. In attempting to define it, you concentrate on your
felt sense of its meaningfulness. Words to define it will arise,
as it were, from this act of concentration on the felt meaningfulness.

In some of these instances, you, the reader, *referred di-*

rectly to the felt meaningfulness that the term "democracy" had for you.

Consider this act of directly referring to the felt meaning. Let us call such an act "direct reference."

Other examples may aid you in performing the act of direct reference, so that you may then take our term "direct reference" to refer to that act. Here are some:

Consider the previously cited case when you have forgotten something—perhaps something you intended to do today. You know *that much* about it, that it was something to do (or a name, or fact, or theory, or whatever you happened to forget). Now, how do you go about trying to remember it? Whatever your own way of doing so is, you will find that it centers around your "feel" of the forgotten thing. You concentrate on that feeling. You relax, hoping that the feeling will open up into the awareness of what it is. You ask yourself, "Was it this?" "Was it that?" and the feeling lets you know that it was not what you proposed to yourself, or perhaps, with a great flood of relief, that indeed it was that. In all these cases, the feeling, although inexplicit, functions centrally in your attempt to remember. And—what for us here is the point to be illustrated—you allow this feeling to perform the described function by your "direct reference" to it as a feeling in your present experience.

The same "direct reference" can be illustrated in very many other cases. Consider one more. You are looking at a painting. It gives you a particular, unique feeling. When you are asked to comment on the painting, you probably will attempt to state in explicit form what this unique feeling is. You may or may not succeed in formulating it. However, even in trying to do, you will give the feeling itself your attention. You will "directly refer" to it as such.

These illustrations show that direct reference to implicit felt meaning is possible.

The term "direct reference" refers to this just illustrated act of referring to a felt meaning. In defining the term we also employed direct reference. Our defining consisted in showing how it illustrates itself. This is often the nature of starting points or principles, and it is precisely as a starting point that "direct reference" is important: Because felt meaning can be referred to directly, it can be a starting point. Because direct reference to felt meaning is a starting point, we may inquire into the relationships between the formal and the felt aspects of cognition, without forcing the presuppositions of either on the other.

b. Feeling as a referent. A referent is an object of reference. By "reference" we mean something very modest and do not wish to involve ourselves in the philosophic discussions implied in this term. We mean only that attention is given to the feeling as such.

In order to refer directly to felt meaning, some terms or symbols are necessary. We use symbols to give a feeling our attention. "This feeling," we say, or "this act" or "what I was going to do today"—these are symbols. These symbols *refer* in these cases directly to the feeling. Let us look at the *objects* to which symbolic reference is possible. Objects of reference can be things, or sense qualia, or thoughts, or—as in this case—feelings. The other sorts of objects of reference mentioned can, of course, be referred to. We are introducing a sense of the term "reference" in which feelings, as such, can be referred to.

It is important to make a special point of "direct reference" *to feelings,* because this might be confused with reference to that which the feelings perhaps stand for, or are caused by. For example, we attempted to refer to the felt meaningfulness that the term "democracy" has for the reader, and, in an analogous manner, to the feeling that contained the meaningfulness of looking at a painting, or to the felt meaningfulness of "what I was going to do today." We were *not* making the equally possible references to democracy as a social phenomenon or as a formal concept, or to the colors of the painting, or to the behavior "I would do today."

By "direct reference," then, we shall mean an individual's reference to a present felt meaning, not a reference to objects, concepts, or anything else[1] that may be related to the felt meaning itself.

1. The reader probably experienced the most difficulty with direct reference to feeling rather than something else in the case of observed sense qualia. Let us then go into more detail here.

In the last chapter we showed that all observation is meaningful and that this meaningfulness occurs to us as felt meaning. The meaningfulness of an observation of red or blue, for example, would thus occur to us as felt meaning. "Direct reference" is reference to this felt meaning.

Whitehead pointed out the error that, according to him, philosophy made in considering sense qualia (of the five senses) as the only "given" for knowledge. Whitehead speaks of the many, many organismic feelings that, as much as those of the five senses, are given for knowledge. The reader thus might grant immediately that what can be directly referred to includes such feelings. However, we asserted that there are such felt meanings even in the case of perceiving a color or some other sensible of the five senses. How can that be?

Let the reader ask himself how he perceives blue differently from red. The difference *to him,* qua his having these two experiences, is one of feeling. It lies neither in the eye nor in the wavelength.

Kant pointed out that even in the perception of a color, the inherent synthetic functions of cognition are already operative, since, if when we see red it is really to be red, not just something quite undifferentiated, then it must already imply the comparison of colors and hence the principle of unity of all cognitions as *our* cognitions, united or synthesized by *our having* them.

Kant defines "our having" them as a purely formal synthetic unity, expressed by his term "unity of apperception." His formal principles point out the function in cognition that, when we look at *our actually experienced having,* we find played by the distinct feel of any perception that is meaningful to us.

Only the reader's own referring, in his own experience, to the feel of perceptions, thoughts, and so on can define, for him, the type of feeling referred to in "direct reference." We mentioned Kant simply for better formal understanding. Kant only cites the function of "our having" experiences, insofar as this function is defined by a critical analysis of cognition, formally considered. This function might, in fact, be performed by anything. He is careful to distinguish the formal function from whatever is experienced as performing that function. We note that felt meaning can be referred to directly as performing this function.

c. The role of symbols in "direct reference." We have shown what "direct reference" is and that feelings can be objects of reference. Let us now examine more exactly the role played by symbols in the particular kind of relationship with feeling that we have termed "direct reference."

We have seen that symbols are necessary for direct reference. The words "this feeling" or "this act" or "what I was going to do today"—these are symbols. What is the peculiar role symbols have in "direct reference" that makes it a particular, distinguishable kind of relationship between feeling and symbols?

In order to clarify the particular role of symbols in direct reference, let us distinguish the role of directly referring from another role symbols may play: conceptualization (we might call it "representation" or "articulation"). Let us, for the moment, consider all manner of conceptualization as one kind of role of symbols, and compare it to their role in "direct reference." In direct reference, symbols (such as "this feeling") refer without conceptualizing or representing the felt meaning to which they refer. Thus the role of symbols in direct reference is distinguishable from other roles symbols can have, because in direct reference there need be no conceptualization at all.

For example, if one says "this feeling," or "what I wanted to do today that I forgot," the meaning of these symbols (that appeared in quotation marks) depends on the felt meaning to which we refer directly. Without that felt meaning the symbols still have a little bit of general meaning, but they are powerless to mean what—in this moment—they are supposed to mean. They depend for their meaning on direct reference to the felt meaning.

(The case is quite analogous to demonstratives. These always depend on present sense perception. In that case their meaning depends on "direct reference" to present sense perception.)

When symbols conceptualize or represent, they themselves "mean" what they represent. We might say that they mean *independently*. Symbols that only refer, on the other hand, *depend* for their meaning entirely on the felt meaning to which they refer.

Conversely, we may speak of the felt meaning in direct reference as being *independently* meaningful. This type of cognition is possible only because the felt meaning functions as an independently meaningful referent of direct reference. For example, "this feeling," or "I am trying to remember what I forgot to do today," or "let me see, what do I feel about the painting" would be impossible without our direct reference to felt meaning as a referent that is meaningful independently of any representative meaning of the symbols (although, of course, dependent on symbols as referring to it).

We have, then, made clear the sense in which the symbols "depend" on the felt meaning—that is the sense in which the felt meaning functions as an "independently" meaningful referent.

On the other hand, we also noted a sense in which the converse is true: the felt meaning can be referred to only with the aid of some symbols, such as the word "this" or some partially descriptive symbols such as "what I wanted to do today."

We note that the only necessary[2] role played by symbols in direct reference is that of referring, that is, of specifying, pointing out, setting off the felt meaning. "This feeling" or

2. The situation is slightly obscured by the fact that we often employ as a specifying marker just such symbols as come as close as possible to the felt meaning. For example, we say "what I wanted to do today, that I forgot." These symbols function in "direct reference" to help us to hang on to the felt meaning. Insofar as they do that, it is accidental that they also symbolize an explicit part of the felt meaning. If we happened to know nothing about the felt meaning, we would employ symbols such as "this feeling" and ask ourselves to concentrate on (that is, directly refer to) "this feeling" to discover what it is.

"a feeling" can occur only if something functions to refer to it, or specify it, or set it off, or mark it off.[3] Later we shall show how a feeling becomes independently meaningful just as soon as it becomes "this feeling" or "a feeling." By being specified as "this" or "a," it becomes repeatable, can return tomorrow and be the "same" feeling and can thus mean itself in many senses.

The referring or specifying need not be performed by a *verbal* symbol. The term "symbol" may be given to anything that performs the function of referring or specifying. (This is a usage of the term "symbol" defined specifically in terms of this one functional relationship, direct reference.) There are visual and kinaesthetic "symbols" and in this sense even actions, objects, and situations can be "symbols." [4] For direct reference, a "symbol" is anything that performs the function of marking off or specifying "a" feeling, and thus making our attention (our reference) to it possible.

Let us apply the name "direct reference" to the whole relationship between felt meaning and symbols, including the roles of both.

d. Direct reference as a functional relationship, and the

3. Throughout this study we shall speak in terms of relationships between feelings and symbols. Feelings will be said to perform certain functions, and similarly, symbols will be said to perform certain functions. Sometimes this terminology may make it appear that symbols are separate agents. We will do our best to avoid this impression by stressing that we are discussing functional relationships in which neither symbols nor feelings are separate. Another terminology might make this clearer: instead of ascribing "symbolic function" to symbols, it can be ascribed to experiencing. One can say that experiencing obtains a symbolic function by means of symbols. This terminology is equivalent to the one being used above. We shall continue to speak of the function of symbols, but this can always be viewed as the symbolic function of experiencing by means of symbols.

4. From now on we shall refer to this inclusive sense of "symbols" as "symbols in the widest sense." This will mean not only verbal and representative symbols, but also objects, acts, and anything that can specify *an* experience.

term "meaning" defined by it. We have noted that "direct reference" is a relationship between symbols and felt meaning, in which each has a role that depends on a role of the other. Hence, we can call these roles "functions" and the relationship a "functional relationship." We have seen the senses in which these functions depend on each other.

Without clear delineation of this functional relationship and interdependence, our analysis would have to duplicate everything. Everything would have to be said once for felt meaning and once for symbols. The symbols "refer" but so does our direct attention. The symbols "mean" the felt meaning, but the felt meaning is also a meaning and hence also "means." [5]

This duplication is avoided when the functions of each are specified and their interdependence is clarified. Without the symbols there cannot be "a" felt meaning, a specific reference, and hence there would be no specific felt meaning to refer to. On the other hand, without the felt meaning, symbols of the sort that only mark out and refer would have no symbolic function at all.

The term "meaning" must be defined for each functional relationship we discuss. For direct reference, what was meant by "meaning"? We note in the very form of the question that our definition will be a kind of examination of *how* we mean when we directly refer.

In "direct reference" we need a pointer in order to refer. We cannot assume that "a" feeling (some unity or reference in any sense) exists without something to mark it off and thus create it as "a" felt meaning. Hence, meaning appears to be generated by the two mutually dependent functions: the function of referring and marking off a referent (performed by symbols), and the function of being a meaningful referent

5. Some of the previously mentioned philosophers struggle mightily with this type of functional relationship between symbolic and felt meaning. Recall Sartre's "debased knowledge" (see Appendix).

with meaning independent of the representative meaning (if any) of the referring symbols.[6]

e. Direct reference as a "general" functional relationship. "Direct reference" is possible in all cases of meaning. It actually occurs only to the extent that the symbols depend for meaning entirely on felt meaning, and only point or refer to it. However, if we wish to, we may refer directly to our felt meaning even in cases where symbols do themselves mean the meaning. For example, take a sentence that symbolizes its meaning quite well: "Democracy is government by the people." Here, we are not normally called upon to refer directly to the felt meaning. Instead, we normally consider the symbols to contain the meaning. In order to become aware that in this case also, our felt meaning can be directly referred to, we must strain the normal experience. We must ask ourselves what we really meant by the word "democracy" or "government" or "people." Then we become aware of the felt meaning of these words for us, and in this becoming aware we "directly refer" to the felt meaning.

We may say with sureness, then, that direct reference is always possible, but it requires an extra willful act (reflection, it is often called) when the symbols appear to symbolize the meaning adequately.

It is apparent that whatever functional relationship normally exists between symbols and felt meaning in the case where symbols do adequately symbolize the meaning, it is a different functional relationship from that of "direct reference." We will have to examine it.

6. This account of the generation of meaning by two mutually dependent functions is not, of course, a satisfactory definition of meaning. Put another way, meaning in direct reference is felt meaning and is defined as that which is set off or marked off as in some sense "one," "a," or "this" referent. Still, we do not understand from this account how feeling is meaningful *by virtue of* being marked off or referred to. We must consider this question later, when we have other functional relationships with which to examine the question (see Chapter V).

f. "Direct reference" defined (a summary). Direct reference is a functional relationship between symbols and felt meaning. The functions of symbols and felt meaning depend on each other. *Symbols function* as markers, pointers, or referring tools that create "a," "this," or "one" feeling by referring to "it." *Felt meaning functions* as containing the meaning (independently of any representative meanings the referring symbols might have), and as referent.

The symbols depend on the felt meaning for meaning. Apart from direct reference to felt meaning, the symbols mean nothing. The felt meaning, thus, has a vital and independent function. It is independently meaningful. There is no meaning in cases of direct reference except its meaning.

The felt meaning depends on symbols to mark it off as a referent. Apart from such a marking off (specification or symbolization defined as a marking off) there is no given felt meaning. Hence, the function of the symbols is also vital.

The function of "symbol" in the sense of direct reference can be performed not only by verbal symbols, but also by kinaesthetic symbols, visual symbols, and by acts, objects, or situations, since these also can "mark off" or specify and thus create "a" given felt meaning.

2. RECOGNITION

a. Description of recognition. Let us turn now to a second, different functional relationship between symbols and felt meaning. It is different in that symbols and felt meaning respectively perform roles different from those examined in direct reference. Thus, there will result different senses of the terms "symbol," "symbolized," "specified," and "meaning."

"Recognition" refers to the case where symbols adequately conceptualize. As was direct reference, recognition is also a "parallel" functional relationship, that is, symbol and felt meaning are in a parallel, one-to-one relationship with each other. What are their functions or roles in recognition?

Let us begin with the case where the symbols exist alone first, as in a page of print that we are about to read. As we read it, the symbols *call forth in us* the felt meanings that constitute our having of the meanings of the symbols, that is our understanding of what is printed on the page. Hearing, reading, or thinking familiar symbols includes—for us—not only the symbols, but also the felt meaning they call forth in us.

(Later we shall discuss the genesis of "familiar" symbols. For the moment we are discussing "recognition," which concerns only such symbols as already are for us in a one-to-one relationship with certain felt meanings in the sense that they call forth these felt meanings when we meet the symbols.)

We do not usually explicate familiar symbols. We say "*they* mean" what they mean to us. However, *they mean,* in that *they call forth* the felt meaning. We hear or see or think them, and in that act feel their meaning.

Let us call the felt meaning aroused by the symbols "recognition feeling," or simply "recognition." We do not mean the feeling *that* we are recognizing something (which is usually absent) but the feeling that constitutes the meaning for us. We recognize the felt meaning, not the recognizing. (It is not like meeting an old, long-lost friend, and being struck by the fact that we recognize him. It is like meeting someone whom we meet every day. We are not surprised at our felt knowing who he is.)

b. Function of symbols and feeling. Here, then, is another *functional relationship* between symbols and felt meaning.

The symbols here have "meaning" in the sense that they function to *call forth* in us the felt meaning.

The felt meaning is capable of being called forth by something that functions as a symbol. Its function is that it *consti-*

tutes our having of the meaning. Without it, symbols would be mere sounds or objects and we would have no meaning.

In this functional relationship, the dependence of symbols and feeling is the reverse of what we found in direct reference. In recognition the symbols appear to mean *independently*. As we noted, we commonly say that *they* (the symbols) mean. This kind of cognition can occur only because the symbols have the power to mean, that is, to call forth recognition feeling. The symbols have this power even apart from the presence of felt meaning. Close the book and open it tomorrow; the symbols will then do their work again. In direct reference the case was reversed. The symbols, "this feeling," mean a felt meaning only while they are employed in direct reference to that feeling. If that feeling disappears, the symbols have no power to bring it back. Hence, in direct reference, the symbols' power to mean depended upon the independent meaningfulness of the feeling, while in recognition the very occurrence of the felt meaning depends upon the independent power of the symbols to call it forth.

c. "Recognition" as a functional relationship, and terms defined by it. Again, it is important to note that the analysis will have to duplicate everything unless recognition is considered as a relationship of interdependent functions of symbols and feeling, respectively. The symbols "mean" what they conceptualize or represent. The felt meaning, however, is our having of their meaning. For example, the discovery that we often behave on the basis of felt meaning is sometimes treated, in psychology, as if symbolized meanings and cognition operated on an unconscious level below cognition. A second analysis of cognition is read into felt meaning "below" symbolic operations. This kind of duplication becomes unnecessary if it is clear that symbols perform the function of calling forth felt meaning, and that felt meaning constitutes our having of meaning or our subjective experience of meaning. Without either function, the other becomes impossible or senseless.

Again, we may define the terms "symbols," "symbolize," and "meaning" precisely for this one functional relationship, "recognition":

Symbols, when presented to us, *call out* felt meanings in us (provided we "know" the symbols). Thus, anything functions as a symbol that is meaningful when "presented to us." For example, a situation can be a symbol in this sense of the term. We enter a situation, orient ourselves in it, and apprehend some of its meaning to us. It can do this without our making its meaning to us explicit in words, or even in other symbols. The situation itself *calls forth* in us the felt meanings (recognition feelings). Hence, it functions as a symbol.

Ordinary sense perception is usually a case of recognition feeling. We see a tree, or we see brown, or we see a shape. "Oh," we say, "that's brown." Or we don't even say that. The recognition feeling is simply called forth and is the meaning to us of what we perceive.

All observation is of this sort. Very little of what we meaningfully observe is put into other explicit symbols. Most of it is experienced by us purely as recognition feeling.

We can say, therefore, that not only verbal symbols but also familiar objects, people, situations, *call forth* recognition feeling.[7] Or, if we prefer a different terminology, we can say that not only artificial symbols but also natural symbols (usually called signs) can *call forth* recognition feeling. Symbolic

---

7. Notice that we found also in the case of direct reference that the function defined as "symbolic" could be performed by things, situations, persons, and acts, as well as by verbal symbols. For direct reference, this function was the setting apart or pointing out as "a" "one" feeling. Things, acts, persons, and situations, as well as verbal symbols, can perform these symbolic functions. In this study, the term "symbol in the widest sense" will be employed to include all these nonverbal kinds of symbols. Note that "symbol in the widest sense" includes persons, situations, things, acts, and words, but does not state whether the definition of "symbol" is that of direct reference, or that of recognition, or a definition connected with still other functional relationships.

function is here defined as "calling forth recognition feeling." This function is performed not only by verbal symbols, but also by things. This has been noted by those who have said that human experience is always symbolic and meaningful.

Of course, we ourselves may "present" symbols or situations to ourselves. That is thought! At least, it is thought seen from the viewpoint of recognition feeling. It is that side of thought called "internal speech," but even symbols we present to ourselves are not always words. Therefore, there can be nonverbal thought. Recognition is that side of thought in which meaning depends on symbols presented and these, in turn, call forth the feeling of what they mean.

We have defined "symbol" and "symbolized" for the functional relationship recognition. Let us define the term "meaning" for that relationship:

A "meaning," for this functional relationship, is a recognition feeling that is capable of being called forth. Something is said to have a meaning if it can call forth a recognition feeling. This recognition feeling is then said to be its meaning.

This definition of "meaning" is the one most widely used. It applies best to the common words of our language and sentences and arguments composed of them, and to familiar situations, actions, and things. Many difficulties in science and philosophy result, however, if this definition of "meaning" is made the only one. In other functional relationships, the definition of "meaning" is different.[8]

8. *Comparison to direct reference:* We have been urging that definitions made in connection with different functional relationships be kept clearly separated. Let us note, however, that interesting, if somewhat complex, results are found if definitions from one functional relationship are applied to another. We could, for example, now look back to direct reference and explain "meaning" as it appeared there by using its definition in recognition. Thus, we could say that as soon as a feeling is generated (made "a" feeling) by direct reference, it becomes capable of also being "such" a feeling, that is, capable of being repeated; in other words, once pointed out as "a" feeling, it has identity and therefore could, in principle, be *called forth* again. However, we must remember that if it is really to be

d. "Recognition" defined (a summary). Recognition is a functional relationship between symbols and felt meaning. The functions of symbols and felt meaning depend upon each other.

Symbols function to call forth in us the felt meaning.

Felt meaning functions as the meaning to us of the symbols. Without it, not only would symbols have no meaning, but we would not be able to think or observe meaningfully.

Symbols (in the sense defined here as calling forth felt meaning) have their power to call forth independently of the presence or absence of the felt meaning.

---

called forth, it will require symbols that will perform for it this particular symbolic function of calling forth. In direct reference there are no such symbols. The feeling (as soon as it is "a" or "this" feeling) could be related to such symbols, but in direct reference it is not related to such symbols. Since we are discussing definitions of "meaning," we note that it could now be argued whether "meaning" is the being referred to as "a" feeling, or whether it is really already the capacity of being called forth repeatedly, Instead of such an argument, however, we may simply note that the respective definitions of "meaning" are associated with two different functional relationships. (Later we may consider the implications of the fact that, when referred to, a felt meaning is already such that—in another functional relationship with symbols—it might also be called forth repeatedly.)

We note then, that recognition and the definition of "meaning" associated with it could be applied to direct reference. Similarly, direct reference, although it does not always occur, *could* occur in all cases of recognition. We can always—if we wish—refer directly to the felt meaning called forth by a symbol. (We did that, for example, when we said, "Now let me see what I mean by the word 'democracy.'") Thus, both recognition and direct reference can be (but need not be) applied to all cases of recognition. For this reason we can call them "general" functional relationships. Direct reference can occur prior to the existence of any symbols that have the capacity to call it forth. Even while a person says "this feeling," he is in danger of losing the specificity of the feeling and if he does, he has nothing with which to call it forth again and may never be able to do so. The function of symbols and felt meaning in direct reference is different from that found in recognition. Their respective dependence on each other is also different in the two cases. The two functional relationships we have so far discussed are clearly different, although once we define terms adequate to one, these terms can be applied to the other.

The felt meaning depends for its occurrence on the function of the symbols.

The function of a "symbol" (to call forth a felt meaning) may be performed by situations, things, persons, and actions, as well as by verbal symbols.

3. EXPLICATION

a. Description of "explication." In discussing recognition we have been speaking of symbols as presented to us first. Felt meaning was called out in us by symbols and did not occur unless symbols performed this function. However, felt meaning, once it is called forth, can itself be prior to other symbols that can explicate the felt meaning.

For example: I enter a situation that is meaningful to me, that is, it calls forth some felt meaning in me. I may wish to explicate this felt meaning in words and may, as yet, have formed no such words. The situation here performed the symbolic function discussed in recognition, in that it called forth the felt meaning. This felt meaning ("symbolized" already by the situation that called it forth)[9] will now be further symbolized by the symbols that will *explicate* it. "Explication" involves functions of symbols and felt meanings differing from their functions in direct reference and in recognition.

Another example: A dramatist endeavors to portray on stage a particular type of human interaction. He expresses this to himself in verbal symbols and they call out in him the felt meaning. He now sets about finding further symbolization of this felt meaning in terms of situations capable of being acted on stage.

Take, as another example, any familiar term such as "democracy." The term calls out in me (and thus "symbolizes") the felt meaning. I "know what it means," and that is sufficient

9. Note again this "widest sense" of the term "symbol," in which situations can function as symbols. Compare footnote 4, above.

if I am reading, thinking, or speaking about democracy. On the other hand, I may wish to define it. In that case, I must let the symbol "democracy" call forth in me the recognition feeling, and then I must find further symbols to explicate that same recognition feeling.

As Peirce pointed out, symbols follow upon symbols endlessly in this way. However, felt meaning functions in each transition! We have seen (in discussing recognition) how felt meaning functions as called out by symbols. The felt meaning functions, as we shall now see, to *select* the further symbols that *explicate* it. Without bringing home to oneself the felt meaning of a term, such as democracy, one cannot define it. The verbal sound alone could not lead directly to other verbal sounds that define "democracy." The dramatist could not creatively imagine a situation to further explicate something without allowing the felt meaning itself to function as we shall now describe.

b. The roles of felt meaning and of symbols in explication. When we begin with a felt meaning (it may be the recognition feeling of some symbol) and seek further symbolization, the proper symbols "come to us." More exactly, we concentrate on the felt meaning itself (thus employing direct reference) and as a result of this concentration upon it, symbols present themselves. The exact process through which this occurs is not well understood, but may be explained in various ways. Our concern here is the relationship of the functions of felt meaning and of symbols in this process. In explication, the feeling has the independent power to be meaningful and to select the symbols. Our term "select" is metaphorical. It suggests that the feeling goes through a card file of all known symbols and selects the correct ones. Another way of metaphorically picturing the process is to speak of symbols associated with (as if they were tied to) feelings. In whatever way this process is pictured, in it one refers directly to a felt meaning which then functions in the process. Without this function of the felt meaning, no further symbolization takes place.

The symbols function to express, delineate, explicate, represent, conceptualize (other words are equally descriptive) the felt meaning.

The function of feeling in explication is quite characteristic and different from its function in direct reference or in recognition. The function of symbols here is to be selected. In that sense they are quite dependent on the feeling. As soon as they appear, however, they are recognition symbols, that is, they now have the power in turn to call out the felt meaning that just selected them.

We are describing both explication and recognition as if there were a time lag. First one feels, then the symbols appear, then these symbols can, in turn, call out the felt meaning that selected them. However, in cases where we well know the symbols, there is almost never a time lag. We no sooner have the feeling than we have the symbols and vice versa. One is almost tantamount to the other. (Later, we will consider the many cases in which no symbols known to the individual exist that immediately symbolize the feeling. Similarly, we are leaving for later the reverse cases in which the symbols are new to the individual and he must work for some time with them in order to obtain a felt meaning for them.)

It was clear what we meant by "meaning," when we spoke of "recognition." We meant that the symbols call forth felt meaning. Now we ask what is meant by "meaning" when a felt meaning is "explicated."

Just as in our other discussions, if we lost sight of the functional relationship we would duplicate everything. We would have to say that there are two felt meanings: (a) the felt meaning to be explicated, and (b) the felt meaning that is the meaning of the symbols we are using—their recognition. When we explicate, we listen to the symbols and if their recognition feeling is really the same as the felt meaning we attempt to explicate, then we consider these symbols as explicating it. If not, then we say, "That's not quite what I mean," and we begin again.

This duplication does indeed occur often. It occurs when one refers directly to a felt meaning and when no adequate symbols are available. But, this is not yet our case. (We will discuss this case later.) Our case is that in which adequate symbols *are* available. It is for that case that we wish to explain what makes symbols "adequate" to explicate a felt meaning. In that case, we don't experience such a duplication. When asked what we mean by such a word, or how a certain situation was, or what we saw, or whatever—we simply say or think what it was, in words.

After we have "explicated," we are just where we were in the case of recognition. We have symbols, and their recognition feeling is our felt meaning. What is more, recognition feelings are already related to certain symbols in the functional relationship we called "recognition." Hence, for explication, the "recognition" relationship must already obtain. Explication depends upon a prior functional relationship (recognition) between certain symbols and certain felt meanings, such that the former can call out the latter. "Explication" is that same relationship, except that the latter calls out the former.

Obviously there are many cases where such a functional relationship does not already exist! Such cases will be examined in the next section.

Provided that this functional relationship already exists, explication adds the further and different functional relationship of a felt meaning selecting the symbols that explicate it. These will be those symbols whose recognition feeling is the felt meaning being explicated.

A note on our definitions of "meaning." We found that "meaning" had to be defined in terms of various functional relationships between symbol and feeling. Since there are a great many other definitions of "meaning" offered by philosophy, why choose this sort of definition?

"Meaning" is defined in this study in terms of functional relationships, because these relationships state the respective functions of feeling and symbol that allow feeling and symbols to "mean." Feelings are "felt meanings" only insofar as they function in such a relationship with symbols. So functioning, their functions are found to be necessary for symbols to "mean." Symbols and felt meanings are really only possible in such relationships. Apart from them, it is not clear what a "symbol" is, nor can we call feeling "felt meaning." Necessarily, therefore, such a functional relationship defines "meaning." It states the functions because of which symbols are meaningful and feelings are felt meaning. These functions must be stated in a "functional relationship" since they depend on each other. If there are several different such functions for symbols and for feeling, then there are several functional relationships and several definitions of "meaning."

A comparative summary of the functional relationships so far discussed. The striking characteristic about "direct reference" was that the symbols themselves, as such, do not mean what direct reference employs them to mean. There the feeling does all the meaning and the symbols only point to the feeling. Recognition is the opposite case: the symbols appear to "mean" in themselves. That is the case in which symbols exist in a functional relationship such that they call forth a felt meaning we named "recognition feeling." Here, symbols depend on felt meaning only in the sense that felt meaning constitutes *our having* the meaning. It is the symbols that arouse the felt meaning, and it is the symbols that continue to function as having the meaning, in the sense precisely, of calling it forth. We moved from that functional relationship to a further one by asking: what if the felt meaning—although called forth by some meaningful experience—is to be explicated further by other symbols? This we found to be a twofold question: either there immediately are adequate symbols already existing in a recognition relationship with the felt meaning, or there are not. If there are, then these symbols select and "mean" the felt meaning immediately, and the previously established recognition relationship is re-established. If there are not, then many questions are raised, which will follow.

Table 1 (p. 112) is a diagram of our analysis so far.

[B]
Creative Functional Relationships ("Specific," Nonparallel")

This half of the chapter deals with functional relationships between felt meaning and symbol, where these are not parallel, that is, where felt meaning does not function simply as the ever-present, general, felt, other side of the coin of all symbolization. Instead, symbols that are already meaningful in the parallel ways described, now enter into a further relationship with a felt meaning that does not have parallel symbols. We thus have a relationship between a partly unsymbolized felt meaning and symbols that usually mean something else (their old meaning, which they already have prior to this new relationship).

What was just said applies to at least two different functional relationships:

1. Symbols that already have parallel felt meaning are put

Table 1. General functional relationships of felt meaning and symbols

FUNCTIONAL RELATIONSHIP	DEPENDENCE OF SYMBOLS AND IN- DEPENDENCE OF FELT MEANING	INDEPENDENCE OF SYMBOLS AND DE- PENDENCE OF FELT MEANING
1. Direct Reference	Symbols do not "mean," only point	Symbols are needed to point or specify a feeling
	Felt meaning re- ferred to directly	Cannot attend to a feeling without refer- ence with pointing symbols
	Maximal	Minimal
"Meaning"	Felt only	
2. Recognition	Felt meaning is needed if symbols are to have mean- ing to us	Felt meaning must be called forth by symbols
	Minimal	Maximal
"Meaning"		The symbols "mean" because they can "call forth" the felt meaning
3. Explication Where adequate symbols exist	Depend on felt mean- ing to select them	Mean the meaning as such, once selected
"Meaning"	Felt, but found to have symbols that "mean it" because they already are related as in (2)	
Other functional relationships: where adequate symbols do not exist.		

together in such a way that a new felt meaning is *created and symbolized* by them. This occurs to some extent in all creative thought, problem solving, therapy, and literature. Its epitome is a metaphor. We shall call this functional relationship "metaphor," using that term to include not only similes and the like, but also all creation and symbolization of new felt meaning.

2. A felt meaning is always *partly* unsymbolized. It can "select" more symbols, and more aspects of it can be symbolized. However, when no parallel symbols are already available to be selected, a new vehicle of symbolization must be created. A metaphor creates a new vehicle of symbolization along with a new meaning. In this second case, however, we already have the felt meaning and seek to further symbolize it. Hence this given felt meaning acts as arbiter of the symbols we use. We listen to them and then feel either that we did, or that we did not, say *what we meant*. Hence, novel symbolization has at least these two sides: let us call the creation of a new meaning (by symbols that thus also newly symbolize it) "metaphor," and let us call the case where a largely unsymbolized felt meaning functions to create a new symbolization *of it* "comprehension."

1. METAPHOR

a. Description. A metaphor achieves a new meaning. It does this by drawing on old experience and by using symbols that already have some other, old familiar meaning. Metaphors differ from ordinary meaningful symbols in that they do not simply refer—as ordinary symbols do—to their habitual felt meaning. Rather, the metaphor applies the symbols and their ordinary felt meaning to a new area of experience, and thereby creates a new meaning, and a new vehicle of expression.

A metaphor, then, contains two relationships between an "old" and a "new": (1) some old (past) experience is affected so that a new felt meaning emerges from it, and (2) old symbols and their meanings are employed in a new way to conceptualize the new meaning.

If we say that the symbols "symbolize" the new meaning, we must be careful to remember that this word "symbolize" has here quite an ambiguous sense. After all, the symbols already symbolize their old meaning. "A red, red rose" symbolizes just that. Yet, when the poet says that "My love's like a red, red rose," what is *newly* symbolized is "symbolized" in quite a different manner than was the old meaning. Our question is: in what manner and in what sense of that word do the metaphoric[10] symbols "symbolize" the *new* meaning? In what relationship do these symbols and their old meaning stand to the new meaning?

Our question about "symbolization" is both about the old and new roles of symbols and about the old and new aspect of experience. How can the symbols (which have an old meaning) now refer to and "symbolize" a new meaning? How does our past experience as called forth by the term "my love is . . ." come to have a new aspect? What is the "new" that now happens to this old "past experience," when it is said that it is like a "red, red rose"?

We are already accustomed to the functional correspondence of symbols and felt meaning. Hence, we need only point out the functional correspondence in this case, to avoid possible confusions of experience (old or new aspects) as apart from symbols (old and new meaning.) The symbols have a new meaning *as* they mean the new aspect of experience. The aspect of experience brought forth by the metaphor is brought forth *by the metaphor*.

Hence, our two questions (the question about the new meaning of already meaningful symbols and the question about a new aspect of old "past experience") both refer to the *one* new meaning that a metaphor means.

How does "past *experience*" obtain a new aspect? How

10. Recall that by "metaphoric" we refer to the creation of a new felt meaning and a new symbolic vehicle. It thus includes the simile in our examples, as well as the many nonpoetic instances of the creation of new meaning.

are old, already meaningful *symbols* employed so as to have a new meaning? To put both questions together: what relation is there between the new aspect of experience and the symbols that, when they are alone, mean something old? What is the new sort of "symbolization" between the symbols "a red, red rose" and the *new* aspect of the old experience: "my love"? This will be the particular definition of "symbolization" in the case of metaphor. It depends on the emergence of a new aspect of experience from past experience. Also, it depends on already meaningful symbols' being capable of a new meaning.

Metaphor involves the functional relationships we have already discussed, and is more complex than these. Let us look at the role of "recognition" and "direct reference" in metaphor:

b. The role of recognition and direct reference in metaphor. We have pointed out that the symbols of the metaphor have *two* different felt meanings—the old one, in general use, and the new one, in the metaphor. The old, felt meaning of the symbols is that of recognition. The symbols "mean" because they call forth a felt meaning. With the metaphor we turn to a new, higher order. A new kind of relationship of "symbolization" is established—now no longer between a felt meaning and symbols, but between a complex of felt meaning and symbols on the one hand, and some new felt meaning on the other. This is the well-known peculiar characteristic of metaphors. Words that are already meaningful can, in a particular metaphor, mean something new, which they again cease to mean if taken out of that metaphor.

The old meaning of the (predicate) symbols is *called forth* by them as a felt meaning ("is like a red, red rose").

The different area of experience is also *called forth* by the symbols of the subject of the metaphor ("my love"). Both are felt meanings. They are masses of felt experience that, so far, are not further differentiated or explicated.

The act of referring the old symbols (and their old felt meaning) to the mass of experience of the other area results in the emergence of a new aspect of this mass of experience.

The old, already meaningful symbols are the metaphorical symbolization of the *new aspect* of experience because they are made to refer to this other area of experience.

Each time they are referred to this partly undifferentiated mass of experience of the other area, they result in the emergence of this (more or less same)[11] new aspect of it.

They "symbolize" this new aspect of experience by creating it anew when so referred.

This symbolization, then, depends on two called-forth felt meanings, on "direct reference" to one of them by the symbols of the other, and on the creation of a new meaning therein.

We have stated the relationship between old and new experience, and between old and new meaning of symbols, as well as the relationship of metaphoric symbolization between the new experience and the new meaning of symbols.

Two questions remain open:

1. How does the reference of old symbols to a different area of experience result in giving it a new aspect?

2. (a) What governs the aspect that will emerge? (b) Can we offer logical[12] principles for this creative referring relationship between the old meaning of the symbols and the new aspect which they now create and mean?

Question 1 is a question about the experienced creative process.

11. One does not create *exactly* the same new meaning each time the metaphor occurs, that is, each time the symbols are applied to this not fully differentiated mass of experience. For this reason, for example, one can read a poem many times and obtain different meanings.

12. The term "logical" in this treatise refers to relationships that are purely between concepts and not mediated by functions of felt meaning.

Question 2 is about the logical relationship or logical determination of the newly created meaning.

2. COMPREHENSION

a. Examples. At the start of Section B we said that novel creation of symbolic relationships could begin either with symbols [(1), metaphor] or with a felt meaning [(2), comprehension].

We could make our transition from "metaphor" to "comprehension" with the following consideration. "Metaphor," the creation of a new felt meaning as well as a new symbolization, really occurs only when one reads or hears a metaphor. On the other hand, the poet himself is in a different position. He is quite likely to have the felt meaning *before* he invents the metaphor. (If it comes to him accidentally as he plays with words, he is, of course, simply in the position of a reader.) Let us say that our poet has a felt meaning or many felt meanings, and wishes to symbolize them. No extant symbols exactly mean his felt meaning. Hence, he seeks to put symbols together in a new way so that these symbols will create that experience in a reader, or in himself qua reader. When he succeeds, he cries out, "Yes, that's exactly what I mean!" To invent a metaphor to express a prior felt meaning is "comprehension."

While reading a metaphor, we experience the new meaning. However, if someone asks us to explain or explicate exactly what the metaphor means, we are then in somewhat the position of the poet. We must find new and different symbols for the felt meaning, which—so far—we have symbolized only metaphorically. Hence, to specify the (usually many) meanings in a metaphor is also a case of what we are calling "comprehension."

Felt meaning functions in this way (comprehension)

throughout psychotherapy, where a client seeks to express his as yet unsymbolized experiences and feelings. A therapist listens to many words, all of which are already meaningful; then he usually shares, although vaguely, the client's feelings and proceeds to symbolize them: he will ask, "Is it such and such and so and so?" trying his hand at finding new symbolization for the feeling. Both persons often struggle quite a while, both feeling the felt meaning concerned and seeking by many words, by metaphors, to symbolize it. It is important to the client that the feeling be symbolized exactly accurately. Classification usually won't do. His experience is exactly this, such and so. Only an accurate new symbolization of it feels to him as the expression of *his* experience.[13] And it makes much difference to a person that his felt experience stands in such a direct relationship to objective symbols. For reasons of great importance to psychology, this new symbolic relationship (which one's feelings may or may not acquire) allows a process of change in these feelings to occur. At any rate, comprehension is a direct relationship of this person's feelings to new symbols. It is not a mere *knowing about* himself *that* he feels a certain class of feelings. Comprehension is a *direct* relationship between feelings and symbols.

One needn't go to therapy for examples of "comprehension." Every report of an experience by the person who had it is "comprehension." We do not have many symbols that exactly call forth in another person an experience we had. Usually we have to create new symbolic vehicles, at least to some extent, to talk about our experience.

Much art is "comprehension," although not always by verbal symbols. Many descriptions of works of art are "comprehension," as we have already said. Such descriptions seek

13. He experiences these feelings moving, flowing, changing, becoming livelier. Hence, the well-known difference between "intellectualized" knowledge, and direct relations between feelings and symbols. See also Chapter VII.

to further symbolize the felt meaning created by the work of art.

b. Comprehension delineated. Comprehension (as was metaphor) is a relationship between felt meaning, on the one hand, and a complex of symbols related to their (usual) felt meanings on the other. When we seek a symbolic expression for a felt meaning, we work with extant symbols. We experience the usual felt meanings called forth by these symbols. Our putting these usual felt meanings together, metaphorically creates a new meaning. However, "metaphor" now is only a part of the process. The felt meaning that we wish to symbolize is chiefly active. It *selects*[14] symbols, as we say. Since there are no exact symbols for it extant, we are likely to make many false starts and say many things that we don't quite mean. As we hear them, we say, "No, that isn't exactly what I mean," or "No, that's only part of it," or "No, it's sort of like that, but not quite." All through this process the felt meaning to be symbolized functions both as selector and as arbiter. We concentrate on (*directly refer* to) this felt meaning and words come to us (*explication*). The felt meaning also enables us to feel whether these words succeeded or failed to symbolize it (arbiter). Only when the felt meaning of the words we used is identical with the felt meaning as we had it do we feel that our meaning has been expressed. At that moment there are not two different felt meanings, that of the words and that which we wish to symbolize. They are identical and symbolized.

Since we wish to distinguish comprehension from metaphor, we described comprehension as if the given felt meaning, which is being symbolized, did not change at all throughout this process. In fact we cannot say that it does not change. Even if we feel that what we finally symbolized is exactly what we meant, it may have changed in the process. Often we

14. See "Explication," Section A, 3, above.

do feel that it has changed. We say, "I didn't really see this about it until I tried to express it." It changes because it interacts with the felt meanings of already meaningful symbols. Insofar as change occurs, the functional relationship of metaphor applies to it. On the other hand, metaphor could not cover instances of comprehension, because in the latter we seek to symbolize what we *already* feel as an experienced meaning. Yet aspects of it, which we did not know it had, do come to light. By the time we say exactly what we meant, it isn't quite the same; it is richer, more explicit, more fully known.[15] We use symbols not only to tell others what we mean; we tell ourselves. The process of "thought" consists of many more felt meanings called forth by any symbol, as these again interact and create (metaphorically) more meanings for us. Such a process occurs also in comprehension and brings about change and development of the felt meaning.

In one important sense, then, the resulting symbolization *does* symbolize the *original* felt meaning. In another sense it specifies it, adds to it, goes beyond it, or reaches only part of it—in short, *changes* it. We are concerned with just this double sense: it somehow accurately symbolizes the original felt meaning while at the same time it somehow also changes it.

We call this kind of symbolization "comprehension." This term puns a dual meaning, which corresponds to the two-sidedness:

1. Only through such a process of specifying aspects and telling ourselves what we mean can we *comprehend* and experience meaning. An idea that comes to us as "Oh-ho, I think I've got something," is a mere feeling, remembered as nothing more than "Yesterday I thought I had it, but then somebody came in and interrupted me." It is necessary for us to symbolize and explicate in order to comprehend what we mean.

15. See Merleau-Ponty in the Appendix, also our section on "Psychotherapy," Section B, 3, Chapter II.

2. Comprehension is a process in which the product some-how includes or *comprehends* the original felt meaning, but is not any longer identical with it.

The term comprehension, then, reminds us that in order to understand ("comprehend") we must encompass ("compre-hend") the original felt meaning, by means of many more meanings.

To encompass with many more meanings is to change, to specify, to form aspects, to create—as well as to stay true to —the original.

Because of this two-sidedness, it is possible to "compre-hend" a given felt meaning in *many* ways, rather than in one way. A given experience can be explicated, communicated, specified into aspects, exemplified, in many many ways, and in each way, although somewhat differently, the experience will be accurately symbolized.

In therapy, for example, one counselor may habitually employ spatial images, another situational ones. One coun-selor may habitually see feelings as pressures and counterpres-sures; another may see them as qualities and savored tastes, another as aspects of a person in respect to situations. Any of the three can help a client symbolize any feeling he has. The words would be very different, yet the counselor could create a formulation in his own language to which the client would, with relief, say, *"That's exactly it."* This doesn't mean that nothing can be wrong. On the contrary, everything ex-cept a correct, accurate symbolization is wrong. But there are many possible exactly accurate symbolizations!

The reader may now feel that "comprehension" is chiefly a question of "illustrations" and will grant that there can be many illustrations of something. But consider how illustra-tions work. Just in this way! They concretize; they symbolize; they select and specify certain aspects of what is to be illus-trated. The illustration symbolizes what was previously inexplicit. It can do so accurately, yet not exactly in the same way as another illustration.

When illustrations are employed to symbolize a felt meaning, it is clear that there can be a great variety of symbolizations. Much would be relative to the illustration chosen, not essential to the felt meaning. Yet that would be a price worth paying for having a symbolization at all, and an accurate one. Thus, illustrations are often cases of "comprehension."

A spatial metaphor for this situation would be the fact that one can communicate a square as two triangles, four triangles, two rectangles, other rectangles, four squares, a hexagon and six triangles, and so on, and it will always *accurately* communicate the square.

The metaphor of the square was designed by the writer as a "comprehension" of—and it may be for the reader a creation of—the experienced meaning that although the several formulations may each involve aspects that are more specific than necessary, there are many ways of symbolizing *exactly* the intended meaning (the square).

Richard McKeon describes a relationship between different valid philosophies, to which "comprehension" also applies.[16] Assuming that nonsubstantive problems (those due merely to peculiarities in the nature of a philosophical method) are eliminated, still, different methods render the "same" substantive experiential facts differently not in the sense that some do it truly and some falsely, but that each can do it differently and truly. If all methods could be reduced, ultimately, the truths of different philosophies would all be the same, but that seems not to be possible. Each formulation gives its own peculiarities to what it formulates. It "comprehends" rather than represents the experiences that it symbolizes.

16. Richard McKeon, *Freedom and History* (New York: The Noonday Press, 1952), Chap. II; "Philosophy and Method," *The Journal of Philosophy*, Vol. XLVIII, No. 22 (October 25, 1951).

c. The functional relationship of "comprehension." A given felt meaning, which is only partly "symbolized," is given (further) symbolic formulation or formulations. The formulation(s) accurately symbolize(s) the given felt meaning.

In the process of comprehension, the given felt meaning is *directly referred* to, and *selects* many different possible symbols.

The given felt meaning, directly referred to, also functions as *arbiter* of the accuracy or inaccuracy of a possible formulation.

The formulation is created from a system of symbols that does not yet contain symbols that mean the given felt meaning.

Hence, new symbolic vehicles are created. This involves a metaphoric process of referring symbols and their felt meanings to the given felt meaning. Therefore, some degree of novelty results. Hence, the meaning that the comprehension (formulation) finally symbolizes is not identical with the original felt meaning. The comprehensive formulation changes the original felt meaning to some extent. It "comprehends" it, rather than being an identical parallel explication of it.

The meaning of the symbols in comprehension *depends* utterly on the roles of felt meaning: selection and arbitration. Without these functions of felt meaning one could neither create further symbolic vehicles for partly unsymbolized experience nor sense whether such new symbols are accurate or not.

On the other hand, the felt meaning *depends* on the symbols for further symbolization. Without them, much of the felt meaning could be had only by direct reference. (One would know that one has "this" experience, but not what it is.)

Once formulated, a "comprehensive symbolization" is capable of calling forth the experienced meaning in another person. In this sense, it becomes *independent* of the felt meaning, although it can call forth in another person only the specifically modified, changed, felt meaning. The other person thus has no way of comparing the comprehensive symbolization with the original experienced meaning—unless he is also given other equally accurate possible symbolizations and told that they refer to the same original felt meaning. In that sense even finished comprehensive formulations are *dependent* on felt meaning.

Comprehension is a functional relationship in which the felt meaning (directly referred to) has maximal independent determination of the meaning of the relationship. The *symbols* and their felt meanings have minimal determination, although this minimal determination is still sufficient to make many different comprehensions possible.

d. Discussion of the creativity of "comprehension." While a comprehension symbolizes the given experienced meaning, it can't help but be creative also. We have avoided a *logical* definition of this creative aspect of "comprehension," just as we avoided it for "metaphor." We won't say that a "comprehension" differs from the original felt meaning in some logically defined way, for example "more specific" or "more extensive" or "more organized" or "more unified." Such logical analyses can be seen as various "comprehensions" of the experienced relationship "comprehension" itself.

The way in which the felt meaning changes as it is being symbolized is crucial for our inquiry. After all, meaning as specified in symbolization must be different from meaning as felt. If it were not so, our inquiry would be in vain and everything would be duplicated: if experienced meaning prior to symbolization were exactly as it is when symbolized, then there would be two meanings, one in experiencing and one in symbols, and two experiencings, one in experiencing and one as our meaning of symbols. Such duplication would be repeated ad infinitum.

Meaning depends on a *relationship* between experience and symbols. Hence, we would expect that experienced meaning is something different when symbolized than it was before it was symbolized. In fact, we should not speak of experienced meaning "before" it is symbolized. We can only speak of an experienced meaning as already "symbolized" in *some* way. Then it can be discussed "before it is *further* symbolized in still *another* way.[17] Since a meaning always exists in terms of a relationship between symbols and feeling, it is clear that a meaning doesn't pre-exist such a relationship. It is a differently symbolized meaning that pre-exists it. For example, a felt meaning to be comprehended may be a "meaning" in the sense of being directly referred to.[18] The given felt meaning must change as it is comprehended because it becomes a "meaning" in a new sense and in a new functional relationship with symbols.

On the other hand, we are not asserting that the felt meaning changes in what might be called its "implicit" content. A good comprehension will be experienced as *accurately* representing the implicit content, rather than changing it.

However, to speak of "implicit" conceptual content appears again to duplicate the functions of felt meaning and of symbols: felt meaning is said to have "implicitly" just that sense of meaning which symbols will symbolize, yet symbols will have that meaning also. Only if the transition from implicit to explicit meaning is viewed in terms of a functional relationship between felt meaning and symbols can this duplication

17. When we have an experience—say with objects, situations, or people —these "symbolize" it (in the widest sense of the word). Then we may seek to symbolize it further, perhaps verbally. Similarly, a dramatist may try to "symbolize" an explicit idea in terms of situations and actions.
18. In discussing direct reference it was found that any feeling is a felt meaning if it is *a* feeling or "this feeling," or if it is "symbolized" by being specified by an action, situations, or object. Hence, it can be said that feelings have meaning, or are meanings. This might also be phrased as "feelings are comprehensible," capable of a relationship with symbols that is here called comprehension.

be avoided. This means that the word "implicit" refers to the possibility of a new functional relationship (comprehension) before that functional relationship actually takes place. When meaning is "implicit," there is the possibility of comprehension. When comprehension actually occurs, the meaning becomes explicit.

When we say that the comprehended felt meaning is the "same" as that which was going to be comprehended (when we still called it "implicit"), we are speaking about the role, in comprehension, of felt meaning. It selects and arbitrates symbols and is experienced as identical with the felt meaning of the successfully comprehending symbols. When we speak of the felt meaning's being different after comprehension, we are speaking about the role of symbols, which comprehend by means of combinations of their felt meanings (recognitions). (The reader can easily ascertain this himself by considering any two illustrations of some same thing.)

It cannot be said that the "implicit" content is changed, since "implicit" can only mean the possibility of just such a (changed, because explicit) meaning.

We may now summarize both the creative and the accurate aspect of comprehension. Comprehension is creative because it creates the felt meaning from combinations of symbols and their felt meanings. It is accurate because it seeks in this way to create just *this,* given, felt meaning.

e. Relation to "metaphor." We must distinguish "comprehension" from "metaphor" since both appear to involve some creation of new felt meaning. The difference lies in that "comprehension" further symbolizes a felt meaning already symbolized. "Metaphor" creates a new felt meaning.[19]

19. Metaphor applies these symbols to an "area of experience." Any area is already partly symbolized, else it would not be *an* area of experience differentiable from other areas. The above distinction between comprehension and metaphor thus disappears. In both we begin with an *already partly symbolized* experience. In both, we *create* new aspects

If we so distinguish comprehension, we may see it as analogous to explication. Explication and comprehension both seek symbolization for *a* given felt meaning. Thus, comprehension relates to metaphor as "explication" relates to "recognition." Explication and recognition follow each other in a process (which could be called "thought"). Explication occurs to further or differently symbolize *a* felt meaning already *called forth* by recognition. Similarly, comprehension attempts to symbolize *a* felt meaning already *created* (perhaps in a metaphoric process).

However, there are many other ways in which these two functional relationships may be related.

3. RELEVANCE

a. Description. In preceding sections, we defined relationships between a felt meaning and one or more symbolizations *of it*.

Sometimes, however, a set of symbols is not fully under-

---

while retaining some of the meaning given in the to-be-symbolized experience.

It is possible to view comprehension and metaphor as a continuum parallel to a continuum between specified and unspecified experience. To the extent that experience is already specified, comprehension applies. To the extent that it is not, metaphor operates.

It is equally possible to view them as identical in extent, and distinguishable by their emphasizing two different ever-present aspects: that which is already meaningful and that which is created from out of the interaction of the already meaningful. Thus, comprehension would be involved in metaphor, giving it determinacy. Metaphor would be involved in comprehension, giving it variety of formulations.

The possibility of comprehension expresses the capacity of experience to *determine* meaning, while the possibility of metaphor expresses new *creation*. In the discussion of metaphor, an unresolved problem was: what *determines* creation of new experiences or meanings? In comprehension (had we not taken up "metaphor" already) our problem would be: how can there be *several* symbolic formulations? What creates many meanings of an experience? We conclude, from this more exact examination of their relationship, that comprehension and metaphor relate in many and problematic ways. Their relationship is one basic way of stating the relationship between determinacy and creativity in experience.

standable without the function of a felt meaning, even though the symbols are not the symbolization of that felt meaning.

In fact, almost all meaningful symbols require the presence, in a person, of many, many *relevant* meanings or experiences. This fact is usually expressed by saying that "past experience" is necessary for understanding. The same fact is expressed by saying that one must understand the "context." If one does not have the felt meaning called "understanding the context," one will only grasp a very limited, superficial part of a symbolization. "Context" may mean the preceding discussion, the preceding actions, or it may mean twenty years of experience shared by some persons, but not by others. In all these examples, felt meanings function to make symbolizations understandable, yet these symbolizations symbolize only some few specific felt meanings, not all those necessary for understanding.

Let us call this function of felt meaning "relevance." This term is a short version of the phrase *"relevant felt meaning, from out of which symbolization is understandable."*

With the consideration of relevance, we again move to another level of complexity. We noted, in discussing metaphor and comprehension, that "other experiences" or "other felt meanings" functioned in these relationships. We did not deal with these "other" experiences, since metaphor and comprehension were chiefly concerned with symbolization and creation *of* a particular felt meaning. We were unable to specify, then, how "other" experiences interacted in (or were part of) the process of creation and symbolization. We also left out of account the functional relationship between these "other" felt meanings and the resulting symbolization. This functional relationship is the "relevance" that experiences may have to each other and to the symbolizations of each other.

b. Multiplicity of relevance. A given felt meaning may

function as relevance toward a great many different symbolizations.

Let us return to the example of a conversation. The felt meaning (relevance) of what has gone before enables one to understand what comes next. Often one has a fairly specific sense of what will be said next, but often one is wrong. Something quite different is said next; something quite different was being led up to. Yet, when the listener hears this rather surprising thing, he can still understand it from out of the same felt meaning that—he guessed—would lead to something else. "Oh," he says, "so this is what you were leading up to!" Both what the listener expected, and what actually was said next, were understandable from out of the relevant felt meaning.

Let us examine this capacity of a felt meaning to enter relevance relationships with many different symbolizations.

In the case of comprehension, *many* accurate symbolizations of the given felt meaning were possible. The various possible symbols that could comprehend the felt meaning change and specify it variously. This also occurs in "relevance," since the felt meaning is modified and specified by the symbolizations that it helps make understandable.

However, such modification is not the only reason why a felt meaning can be relevant to *many* symbolizations.

Relevance concerns the *other* meanings that function in such cognitions as we have described. Anything meaningful always involves many "other" meanings. Whenever a given meaning is related to another given meaning in a given way, we may reflect upon how this relationship was experienced and find countless other meanings implicitly involved. To say this in our terms, comprehension and metaphor applied to the experience of such relationships will give us many other meanings.

Not only are many different symbolizations capable of

being understood from out of a felt meaning, but the converse is equally important. The same symbolization (one set of verbal symbols) may have quite different meanings, and quite dfferent degrees of meaning, if different felt meanings function "from out of which" this one symbolization is understood. For example, the experienced and the inexperienced person will have, for a given set of words, quite different understandings. An apprentice may learn a maxim. After twenty more years of experience he may come to a much different and fuller understanding of the meaning of that maxim. When he then comes to teach his apprentice, he may be unable to find any better symbolization of what it means than the original words he learned twenty years earlier. Another example:[20] a client in therapy may be able, in his first hour, to symbolize certain insights about himself. When, after many, many hours, of therapy, he arrives at the experiencing in himself, of which these insights are the symbolization, he may not be able to symbolize the experiencing any better than in the same words. Often he will feel that the therapist can't possibly understand, because the words are the same old words, but the experiencing to which they now refer is new. With this new experiencing as relevance, quite a different understanding of the old words is possible.

These two examples demonstrate that the same set of symbols may be understood differently and to a different degree, given different felt meanings from out of which they can be understood.

c. Definition: the functional relationship of relevance. A set of symbols is understood by means of many experienced meanings in addition to the one felt meaning that the symbols symbolize.

Experienced meanings function as "relevance" feeling, from out of which the given set of symbols becomes meaningful.

20. See further discussion of this example in Chapter VII.

Without a relevance feeling, from out of which the set of symbols is understandable, the symbols mean only their particular meaning. With this feeling present, the symbols can mean what they are intended to mean in this context, and can have their intended richness of reference to experience.

The experiences that function as relevance feeling may themselves be unspecified. Often only a small part of (a few aspects of) this felt meaning can be comprehended.

The understood symbols modify the "relevance" felt meaning. Hence, the symbols that will be understandable are often unpredictable, yet once they occur, they are seen to follow from out of it.

Any experienced meaning can function as a relevance. All kinds[21] of symbolization can be understandable from out of a relevance.

Very many different symbolizations could be understandable from out of the same relevance felt meaning, and could modify it.

The same symbolization can have very many different kinds and degrees of meaning if different relevance feelings function.

d. Relationship between relevance and other functional relationships. In a sense, relevance is a kind of symbolization. Often all the experiences from out of which some symbolization is understandable cannot be conceptualized themselves. Comprehension of the relevance felt meaning can, of course, be attempted. But usually the result is not a comprehension of the felt meaning at all, but simply another symbolization capable of being understood only from out of it. For example: a painting may be decribed by many critics. An excellent job of symbolization of felt experience may be achieved. Yet even these descriptions are usually quite meaningless if one does

21. "Symbolization" here is used in the widest sense—for example, as including situations, objects, persons, as well as gestures, acts, verbal symbols.

not first obtain a direct visual experience of the painting, so as to understand the symbolizations from out of one's own, present, felt meaning of the painting. Hence, even these symbolizations of the critics are really "symbolizations" of the relevance sort, rather than comprehensions that (as we defined comprehension) can call forth the felt meaning in someone who does not yet have it.

The relationship of relevance to other functions has the same ambiguity we previously found between metaphor and comprehension. All functional relationships seem to be involved in each other. We have seen that relevance is involved in metaphor and in comprehension. A case could be made of calling them all relevance, since even a comprehension will not be understandable without *some* other experienced meanings. On the other hand, we must look at our subject matter (symbolization of experience) from both viewpoints. Both viewpoints are capable of being applied to every case, yet both are necessary.

e. Impossibility of logical definition of relevance. As in metaphor and comprehension, logical definition of what will be relevant is impossible prior to the functioning of a relevance. Let us look briefly at what kind of logical definition relevance may have.

Traditional logics offer two broad ways of viewing relations between conceptualized meanings: meanings may be viewed as entities that determine what they can be related to; meanings may also be viewed as themselves determined by interrelations of many "other" meanings. If we now compare relevance with both metaphor and comprehension, we note that relevance represents this latter view of meanings. By means of experienced "other" meanings, we come to understand a given meaning. Metaphor and comprehension, on the other hand, represent the view that a meaning determines its relations to other meanings.

In this essay we do not decide among these kinds of logical formulations. Either formulation is applicable once experiencing has performed its function in the experienced creation of meanings. Only later can logical analysis inquire how it was relevant in a logical sense of relevance. This logical inquiry will itself be based on further creation of aspects of the felt meaning that can then be seen to be related to the newly understood meaning in terms of old and new kinds of relationships.

Hence the question is not: what logical relationships determine when a felt meaning is relevant? The question in a given case is rather: what new aspects can we create or comprehend, to formulate how this felt meaning functioned relevantly?

Relevance thus represents the function of experience in making anything understandable. In principle (as we shall see later), any person's experience could function to understand anything, if the experience were sufficiently modified by so functioning.

f. Importance of relevance to the relation between philosophies. Comprehension showed that *many* accurate formulations of a given experience were possible. Relevance shows that a given experience can be relevant to *many* different other experiences and their formulations. Experiences can be relevant to each other and affect the myriad ways in which they may be symbolized. Among these, many will be equally accurate, although different meanings will result. Hence, not only are various comprehensive symbolizations of one felt meaning possible, but a great variety of *other* experiences may be drawn in relevantly. The result is very many different ways to symbolize experiences and make them understandable.

Different philosophies (different basic schemes of symbolizing experience) may thus not only provide equally accurate "comprehensive" formulations of a given experience, but also may imply equally accurate, but different relevances of other experiences.

a. Description. In our discussion of relevance, the felt meaning was assumed to be already present. How is such a felt meaning of relevance created in a person, if it isn't already present?

Basically, the answer is that one must experience first. Only then can experience function and be modified in the understanding of other experiences or symbols. However, this answer is tautological, since one must therefore have experiences one cannot understand, in order to use them to understand other experiences. We are thus confronted with the problem of the creation of meaning in experience. We have noted this problem already when we said that meaning (for example, symbolization of one sort or another) always exists, since not only verbal symbols, but also things, situations, persons, acts, may "symbolize" in the widest sense of that term.[22]

Granting meaning in experience, how are further novel meanings created? In the process of creating novel meaning, not two but many experienced meanings interact. In discussing metaphor, we left the many "other" interacting experiences out of account, since we were interested in how symbols that have a given "old" meaning can create and symbolize a second, "new" meaning. We must now look at the process from the viewpoint of many, many relevant meanings interacting to form a new felt meaning. For example, one comes upon a metaphor in a poem. All the preceding meanings of the poem are fresh in one's awareness and function in the interaction of the two areas of experience of the metaphor. We saw in the discussion of relevance that many and different felt

22. See Section A, above.

meanings can become relevant (through a creative modification). These many relevant felt meanings function in the creation of the new meaning. In discussing relevance, we were chiefly concerned with the function of relevant felt meaning in *understanding* a symbolization. Now, let us concern ourselves with the *creation* of such a felt meaning. Let us therefore focus on the *creative modification* of relevance.

Let us return to the example employed in the discussion of relevance:

If someone tells a story, describes an experience, or continues for any length of time on one discourse, or one context, all his meanings *create in us* a felt meaning of relevance, from out of which we understand the next thing he says. As he talks, he creates in us, and continually modifies in us, the felt meaning necessary for our understanding.

This creative modification and creative building up of the felt meaning needed for understanding is an aspect of relevance. Let us call this aspect of it *circumlocution* and treat it as a separate functional relationship, since we are concerned with the creation of such a relevant felt meaning, not its coordinate function in understanding symbolizations.

Although "circumlocution" is a term usually reserved for verbal symbols, let us employ it for all kinds of symbols, including things, people, situations, acts, and so on. Thus, direct experience in a field, or with a person, will also creatively build up and modify one's felt meaning (necessary in understanding that field, person, or situation) just as a person talking about it would creatively build in us the felt meaning by means of verbal symbols.

b. Definition: the functional relationship of circumlocution. A felt meaning is created in a person by means of symbols that do not symbolize that felt meaning.

The creation of the felt meaning occurs over many steps, each step being a creative modification of the felt meaning (which, at the same time, functions as a relevance, from out of which this next modifying step is understandable).

Each of the symbols (including things, persons, situations, acts, and so on) is already meaningful in itself (recognition) and these felt meanings interact (as in metaphor) creatively to produce new felt meanings, that is, modifications of "the" felt meaning being gradually created.

The felt meaning can be referred to directly (as with phrases such as "I think I know what you're getting at" or "this field is so and so" or "let me see now if I know what you mean.")

All experience (of things, persons, situations, and so on) may be seen as circumlocution, although presumably no one sets these experiences up in order to communicate a felt meaning. For example, a person long in a certain field of endeavor comes to have many felt meanings owing to his experiences in the field.

Art may be viewed as circumlocution in which someone actually does arrange experiences for someone else, in order to create in him a given felt meaning.

Most verbal communication is, or depends on, "circumlocution."

All *continuity* of meaning in experience, verbalization, thought, involves "circumlocution."

Circumlocution and relevance imply each other. Both imply the creativity of relevance (between experienced meanings), which, as we have seen, is a creativity of meaning.

The functional relationships do not relate to each other in any unique way. We have drawn many different relationships between metaphor and comprehension, and between these and relevance.

Circumlocution could be placed in relation to the others in many ways. One such way of relating the functions follows (see Table 2).

Relevance is parallel to comprehension, since in both a felt meaning is *given* rather than *created*. It differs from comprehension in that the symbolizations it relates to are not *of* it, but merely understandable from out of it. Circumlocution, then, is the creation, with symbols, of just such a felt meaning of relevance, from out of which some other symbolizations will be understandable. In this sense, it relates to metaphor as comprehension relates to relevance.

Table 2. A way of relating the functional relationships

	GIVEN FELT MEANING	SIMULTANEOUSLY CREATED
Symbolization of felt meaning	Comprehension	Metaphor
Felt meaning functions relevantly, but is not symbolized by the symbols	Relevance	Circumlocution

CHAPTER IV *Characteristics of*

Experienced Meaning as

Functioning in New Symbolization

Brief   Section A concerns the question: do conceptual
Statement   meanings become illogical and arbitrary, are they lost
             in complete relativity, if felt meanings function in that
             variety of ways with symbols which has been set forth?

It is true that the relations between symbols and felt
meaning are more fundamental than logic, for meanings and logical patterns are first formed in the interaction of symbols and felt meaning. Logic is therefore
secondary and operates only after the formation of
meanings.

However, the logical use of concepts must and can
be differentiated from the role of felt meaning in the
creation of *new, further* meanings.

The question is now posed: can these further meanings be "anything at all," are they arbitrary, since
felt meaning can help produce so *many different* symbolized meanings? In short, can you make a symbolic
"silk purse" out of a "sow's ear" felt meaning? Can
you interpret it to be anything at all?

It is shown, on the contrary, that one always refers
to a very particular, finely determined felt meaning
whose multiplicity of potential symbolic meanings is
the opposite of arbitrary. A felt meaning is not any-

138

thing you please. The multiplicity of its possible symbolizations is due to the fact that it has a very complex determination. Therefore only some of the many preconceptual meanings of a felt meaning can ever be symbolized (created, finished, completed, discovered, differentiated, specified—choose your term and scheme, for these functional relationships are more fundamental than the scheme you use to logically describe them).

A radical empiricism will not assume logical patterns of any sort to precede the creation of logical patterns. A radical empiricism will not read into preconceptual experiencing any conceptual patterns (since these were themselves created by interaction of symbols and experiencing). It will retain fully formed and defined concepts and logical deductions, but will not confuse these with the experiencing process functioning in the creation of new meanings.

Section B gives the characteristics of felt meanings as they function in the creation of new or further meanings. These characteristics are very different from those of finished and defined concepts. It must be borne in mind that they apply to the creation of *new* or *further* aspects. Once the new aspect is created, it has number, scheme, necessary logical implications, and limited applicability, and only certain statements can be applied to it. However, as the aspect is being created, its creation is not determined by the character it will have once it is finished. On the contrary, its creation involves felt meaning whose character it is to have no given number or units, no predetermined scheme, no necessary logical implications. These must first be created. They are created by creating a new meaning, a new aspect of experiencing—and this it is that has these defined characteristics.

One may always take a defined meaning or concept (at any junction of a discourse, or in any theory) and refer directly to the felt meaning one has for it in that context. One may then employ the open preconceptual characteristics of this felt meaning to create many important new meanings whose number, scheme, and logical implications will be quite different and independent of the first given meaning. Of course, we then still have available the original, precisely defined concept, as well as our new concepts which we may now define. The result is that we can illuminate any concept of a theory by use of the creative characteristics of felt meaning. And, although this is so for theory on any subject, these characteristics themselves constitute a basic theory of the nature of human phenomena.

[A]
Experienced Meaning Is Not Determined by Logical Relationships, But Does Not Function Arbitrarily

1. REVERSAL OF THE USUAL PHILOSOPHIC PROCEDURE

In each of the nonparallel functional relationships we have met questions regarding logical determination and we have left such questions open.

For example, in metaphor the logical question was, "what determines the new meaning?" This question seemed to imply a prior logical relationship of "likeness" between the two interacting old meanings from which the new metaphoric meaning comes.

In comprehension, from a purely logical point of view, the symbolized comprehended meaning ought to be uniquely equal to the "implicit" meaning.

In relevance, again, it might have seemed that some logical relations determine which felt meaning will be relevant to which other meanings and in just what respects. Finally, in circumlocution, the meanings that gradually build up a relevant felt meaning might be seen to stand in some logical relationship to it.

In each of these cases, we were careful not to let the functional relationship depend on one or another sort of logical relations. Instead, we noted that such logical relations themselves depend (a) on the prior creation of the symbolization and (b) on still further creation of aspects of the experienced creation, which can then be seen as applicable logical relations.

We are employing the term "logical" to apply to uniquely symbolized concepts. A "logical relationship" is one that is entirely in terms of uniquely specified concepts. Whatever occurs in the creation, specification, or symbolization of concepts is obviously prior to their properties as finished products. Also prior is whatever must occur in the creation of the concept of a logical relationship itself.

The functional relationships formulate how felt meanings function before logical relationships either apply or are created.

Let us illustrate this in the case of metaphor. We will illustrate it by showing that the logical relation of "likeness" does not determine the metaphoric creation, but is itself based both on that creation and on a further creation of the aspects that the logical relation formulates as "like." As our example of the functional relationship "metaphor," let us again take the simile "my love is like a red, red rose."

The old philosophic procedure tempts us; we ask: what determines the new meaning of the metaphor? The most immediate answer will be: it is *like* the old meaning. The *like-*

ness to "red, red rose" appears to determine just what aspect of "my love" will be newly created by the metaphor.

Many philosophic formulations tempt us to say: relations determine meanings. Comparisons determine meanings. Similarity is the fundamental relation.

It is clear that roses and girls are different. In what way, then, can a rose and a girl be alike? Not in every way. We must first find, create, specify the likeness. Perhaps the girl and the rose are both fresh, blooming, eventually passing, beautiful, living, tender, attractive, soft, quietly waiting to be picked, part of greater nature—each time we feel that we have not stated the metaphoric meaning completely, but have only drawn out some true aspect of it. Our drawing out these meanings was a further creative process, for we did not *explicitly* note any of these even when we read the metaphor. It is clear that, *for us,* the metaphor *was not based on these* likenesses. Rather, the likenesses we drew out were based on the metaphor—on the experiencing together of "my love" and "red, red rose." The likeness is creatively specified and symbolized by the metaphor. Particular likenesses can then be "found" or "created," as aspects of the metaphoric meaning.

We have considered the *reader* of the metaphor in our example. The first *creator* of the metaphor begins with his undifferentiated experience (of his girl), which the metaphor will help him specify. He specifies his experience by asking himself, "Now what is that like?" He, too, does not yet have the likeness at that point. He asserts that there is a likeness between something unspecified in his present experienced meaning (of the girl) and something (as yet not found) in his experience in general. When he finds it (a red, red rose) he has *only then* fully created *the specific aspect* of the experience of the girl. Thus, he specifies it out of the undifferentiated experience. In other words, the likenesses exist only as the new meaning is created. The likenesses do not create the new meaning. He does not pick "red, red rose" because it is just like his girl. He newly specifies something about the girl by means of the experience and symbols: "red, red rose."

Hence, a metaphor is a *creation* of meanings *and* of likenesses. One of these does not create the other, but they are tantamount to each other.

Every likeness is itself a meaning and must be created and specified in experiencing. In the specific case before us, we note that there is no likeness before the meaning is created. After the metaphor is created, the new felt meaning is symbolized only by the metaphor. It can be further symbolized in a comprehension. That is done when implicit likenesses are formulated from it.

It is for this reason that a metaphor is so rich, so full of many, many possible meanings and likenesses. It can never be exhausted by stating or analyzing the likenesses on which it is supposed to be based, but which it really is in the act of creating.

Other philosophers have shown that relations themselves depend on prior meanings. I. A. Richards is one of the latest to show that "comparing" must always occur in certain "respects" and hence depend on these "respects." [1] All concepts are the result of comparing and are relative to the choice of "respects." With the term "respects" he states that likenesses are themselves meanings that must be created.

The same problem can also be found in an old argument against Aristotle's theory of abstraction. Whewell pointed out that a definition, for example, of "horse," could be abstracted on the basis of the likeness of many horses if one were fortunate enough to have a group of horses already selected. Otherwise, one is likely to abstract "brown with short hair" which would include certain kinds of furniture as well as omit many horses. In this argument, again, it is pointed out that

1. See Appendix.

comparing depends on respects that must already have been created.

Conclusions: 1. A likeness is a meaning, that is a *respect* in which two things are said to be alike. Such a respect can be newly created by a metaphor and further specified by comprehension.

2. The creation of the metaphor is not determined by the likeness. Even after it is created, the likenesses implicit in it still wait for further creative symbolization (comprehension). The likenesses are formulated only after both these creative processes.

2. WHAT DETERMINES THE CREATION OF MEANINGS?

We have now reversed the traditional philosophic order. Contrary to that order, logical or conceptual relations do not determine the creation of meanings. What does determine it?

a. Direct reference. Logical relationships are secondary and dependent on something else. If we could not have direct access to the functioning of this something else, knowledge would become equivocal and arbitrary. But we do have such direct access in direct reference and in all the functional relationships since these involve direct reference. Hence, we can directly refer to felt meaning and examine and employ its prior functioning.

b. Distinction between concepts and felt meanings. We sharply distinguish between uniquely specified (logical) concepts on the one hand and the functioning of felt meaning on the other. Without this sharp distinction, all knowledge would also become equivocal and arbitrary. For example, we said that a felt meaning could be symbolized in various different, equally accurate comprehensions. This must not be taken to mean that these comprehensions, as uniquely specified concepts, are equivalent. If that were so, explicit meanings would become equivocal and arbitrary. Rather, a felt meaning can function so as to be accurately comprehended in various ways by *different* symbolic comprehensions. The formulations are equivalent only with respect to this functioning felt meaning. Each of these different formulations will accurately symbolize the felt meaning. On what basis is such accuracy asserted? On the basis of the direct reference to this felt meaning.

c. Felt meanings function determinately. The term "creation" does not imply a creation ex nihilo. It is a creation in which experienced meanings function. Also, we do not mean an arbitrary or indeterminate creation—a creation of just anything. The experienced meanings to which one directly refers have certain determinative roles in the creation. We have attempted to state these in the case of each of the functional relationships.

We can put this another way: the "creation" is not of just anything. The felt meanings that function in it are *these* (direct reference), not just anything. Each functional relationship is a formulation of how some "this" felt meaning functions to determine a creation of new meaning.

Thus, although creation of new meaning is not determined by logical relationships, neither is it simply indeterminate. It is determined by the functioning of certain directly referred-to felt meanings. We have been attempting to formulate how these function.

The functional relationships have different degrees of creativity. However, all the nonparallel ones have some degree of creativity.

Similarly, the functional relationships have different kinds of creativity, because they do not concern the same functioning of felt meaning and symbols. In metaphor and circumlocution the felt meaning itself—as well as a kind of symbolization of it—is created. In comprehension and relevance, a *given* felt meaning is creatively modified by symbols, rather than newly created. Whatever the degree or kind of creativity involved, in every case *certain given* felt meanings are directly referred to and function in the creation of new meaning. It is always just these given ones that so function. They are always directly referred to. Their functioning is both creative and determinative.

We have inverted the usual philosophic procedure. Instead of seeking certain conceptual presuppositions that determine all experience (and knowledge) we have sought to formulate the function of directly referred-to experiencing in the creation of concepts.

The usual philosophic procedure is to lay the conceptual into the preconceptual. The raw material of knowledge is controlled by conceptual rules. Conceptual relations thus determine concept formation before these conceptual relations are ever created or symbolized.[2]

2. Put most broadly, the usual philosophic procedure is to lay the conceptual into the preconceptual. Philosophy usually asserts that the order, nature, rules, intelligibility of fully formed knowledge are properties of the raw material of knowledge. Of course, philosophies differ greatly in how they do this. In every philosophy there is a raw material of knowledge —for us—but philosophies differ on the status they give it. Empirical philosophies show that all our knowledge is based on this raw material, that is, on certain principles they attribute to it. Rationalistic philosophies place the principles of intelligibility in us (mind, understanding, language) and give the raw material a much more arbitrary status. For us the difference is not relevant because the raw material must dance to the tune of philosophy's rules of intelligibility in either case.

A few examples may clarify this. For Aristotle, the rules of intelligibility lie in nature. Of course, he accounts also for our attempts to grasp them. This occurs through abstraction from sense perception, since they are in nature.

For Plato, similarly, perception, experience, knowledge are all imitations crudely following the principles of being. Hence, perception can be "examined" and just these principles of being can thereby be approached.

For Kant, the sensible raw material of our experiencing apparatus is quite unformed. All forms are attributes of knowing apparatus. However, this unformed material *must* be subjected to the forms of our knowing apparatus. It can in no way be referred to, except by means of just these forms.

For Russell, perception is analyzable according to certain basic logical principles, which are also the basic principles of all linguistic and mathematical formulation of meaning. These basic forms can be called "the furniture of the world" or such assertion can be denied. But the only status sense-experience has for Russell is to be so analyzed and to so fit into just these basic forms.

We find, instead, that whenever logical relations are said to apply to an instance of concept formation, they really are posterior to two experienced creations: (a) the experienced creation of the concepts to which they are said to apply; (b) the experienced creation of certain further aspects of these concepts which are then formulated as these logical relations themselves.

SUMMARY

We have inverted the traditional philosophic procedure.

Logical relations do not determine the creativity of new meaning and new symbolization. The preconceptual is not determined by the conceptual. We are inquiring into the functioning of the preconceptual itself. We can do so because the preconceptual, when it functions in symbolization, can be directly referred to. Its various functions, as well as the roles of symbols, have been formulated in the functional relationships.

For Dewey, experience involves the principles of knowledge in its very production. The process of inquiry can move on, but there is no past (raw material or experience) that is not already a product of just this process of inquiry.

We note that in all these philosophies the raw material, for us (our experiencing) is already controlled by the principles of knowledge according to the given philosophy. This is the case whether the philosopher asserts that the origin of these principles is in nature or in knowledge.

But we know that all this cannot be as they say, because they do not agree on just what are the fundamental principles of intelligibility. They offer us many different sets of fundamental principles, each controlling their notion of experience, as well as knowledge.

In this essay we have reversed the procedure by finding a way of referring to experiencing directly. Of course, in doing so, we have had to remain neutral toward all the many various sets of principles of intelligibility. Each philosopher has convinced us that the raw material of experiencing *can* be seen to have each of these sets of principles. The fashion in which we have shown the possibility of reference to experiencing directly also supports this variety: "this feeling," to which I refer by "direct reference," can enter into symbolic relations with any set of principles of knowledge. Furthermore, our own very reference to the experienced creating of a new meaning is in the same position: it *could* be symbolized and specified so as to create any one of many possible principles of intelligibility. The experienced process of creating meaning also creates meanings that *can* be seen as fundamental principles of intelligibility.

Knowledge does not become arbitrary as a result of the broad possibilities for creation of meaning that felt meanings offer:

1. Felt meanings can be directly referred to when they function.

2. Logically specified, symbolized, unique concepts are not felt meanings and do not have the creative characteristics of felt meanings. Our having of concepts involves felt meanings, which can be directly referred to. They make their creative functioning available to concepts without destroying the logical relationships of concepts as uniquely specified products.

3. The felt meanings that function in experienced creation of meanings are always just *these* (directly referred-to) felt meanings, having whatever meaning they have. They are not indeterminate, they are merely capable of further symbolization. Their functioning in symbolization is our subject of inquiry. Although this functioning is not logically determined, it is not indeterminate. If this felt meaning functions, the results will be different than if some other felt meaning functioned instead.

In the following section we inquire more exactly into the characteristics of felt meanings so functioning.

[B]
Characteristics of Experienced Meaning as Functioning in New Symbolization

INTRODUCTION

Our experienced having of concepts involves functions of felt meaning. Behind the logically specified concept, therefore, lie the immense creative possibilities of felt meaning. One of the aims of this treatise is to examine, and to systematically employ, this creative richness.

We have seen that insofar as it is symbolized, felt meaning is simply our having of the meaning of a given symbolization. Uniquely specified concepts have kinds of relationships and necessary implications that the present treatise does not disturb. The vast creative possibilities that felt meaning gives to concepts concern *further* symbolization.[3] The felt meaning of any symbolization is still capable of further and different symbolization in all seven functional relationships.

We will now examine some characteristics of felt meaning qua functioning in further creative symbolization. It is important to keep in mind that these characteristics apply to the creation of further symbolization, not to given symbolized products. The latter simply have the necessary attributes defined in logic. Hence, we shall call what we are about to examine the "characteristics of experienced meaning functioning in new symbolization."

To view experiencing as capable of various symbolic relationships, but without specifying any particular one of them, raises some problems. Experienced meaning functions differently in different functional relationships. Thus, there is a twin danger: either (1) we will take *one* of these functional relationships as crucial and ignore the fact that felt meaning functions in others, or (2) we will speak of felt meaning as an occurrence altogether apart from such relationships with

3. For example: Some familiar symbols are in a functional relationship of "recognition" with some experienced meaning that is called forth by them and constitutes our having of the meaning of these symbols. But this experienced meaning is not only the experienced side of the functional relationship just stated. It is an experienced occurrence capable of entering into many other functional relationships with symbols. Hence, we say that the experienced meaning that is "involved" in this specific meaning is capable of the creation of other meanings, aspects, relationships. (For example, further "explication," see Section A, 3, Chapter III.) Of course, it realizes this capacity only as it enters into some other functional relationship with symbols.

symbols, which will be quite a questionable thing to talk about. Can there be experienced meaning without symbols of any sort? Not, at least, on the basis of our definitions, for we defined "meaning" in terms of relations between experience and symbols.[4]

Nevertheless, we must accept both dangers. In reference to the first, we must always discourse under one or another of these functional relationships because we are discoursing, that is, making meaning, specifying, and so on. We cannot discuss *our* experienced meaning of experienced meaning without putting it into one or another of these functional relationships.[5] Thus, the best we can do about danger 1 is to accept it, know it, and look back on ourselves often to note which relationship we employed in saying what we wished to say, and to note whether the same thing, or something else, would be said under another relationship.

Danger 2 can be escaped, since our whole inquiry is based on the possibility of "direct reference" to experienced meaning. (Since direct reference is only one of our several functional relationships, we have incurred danger 1 already.)

In whatever relationships a given felt meaning functions, it can also be directly referred to. Thus, it can function in at

4. Or as "symbolic functions of experience," that is, experience functioning as standing for *such* an experience. This is the same idea without the "relationship logic" implied in the first statement.

5. What we are saying applies to our own saying of it. We must formulate and deal with specified aspects of experienced meanings that could be specified in other ways. Hence, what we say must be taken to refer to the felt, "directly referred-to" meaning. Our logical formulations, here and all along, are quite relative, that is, could be specified differently. Only if our formulations, metaphors, explications, and specifications are taken as directly referring to our own concretely present experienced meaning can they all be on a sure footing despite their relativity.

Experienced meanings to which the reader may directly refer were described in Chapter II. The reader is asked to refer directly, as he reads this chapter, to his own experience of thinking, speaking, problem solving. As we discuss characteristics of experienced meaning, the reader's own experienced meanings will thus be in at least one functional relationship, that of his own direct reference.

least one other functional relationship, namely direct reference. It can also come to function in still other functional relationships.

This gives us a safeguard against danger 2 (the mistake of speaking about experienced meaning totally apart from symbolization). This safeguard lies in our purpose; we are, after all, not concerned with felt meaning as *separate*. We are only interested in it as it can enter more than one functional relationship. Thereby it makes further creation and symbolization possible. This capacity of felt meaning lies behind specified logical meanings and can enrich philosophic method.

We shall now consider characteristics of experienced meaning in terms of capacity for further functional relationships.

1. THE NON-NUMERICAL CHARACTER OF EXPERIENCE

If we say the word "life," a large mass of undifferentiated experience is called forth as the felt meaning of that word. If we say the word "now," the same happens. And the same goes for "yesterday." It does not really seem that there are *fewer* experiences in the undifferentiated mass called forth by "now," "yesterday," or "life." We could differentiate and create an endless number of specific experiences from out of either "life" or "yesterday." It does not seem that logical extension bears any relationship to number of experiences called forth in a felt undifferentiated mass.

As Plato pointed out in the *Meno, any* experience can be related to anything else, or at least to something else, which in turn can be relatable to something else. In this way everything could, in principle, be "recalled" by our thoroughly comprehending even one experience.

(Comprehension involves other experiences as well as the creation of other aspects of experiences. Note our discussion of relevance in the last two functional relationships.)

The meaning-to-us of terms and things involves the felt meaning in us. This felt meaning is always only partly differentiated. Hence, the meaning-to-us offers endless potentialities of relations and differentiations.

The word "differentiation" above implies a particular type of philosophy and its further implications. Let us try to say only what we may say about felt meaning, if necessary by saying it in terms of several philosophies and then "directly referring" to the experienced aspect we mean.

Anything meaningful calls forth a mass of "associations."

Anything meaningful is experienced by means of *a mass of* past experiences and action tendencies derived from past interaction with the environment.

It is therefore a conception only because other representations are contained under it, by means of which it can relate to objects.[6]

Concepts are abstracted from countless experiences.

We note, then, that many philosophies give us terms for asserting that a meaning-for-us is grounded in, or associated with, or relatable to, *countless* other meanings without which it would not mean anything to us. Hence, we can use any of the above terms to refer to this aspect of any experienced meaning. Any experienced meaning will be differentiable into *countless* experienced meanings, each of which, because it is a meaning, will again be differentiable into countless meanings. Therefore, there is *one* experience, or *an* experience, or *a* meaning only, if one takes into account that it must already have been specified, selected, created, as *an* experience. Apart from this specification, it is always multiple. Experiencing is multiple, non-numerical. *An* experience is a symbolic crea-

6. "Er ist also nur dadurch Begriff, dasz unter ihm andere Vorstellungen enthalten sind, vermittelst deren er sich auf Gegenstände beziehen kann." Immanuel Kant, *Kritik Der Reinen Vernunft*, ed. Felix Meiner (Leipzig: Raymund Schmidt, 1944), p. 109.

tion.[7] Nor is it made up of two, five, or a million other unit experiences. There are no units. Anything like a unit experience is always a product, embodying its experienced production and selection. Conversely, a unit experience can always be differently symbolized as an aspect of many other experiences. A given set of "many" experiences can be differently symbolized as "one" experience.

Let us call this the "non-numerical" character of experience as functioning in the creation of new aspects.

A corollary. Accordingly, external and internal relations of experiences are basically not distinguishable. There are no initial units, but these must first be specified. Hence, they can be specified as aspects of one experience "within" which they are to be found—or nearly the same finding can be specified as two experiences related one to the other. Both ways, the "finding" is creative. (When Plato reminisces, he creates either the new whole of the first experience within which all is to be found, or the related experiences and their relations to the first experience.)

2. THE "MULTISCHEMATIC" CHARACTER OF EXPERIENCE

If experiencing is not constituted of unit experiences (but only symbolizing makes it so), then it follows that experiencing is not organized in schematic relationships of units to each other, but only symbolizing makes it so. For example, experiences are not—in experiencing—already "within" each other, or "close to" each other. The term "differentiation," for example, implies a scheme of experiences within experiences. In applying it in our discussion of units in experience, we schematized experience.

Since we wished to discuss experience prior to any one specific symbolization, we provided several other schemes with

7. See Section A, 1, Chapter III, "Direct Reference."

which we could also say what we had first said in terms of "differentiation." We could then employ all these different formulations to refer directly to the experienced meaning we wished to formulate. Thus, although each formulation had its own set of philosophic implications, we were not obliged to accept any of these.[8] Instead, we directly referred to something experienced that *could* be creatively formulated in various ways. We referred to it without destroying its multischematic character.

Very many kinds of schematic relationships *can* be seen to apply to experiences that have been specifi*ed,* symboliz*ed,* and so on. Rather than saying that experience is not constituted of experiences in schematic relationships to each other, let us say that experience is "multischematic."[9] It is capable of many different specifications, many units, and therefore many different kinds of relationships between units. By "capable of," we will mean that experiencing as such is not patterned in any *one* of these schematics, but that when experiences are specified, then schematic relationships between experiences are likewise specified.

Our second *characteristic of experience as functioning in the creation of new aspects,* then, is that it is "multischematic." That is, to-be-specified experienc*es* are capable of being specified according to many schemes.

Definition of "aspect of experience." The term "aspect of experience" will be employed to name the specification of experience that results from its functioning in creative symbol-

8. We choose to call this use of terms "functional equivalence" both because all the equivalent terms can "function" to refer to the same experience, and because the experience to which they can all refer is a "function" performed by experience, which can be variously symbolized by these equivalent terms. See Chapter VI, Section A, 7.

9. This allows our later assertion that all experience is already *partially* symbolized, "preconceptual," and therefore capable of partial determination of its aspects.

ization. Prior to a given instance of so functioning, experience is non-numerical and multischematic. Any given instance of this functioning creates or specifies an "aspect" of the experience. Depending on the other experiences that also function in the creative symbolization, different "aspects" will be specified. (Such symbolization involves "aspects" both of the given and the other experiences.) One may always creatively specify what aspects of these other experiences "were" involved in this creation. If the creation has already occurred, then such a specification is a comprehension. We placed the term "were" in quotes because these aspects are specified only when the comprehension is undertaken. They will *then* be said to have already been there, when the experienced process occurred.

a. Experience is time-inclusive. Since unspecified experience has no unique unity or units, it does not have unique temporal units. Any schematic relationship between experiences implies units (and is specified simultaneously with such units, if they are specified). This is true also of temporal units. Theories of time, moments, before and after, and so on are schematic relationships of units, into which experience can be specified. Experience apart from such specification cannot be considered as temporal units or as in a temporal scheme.

We have seen that, in order to speak of "two experiences," a specification must have taken place, giving unique unity to these two experiences. They may be so specified as to have some given schematic relation—for example, before and after in an irreversible temporal sequence.[10]

Now, the present essay is about relationships between experiences—for example, between the preconceptual, felt, experienced meaning and its symbolization, or again, between a symbolization and the felt experienced meaning it calls forth,

10. It is not implied that such temporal specification—or indeed, any specification—is arbitrary. (See pp. 118, 145 on accuracy in comprehension of "implicit meaning.")

or again, between "old experience" and a "new" aspect said to be "of" or "already in" it.

The temporal relationship between such experiences (we first have one, then the other, and looking back from this other experience we assert that something was "already in" the one) is specified along with the specifications we are making, when we symbolize other aspects of it. To say that "this" came before something else is more specification than merely to call it "this," which, as "direct reference," we have already shown involves specification. Hence, experiencing *includes* the capacity to be temporally specified. (An error is just as possible here as in any other specification and raises the same problems—see footnote 4, p. 75.)

For the present treatise the importance of this characteristic (a corollary of characteristics 1 and 2) is as follows:

All our subject matter, including characteristics of experience, refers to the *experienced* process of symbolizing, creating, specifying meaning. This experienced process involves relationships between experiences, between unsymbolized and then symbolized versions said to be of the "same" thing but, of course, themselves two different experiences. If we chose a temporal scheme as fundamental to experience, we would say that it always involves looking back from one moment to a preceding one.

If the distinction between experiences could not be made as we are making it (between the unspecified or unsymbolized and the symbolized) then the symbolized and the unsymbolized would be the same thing. We could then not say that a symbolic meaning *involves* felt experiencing; we would have to say that it is nothing but felt experiencing. Its unity, schematic relations, and the rest that it has qua specified symbolized meaning would be utterly lost. We obviously must distinguish between the formed, unified, schematic, logical specified meaning and the not fully determined, un-unified, multischematic experiencing *involved in having* that logical meaning. For this distinction we *may* employ a temporal scheme and speak of moments of experience, the latter being the one in which we look back reflectively and note what the former moment "already" involved. However, we must not accept the temporal scheme as fundamental. To note *a former moment* as "involved" is precisely the experienced relationship (of specification, symbolization, function in creativity) of which we are here investigating the variants: the *many functional relationships.*

It is possible, therefore, to formulate all functional relationships in a temporal scheme. The unspecified experience and the symbols can be viewed as occurring after each other in time (in either order). Symbols then involve simultaneous experienced meaning that can be seen to be in a temporal relationship to experienced meanings preceding or following it. The experienced meaning of the symbols, on that showing, could always be related to them in some temporal scheme. On the other hand, the meaning-to-us can occur simultaneously with the symbols in one experience (as Merleau-Ponty emphasizes).[11] The experience to be explicated (or to be created) can occur earlier or later. If one were interested chiefly in temporal relations and the various ways in which they can be specified, a whole philosophy of temporal aspects of experience could be written. Finally, if one were interested in temporal relations *and* in the functional relationships here elucidated, one could create a multiple scheme in which both functional relations and temporal relations were distinguished and determined each other. However, we are mentioning all these possibilities only to show that the temporal schemes are merely one group of very many kinds of schemes that can be aspects of experience. The functional relationships of experience to symbols—which are kinds of schematization or specification—

11. See the Appendix.

can be seen as fundamental to any particular scheme, including the temporal.

   b. "Things" and "process." What we said of temporal schemes is, of course, applicable to all schemes. For our purposes we might mention two other schemes of importance: "thing" and "process." These involve different temporal schemes. Of the many possible versions of "thing" schemes and "process" schemes, we are here concerned only with the following difference between them: "things" are in one *place* during many *times,* whereas "process" (as conceived here) is in many *places* in one *time* (like a river flowing at many points simultaneously). Both schemes can be aspects of experience, as can all schemes. For us, it will later be important that both these schemes can specify experience. Thus, we may speak of experienced meaning as an occurrence (thing) or as a process. For example: "While a given experienced meaning may be in a functional relationship with some symbols, it has the capacity to enter into other functional relationships with other symbols." This sentence specifies "experienced meaning" as an occurrence or thing. Presumably "it" enters into another functional relationship at another time. Although unspecified, the capacity to so enter is part of that experienced meaning (for example, in therapy, problem solving, art); this unspecified capacity of "it" is quite an important part of the occurrence. On the other hand, and with quite a different temporal scheme, we may specify experiencing as a process. We can then assert that the process of experiencing a specified meaning (for example, a certain "functional relationship," now better stated as: a symbolic functioning in the experiencing process) can be referred to directly. Experiencing is easy to conceive of as "going on" in many respects (places) at once. Therefore, if experience is specified as "process," it is easier to conceive the fact that an experienced meaning includes not only the aspect of it that is specified (in functional relationship) but also much more. For any specified meaning we can always refer to the process of experiencing as a changing, of which one specified meaning is only one of many simultaneously changed aspects (see Chapter VII).

3. MEANINGS ARE LIKENESSES AND VICE VERSA

We have seen that a likeness does not determine a newly created meaning. Rather, a likeness is itself a newly created meaning. Conversely, any newly created meaning (whether it be called a likeness or a meaning) can be further found to be "like" all the many meanings that functioned in its creation. In fact, the two are tantamount to each other: one may first find the new meaning, then look back to find a likeness that appears to have determined the new meaning. Or one may first find the likeness (in a particular respect) between some meanings, then consider that likeness to be a new meaning. In either case, the given meanings function in the creation of a new meaning, and can be created or explicated.

Since experience is "non-numerical," it can be specified as one or as many experiences. Therefore, it can be specified as a meaning, or as relations between other meanings. It can be likenesses to other meanings.

A felt meaning is general; it is a "such," not only a "this." As general, it can occur more than once. It is applicable to two, otherwise diverse things. Therefore, it can be a relation of likeness between them. Any meaning is therefore a case of a possible likeness. The likeness is a likeness in the respect of just this meaning. It is itself a "meaning" precisely because it can be an aspect of more than one experience. Hence, it again can be more than one relationship; that is, it can function in specifying.

Thus we have our third characteristic of experienced meaning functioning in creative symbolization: a meaning can be specified as likenesses, and likenesses can be specified as meanings.

4. RELATION OR RELATA

Since meanings can be seen as relations between meanings, a creative process is possible in two directions: a given experienced meaning may function in (a) creating relations to (new aspects of) other experiences; (b) creating other experiences between which this given one is a relation. Thus, an experienced meaning may be viewed as giving birth to a new meaning, or as aiding in the search for its parents. (From the viewpoint of experienced meaning, the metaphor of birth is as fitting as the spatial metaphor of relations "between" meanings.)

New aspects can be specified either as a relation "between" it and something or as aspects both "of" it and "of" that other something. As experienced meaning, it is all three.

Note that more than one meaning must function in such a creative process. We have mentioned this earlier. We can call the process one of "interaction of experienced meanings." What if one has only one meaning? But we already know that this is never the case (meanings being non-numerical and implying, including, "already" having, relations to many, many meanings). Let us deal with this multiple aspect in more detail.

5. MULTIPLICITY

Several factors operate to make all meaning-to-us capable of being multiple. (We noted, in discussing metaphor, that there were always many more than one meaning, that is, many more than one likeness between the new and old meaning.) Let us draw together here some of the characteristics of experience that make for the multiplicity of any meaning qua had-by-us.

a. An experience is multiple. The "non-numerical" character of experienced meaning implies that *many* meanings are "already in" any experienced meaning (that is, they are capable of specification). These meanings "already in" it denote functions of felt meaning. We have seen that in each functional relationship the meanings said to be "already in" an experience are a myriad of specifiable meanings.

b. Experiences have multiple interactive relationships. In discussing "recognition," we noted that the felt meaning that stands in a relationship of being "called forth" by symbols is capable of being *further* specified by other symbols as well. The felt meanings that are called forth are capable of "selecting" other symbols (including objects, situations, and so on). We noted that "recognition" and "explication" engender each other, and that this process of engendering more "recognition" and more "explication" could proceed in both directions from any given point: a given felt meaning can function to select symbols that call forth more (because they call forth a felt meaning capable of more specification). A given felt meaning can be called forth by symbols, situations, or objects ("symbols" in the widest sense). These could "call forth" other felt meanings, which in turn could select other symbols. The processes of "calling forth" and of "selecting," which were perfectly parallel relations of felt meaning and symbols, can be set in motion and can have many steps. This is the case because a felt meaning is capable of more than the one aspect that is specified in each of these parallel relationships.

c. The equivalence of (a) and (b). We noted that there was a limit to the applicability of the parallel type of relationship. Hence, we moved on to the relationship of "metaphor," in which we focused on this multiplicity as capacity for the creation of meaning, and the *many* likenesses implicit in it.

What we said under (a) is not essentially different from

(b). After all, the difference between (a) and (b) is that in (a) we considered the multiplicity as internal to an experience, in (b) as external. But, characteristic 1, the non-numericality, was precisely the finding that there is no real difference between internal and external multiplicity, that is, between "within the experience" and "among experiences."

We can say that these two, (a) and (b), are functionally equivalent, since they refer to the same experienced aspect of experience. However, they are different qua logically specified formulations.

d. The as yet unspecified is multiple. The multiplicity of felt meanings generates the process or movement we noted in (b).[12] Before they are explicated, very many unspecified meanings are "in" the felt meaning that is "our having" of the specified aspect of it. These unspecified capacities of felt meaning function in cognition. In recognition and explication, we found a movement through successive recognitions and explications, brought on by the multiplicity of the felt meaning. It could be specified in multiple ways as more than was specified.

The movement we are describing is ordinarily called thinking. Thinking is the process of successively "selecting" symbols for present felt meaning, finding that the symbols "call forth" more felt meaning than one anticipated, than "selecting" more symbols for some of this excess. This excess can be specified in multiple ways.

We note, then, that (a), the "non-numerical" character of experience, (b) and (c), the creativity of many new aspects of experience through the interaction of experiences, and (d), the multiple possible specifications of any unspecified experience, all show *our fifth characteristic of experience*: "multiplicity."

12. Although it can also be specified as a "thing" capable of entering many relations.

6. ANY CONCEPT IS ONE OF MANY

From characteristics 1–5, it follows that a newly created aspect of experience will be only one of very many that might have been created ("created"—that is, specified, differentiated, synthesized, and so on) as an aspect of that experience.

This characteristic of experienced meaning has been already stated, especially in 1 and 5, where it was noted that an experienced meaning is always a multiplicity of aspects that could be created or specified.

However, all the experienced meanings that function in a creation of a new meaning determine the newly created aspect. Hence, it might be thought that *only one* aspect so determined could result. Thus multiplicity might be questioned. Yet, all these experiences are themselves multiple in the same sense. Very many aspects *of them* could be specified. Hence, it follows that although what is created is not arbitrary, but a very highly and finely determined product, a very great variety of new aspects might have been created.

It is speculative to say that if *all* the interacting experiences were known, the product could be seen to be uniquely determined by them. These experiences themselves are capable of multiple specifications. Hence their possible influence on what is created is also multiple. Yet this capacity to be specified in very many various ways functions vitally in the creation of new aspects.

Our sixth characteristic of experience (as functioning in the creation of new aspects of meaning), should read:

6(a). Any *newly* specified aspect of experience (new meaning) is only one of very many that might have been specified (created) from the same given meanings.

6(b). From 6(a) it follows that any meaning can be seen as only one of the very many aspects of some specified experiences. This means that one can consider any specified meaning as if it were a newly created aspect of the experiences, which it specifies. The given specified meaning is not the only way one can refer to or specify these experiences. Any meaning can be viewed as one of many possible meanings "relative to" certain referrable experiences.[13]

Another way to express 6(b) is to say that all specified meanings are metaphoric. (I. A. Richard's discussion exemplifies this very well.[14]) Any specified meaning is one of many possible creative specifications of some experience. For it many other meanings as a group are functionally equivalent (or seem so, temporarily, for certain purposes—"purposes" being another term like conditions, relevancies, contexts, experiences) (see Chapter VI).

Another conclusion from 6 is that only *after the creation* may logical analysis validly set forth the relations, forms, systems, contained in any creation of meaning. Logical analysis can say nothing about kinds of meaning not yet created. Therefore, it can say nothing about meanings that might have been created instead of those which were. But much of what follows from a given meaning is due to the peculiarities of how it is specified, not to the experiences. These could have been specified differently. Therefore, the relativity of any specified meaning will always be beyond logical analysis and its products.

7. ANY EXPERIENCED MEANING CAN (PARTLY) SCHEMATIZE (CREATIVELY DETERMINE) A NEW ASPECT OF ANOTHER EXPERIENCED MEANING

We have already noted that "other experienced meanings" were involved in the creation of the new aspect. We showed that the new aspect of A can be a relation between A and

13. "Relative" is thus defined as "relative to" certain experiences to which one can directly refer. Also, "relative" always implies other possible meanings (specifications) that refer to the same experience.
14. See the Appendix.

"others," or it can be related to A by "others." *BCDE,* the "other experienced meanings," partly determine the nature of this new aspect.

We didn't consider this determinacy of the "other experiences" under characteristic 4, because any of them could also be taken as A: any of them could be taken as "the" experienced meaning, of which a new aspect is being created. The functioning of the "same" experienced meanings could have created a new aspect of any of these other experiences. The experienced creating itself could be specified as a creation of an aspect of B or C or D or E, instead of A. We would do this if we tried to show how B functioned in the creation of an aspect of A. This would be done by specifying an aspect of B. "How B functioned" means the same as "an aspect of B," since the experienced creating could be specified as a functioning of B only by specifying an aspect of B. Since it was an aspect of A that was actually specified, this didn't occur. We thus never answered the question of how B functions when no aspect of B is specified, either as such, or later when one wants to show that B did function.

Let us now (characteristic 7) focus on the function of these "other experienced meanings" in partly determining a new aspect of A.

We will continue to let A stand for the experience whose aspect is being newly created; B, C, D, E will stand for the "other" experiences in interaction with which this creation occurs.

A, B, C, D, and E are multischematic; that is, they "already" contain an endless number of possible schemes, relations, aspects, *capable of being created, specified.* Since B functioned when an aspect of A was created in interaction with B, some possible scheme "already" in B can later be seen to have determined the new aspect of A. This scheme can then be separately specified of B or of the new aspect. Let us express this by saying that *B* can later be seen to have "*schematized*" the newly created aspect of *A*.[15]

For example, we ask: what in *A* is like *B*? Or, we ask: what in *A* could answer question *B*? We let *B* determine the aspect of *A* we seek to create. Of course *B* doesn't "determine" it *fully*, because that would just be *B*, as it stands. We instead seek some new aspect *of A* that is "already" in *A*, but that will fit *B*.

Many, many experiences (*B, C, D, E*) function in such a creative act. For example, the "context" is a whole mass of experienced meanings including what we really mean, why we ask, what we will accept as an answer and what not, and the purpose of the inquiry. Any question we ask, as well as many other meanings, all function to help schematize the to-be-created aspect of *A* that is "like" *B* or that fits the specifications of problem *B*.[16]

15. The principle that an experience can be schematized by another also implies that the "other" can be schematized by the first. However, the "schematiz*ed*" experience is the one of which an aspect is being specified. If it schematizes, instead of being schematized, an aspect of the other experience will result. (If, after the creation of meaning, we seek to explicate how *B* has functioned, we create an aspect of *B*. In that act of explicating how *B* schematized *A*, we are now really schematizing *B*, using the created aspect of *A* as the schematizing experience.

16. Here is some discussion related to the seventh characteristic.

(a) *Philosophies*. The ways in which experiences can schematize could be (and have been) used as a basis for philosophies of relations between concepts. Any such philosophy is an analysis of schematizings that have already occurred. However, there is no meaning that could *not* be used to schematize experienced meanings. Any peculiar aspect of any meaning is itself capable of being specificed as a meaning, as a relation, as a scheme. Hence, there are as many different ways of schematizing some meaning as there are other meanings and possible aspects of other meanings. The ways of schematizing are quite evidently countless.

A good philosophy of such relations between concepts is quite valuable and useful. However, it must be interpreted not as rules for concept formation, but as an analysis (one among countless possible ones) of some relations (some among countless ones) between some kinds of concepts (some kinds among countless ones). Of course, this fact is no reason why we should have no analyses at all. The *possible* richness and relativity would be a poor reason for depriving ourselves of some few such principles.

Seventh characteristic of experience (functioning in the creation of new meaning): Any experiened meaning can *schematize* another experienced meaning, or be schematized by any other experienced meaning.

8. EVERY EXPERIENCE IS CAPABLE OF HAVING AN ASPECT SCHEMATIZED BY ANY OTHER EXPERIENCE

The seventh characteristic implies the eighth. The seventh (that any experience can schematize or be schematized by any other) viewed creation of new aspects from the point of the *schematizing* experience. Let us now look at it from the viewpoint of the *schematized* experience of which it creates an aspect. Seven implies that any experience can be seen as having "already in" it an aspect that is schematized by any other experience.

If you think of two meanings *A* and *B,* you can find (create, specify) an aspect of *B* that is schematized by *A*. Since experienced meanings are multischematic, the schematic relation between them is created along with the new meaning.[17]

In our own task we have noted that, at every step, we must use some concepts, some principles, some schemes. We never tire of pointing out that these, too, are relative to the very characteristics of creative functional relationships of experienced and specified meaning, which they formulate. Without the employment of specified and schematized meanings, however, there could be no functional relationships and no philosophy or thought, either about such relationships or about something else.

(b) *The many are experienced as one.* We have been speaking of "two" meanings interacting as "two" experienced meanings. Actually, we experience them (and all the other meanings that could be specified as also functioning) in *one* felt experiencing, which is "our sense of" the problem, or the question, or the something we mean, or seek, or think. Of this felt (experienced) meaning we specify aspects. It is up to us—that is, up to the many meanings playing into this *one* felt meaning—whether the aspect we specify will be "of" one or another of these meanings. Hence, experientially, we can refer to the one interaction experience.

17. Seven and eight will hold true so long as some experienced meaning, that is something multischematic, can intervene. Seven and eight cannot hold true of two specified meanings, unless their experienced meanings can function in the creation of new aspects.

But suppose we begin with a given specified relationship, an instance of which is to be created between two other also specified meanings, *A* and *B*. The multischematic nature of experience can allow us to find an aspect of this given relationship. This new aspect can be schematized by both *A* and *B*. Therefore, its to-be-created application between *A* and *B* is multischematic, even if all three terms are uniquely specified.

Of course, neither 7 nor 8 (nor any of these characteristics) is possible of *specified* meanings, as such. They are only possible of *experienced* meanings qua what may be created (specified) of them. Hence, they refer to what is left open to creation —either a new relation, or a new thing, or some other new thing, found between given things and given relations. Thus, some new aspect of *A* can always be found, even if it must be related to *B* in a specified way, fit *C* for a certain problem, *D* in a certain relevance, *E*. . . . This is thinking. If nothing is left open for creation, any problem can be stated so that it is unsolvable and no thought can occur.

Nevertheless, it appears at first blush that our eighth characteristic is quite metaphysical. In fact, it is most neatly stated in a metaphysical way: "Because all possible schemes (all intelligibility) come from a metaphysical source *X*, therefore any scheme or meaning will embody some scheme that is a creation of *X*. Therefore, any scheme or meaning can be found again in any other meaning, since it is also a creation of *X*." In various philosophies, *X* has been God, nature, conditioning, the mind, and so forth.

However, we can leave the metaphysical answer quite open by using all these answers as functionally equivalent,[18] since they *can* refer to the experienced creative process. We can restrict their use as functionally equivalent, so that they refer only to the experienced creative process. Whatever is sup-

18. See p. 214 for definition of this term.

posed to control that process, that process does so function. We are only concerned with this function.

If we use these theories as functionally equivalent, we have no warrant on the basis of which to assert that there is one common determinant and that *therefore* any meaning can be found again in an aspect of any other meaning. Nor are we asserting that. We are asserting that such an aspect can be *created*. "Aspect" refers to what can *then* be seen to have been "already" in the experience.

It should be quite clear that we are not saying that any form will fit—or really be "already in"—anything. That would make all meanings arbitrary. On the contrary, a *new* aspect has to be created, precisely because a given meaning will not fit another given meaning in the given ways in which it may be asked to fit. Only the then created new aspect will so fit. Hence, this creative process is highly and finely determined by all the meanings that go into it.

For example: when the poet asks himself, "What is my love like?" he finds that some of what he experienced can be specified by calling it "like a red, red rose." With this specification he has created a new aspect of his experience of her—just what in her is like a red, red rose. Undoubtedly, he began with not exactly that aspect of her, but both more and less. Now let us look at how "like a red, red rose" can be found in "my love." It can be "found" in it, because a new aspect of it is created, and "like a red, red rose" can be found in that new aspect. For example, my love does not grow out of the ground. Thus, "red, red rose" doesn't fit the girl, but perhaps it fits her freshness. But our eighth characteristic demands that any meaning can be found in an aspect to-be-created of *any* other meaning. Very well, how does my love grow out of the ground? We create still another new aspect of her: she is deeply rooted in her native country and its culture, she is earthy, she appears suddenly and noiselessly as if out of the ground—so long as we play with only two meanings, we can, in fact, create very many new aspects of a meaning that will be schematized by the other meaning. Usually, in serious thought, very many experiences are interacting to finely determine the aspect to be created—and it may require genius to do it then.

We note that if B schematizes A, then there are aspects of B that fit and aspects of B that do not fit. If in turn we take these aspects that do not fit, we can again create new aspects of A, of which there will be aspects that these do fit.

The eighth characteristic is possible because any amount of intervening aspects and aspects of aspects can be created. To illustrate, let us ask: how can you be sure that any meaning N can be a relation between A and B? Only certain relations are possible between specified meanings. How does the endless multiplicity of experienced meanings enter this determined, limited relation between specified meanings?

A new aspect of A can be created with N; in fact, very many such "NA" aspects can be created. Between each NA and B, at least one relation is possible and this can be found. It is a relation between A and B. It is an aspect of N.

Note that as soon as we created the aspect of "my love" that "grows out of the ground," we could then inquire just what it meant and didn't mean. It related to the rose's growing out of the ground only in certain ways. (For example, not necessarily rooted to a spot. If this is to be said of "my love," still newer aspects must be created.) The logically necessary implications of specified meanings are not obviated by creativity.

If we can assert that any meaning can be a relation between any other meanings, we have covered all the other possible ways in which a new aspect schematized by any one meaning can be found in any other. Seven implies eight. If the creation is possible, the finding "in" is implied. The creation is possible and determined (schematized) by all the interacting experiences. Because they determine the creation, an aspect of them can be created that can be seen to have determined it, that is, that can be seen to be related to any (new) aspect of any experience, or indeed to any experience considered as being determined by it in the creation of aspects of it.

All these characteristics are possible because the multiplicity and multischematic character of experienced meaning enters and offers its capacities for countless new[19] aspects, whenever experienced creating of meaning occurs.

9. CREATIVE REGRESS

We must list as a ninth characteristic something we have spoken of many times in the foregoing: in the case of any given specified meaning, one may directly refer to the experienced meaning involved in it, and one may then specify that experienced meaning in a different way than the first given meaning had specified it.

This fact is a ninth characteristic, because it is applicable to experienced meanings qua capable of further symbolization. It applies no matter what functional relationships occur before or as a result of this transition from one to the other.

We experience transitions from one specified meaning to another, and from given specified meanings to new ones, via experienced meaning. At such transitions we *refer directly* to the experienced meaning (that is, to our having of the specified meaning), and we say something like, "Let me see, what did I mean by so and so?" or, "Now, what did I bring this up for?" or "What do I really mean by *X*?" Then we specify the felt meaning another way, or allow it to function

---

19. From this eighth characteristic it is especially clear that systems of formal logical relations can only offer *some* versions of the kinds of relations that *can be created*. We have shown this at the beginning of this chapter (p. 141) and will discuss it again in Chapters V and VI.

together with other experienced meanings, to create new aspects.

Let us call this deliberate "direct reference" to "what we meant," that is, to the experienced meaning, "creative regress." By "regress" we mean leaving the specified meaning and turning to the felt meaning—to our having of the meaning. By "creative" we indicate that we regress to the experienced meaning in order to create (specify, discover, or whatever) new aspects.

We are here concerned with the experienced fact that, in such a transition, an experienced meaning plays several roles: first, it is our having of a specified meaning; then, secondly, it is "directly referred" to in "creative regress"; then, thirdly, this (same?) experienced meaning is specified in a new and different way.

One cannot assert that the experienced meaning really is the "same" throughout, although one can't assert that it is not. However, it is an *experienced characteristic* of experienced meaning, that it may function in transitions as described, and that it is a present, concretely experienced fund of many possible specifications of it. Although the formulation of how we experience this presents theoretical problems, everyone will readily notice that he experiences it. We call it "creative regress," characteristic 9.

CHAPTER V

The Principle of

Universals: "IOFI"

Brief	In this chapter the basic principles of this philoso-
Statement	phy are discussed and illustrated.

Introduction

One may always stop in the midst of a discourse and ask, in reference to any given meaning in it, just what methodological considerations are involved in it and in its role in that discourse.

For example, one may consider how any meaning follows logically at the point in the discourse at which it arose, and thus engage in an examination of logical connections and problems. Or again, one may inquiry into the sort of meaning it is, the sort of defining it represents, the kind of conceptualization it is an instance of, the type of observations it is founded on, and so on. Then again, one may discuss the intent, in the discourse, that motivated its being mentioned, or again, the type of argumentative role it plays.

All these examples could occur on various levels of specificity or generality. For example, if the discourse is about democracy, one may stop at a given meaning and inquire into either what sort of definition of democracy it is an instance of, or what sort of definition of a state or citizen or political function (whatever it happens to be) it is an instance of.

Similarly, one may inquire into its role in the discourse insofar as it proves anything, or again insofar as it proves some more specified type of conclusion, for example, insofar as it proves something about a political function, or even insofar as it proves some type of peculiar aspect of political functions. It is evident that such methodological considerations can be extremely specific, yet always the methodological discussion is on a more general plane than was the original meaning. Methodological discussion is a reflection upon meanings in discourse, although, of course, this reflection involves its own meanings as well.

For example: "democracy is government by the people" might be cited—depending on how it appears in a particular discourse—as an instance of the following methodological considerations: definition; definition of democracy; the sort of definition that involves an identity of object and subject, since the people—if they govern, govern the people; and so on. Clearly countless methodological considerations on all sorts of levels of generality and specificity could be raised about any one meaning. If a meaning or several meanings appear in a discourse, some such considerations will be relevant, others irrelevant. Even so, countless relevant methodological considerations may be raised.

The meanings involved in raising the methodological considerations are themselves important. Often they are new meanings resulting from the asking of methodological questions about some meanings arising in discourse. Of course, methodological questions may again be asked of *these* meanings, and again of the meanings involved in asking these questions. Hence it is possible to create levels upon levels of methodological considerations of methodological considerations. Furthermore it is possible to raise immense schemes of such levels at *any* point in a discourse. At another point in the discourse similar but different schemes of such levels could be raised by inquiring in this fashion. Schemes of levels have been systematized by philosophy, but it is evident that no limit can really be placed on the kinds of levels and kinds of schemes that may result, since at any point, any meaning can be inquired into with methodological questions of very many sorts and levels of generality.

We may conclude: any given meaning may be reflected upon with methodological questions of all levels of generality, and, in turn, this reflecting may be reflected upon again with methodological questions of all levels of generality.

1. METHODOLOGICAL QUESTIONS CAN REFER TO THE KIND OF EXPERIENCING INVOLVED IN A MEANING AND ITS ROLE IN DISCOURSE

The present essay brings to this well-known methodological situation the additional consideration that any given meaning may be inquired into methodologically *as an experienced meaning.*

Everything that has been asserted previously about methodological reflection still holds. Now we add that one may ask methodological questions of any specified meaning *as* one specification of an experienced meaning.

We may ask our methodological questions as follows: what *kind of* experienced meaning is this? What kind of experienced "following from" other meanings is involved in this experienced meaning? What kind of experiencing does having this meaning involve? (We have often asked this methodological question in this essay.)

As has been shown, all meanings, relationships, logical connections, and so on have meaning *to us* as experienced meanings (that is, specifications from experienced meanings). Therefore: all methodological questioning can be considered in terms of specifying the experienced meanings that are (reflectively) seen to have been involved in the given meaning about which one asks methodological questions.

Let us therefore consider the many levels and kinds of methodological questions that can be asked of any meaning in a discourse, now in terms of specifying the experienced meanings seen to have been involved in the given meaning. Our present task, then, is an instance of creative regress, where a transition is made from a given meaning to the "direct reference" to the experienced meaning involved, and thence to a new specification of it. In our case the new specification of it will be one of methodological significance, that is, it will be the answer to some question about what *kind* of methodological entity the given meaning was.

Now, we have seen that methodological reflections always refer to some more general meaning, to some *kind* of meaning, rather than to the given meaning itself. They refer to the *kind of* thinking, questioning, "following from," defining, or whatever, of which the given meaning is an instance. Any methodological reflection considers the given meaning *as an instance* of some general, methodological category.

Various formulated logics and philosophies offer various groups of such basic methodological categories. Our examples (defining, thinking, cognitive activity, "following from," questioning, and so on) are examples of such methodological categories.

Principle. One may creatively specify new methodological categories by considering any given specified meaning as an instance of a (new) kind of methodological category in any (relevant) aspect of it or its role in the discourse.

Although this principle is perfectly obvious, it is not generally known, stated, or used. It is usually assumed that methodological categories are purely conceptual and uniquely determinable, although of course everyone admits their controversial nature. On the contrary, we find that *any* aspect of a given meaning or of its role in a discourse can be considered as an instance of that kind of *experiencing*, and it can be specified as an instance of many procedures, methods, kinds of concept, and the like.

Note that this principle is an instance of the conclusion of Section A, Chapter IV, where we asserted that relationships and meanings are created simultaneously and are two kinds of specification of one same experienced meaning. Thus relationships are tantamount to meanings and vice versa. Here, again, we find that any meaningful methodological aspect of a given meaning constitutes the discovery of a general (capable of recurring) methodological consideration (or concept or category). In other words, just as relations do not create meanings, so methodological categories do not create methodological meanings about a meaning in discourse. Instead, the discovery of meanings and methodological aspects of a given meaning is already tantamount respectively to the creation of new relations and new methodological categories. Of course, one may begin with an extant methodological category and inquire into a given meaning from its point of view. (Example: "What sort of definition, or what sort of essential definition, or what sort of definition of a state, is this?") But one may also inquire into "what sort of experiencing was involved in having this meaning," and thus discover simultaneously a methodological aspect of the given meaning and a new methodological category.

To apply this principle is to make a meaning deliberately reflexive. Some meanings are obviously reflexive: obviously instances of themselves as *such experiencing,* for example: "word picture" or "direct reference." Such meanings mean a class of experiencings of which they themselves, as experiences, are members. But, for any meaning (even those that do not already mean kinds of experiencings) we may seek a class of experiencings of which they are members, when considered as experiencings.

For example, let us say I am thinking, "Democracy is government by the people." I then refer directly to my experienced meaning. Let us say I was engaged in thinking about the problem that in democracies tyrants, demagogues, presidents—in short, individual powerful leaders—usually represent the popular interest against some ruling class, oligarchy, or aristocracy that has control of the democratic institutions. I *then* thought: "(but) democracy is government by the people!" After a while, I ask myself: "Now what was it I was after—or what did I really mean when I thought 'democracy is government by the people?'" Or suppose someone says, "What do you mean?" and I, knowing perfectly well what I mean, have creative regress to what I mean, because now I must make it explicit in other words. I refer to and grasp the felt meaning, and not only do I find and grasp it, but I consider it now from a slightly different, and further, viewpoint; for example: I want to know what its point or drift, or relevance, was at that stage of discourse ("what was I after?"); or I want to state more exactly what I meant, or I want to examine what kind of meaning I introduced, and what kind of introducing it was. One way in which the experienced meaning (which was involved in my thinking "democracy is government by the people") can be further specified is, "I brought up democracy, defined as popular government, as a contrary indication to what I had been thinking about democracy, since this usual definition is contrary to my thinking that the popular interest is usually represented by powerful individuals who tend to destroy democratic institutions."

We don't have many terms for this kind of experienced cognitive procedure. Here the term we would need might be "contrary indication raising," an essential activity in problem solving. Some terms of this kind that we do have are: questioning, answering, disagreeing, generalizing, illustrating, limiting, applying.

Definition of "experiencing procedure." The terms just mentioned specify different *"experiencing procedures,"* that is, experienced transitions between one step of thought and another.

In discussing such transitions, we have already mentioned (Chapter IV, Section B, 9) that the experiencing in a transition in thinking may be viewed as "one" experiencing of which the two steps of thought are simultaneous aspects (although they are specified at successive times). The specifiable "experiencing procedure" is a third aspect. In principle one might specify these aspects in any temporal order. For example, one may begin with a given meaning and seek the "experiencing procedure" involved in it and thereby find a more general meaning that also specifies the experienced meaning, that is, one that is another specification like the given one. Or, one may reflect upon a transition that has already occurred in thought, and seek to specify the "experiencing procedure" that has occurred between the two steps of the given transition. In either case, the experiencing may be conceived of as "one" with several specifications of it.

Although, as we have already noted, this specification of the experiencing as "one" is only a matter of our specifying, that is, is relative (it could have been specified as three different occurrences), the fact that we may do so in the case of any given specified meaning—or any given transition—*can* always be *experienced* and constitutes a principle of importance. To repeat this in different words: we can assert the identity of the experiencing of several aspects of such a transition, only in the sense that we may specify the experienced meaning involved in it as an "experiencing procedure." Hence, this is not a principle of what experiencing is, in some absolute sense, but rather a principle of what we may always do (always experience) with any given meaning.

The principle is this: in the case of any given meaning, the directly referred-to experienced meaning involved in it may be specified as an "experiencing procedure," that is, as a certain kind of more general meaning. *In the sense that this can always be done,* "experiencing procedure" and both given and other meanings in a discourse are aspects of the "same" experiencing.

It is not mysterious that (via the experienced meaning) it is possible to specify any meaning as an "experiencing procedure" and vice versa. A meaning (in a discourse) is intimately tied up with other meanings. Also, it *is* the meaning of the activity or "experiencing procedure" through which it rose. At some point in a discourse we say, "I've just had a thought." The experienced meaning of this "thought" is all of the following: (a) meaning(s) at that point in the discourse, (b) the given meaning (that is, the "thought" I've just had), and (c) the "experiencing procedure" or activity that constitutes this thinking (that is, this moving "from" other meanings "to" this one.) ("Moving from one to the other" is a spatial metaphor that can be used to specify this experienced "transition." The term "transition" is likewise a spatial metaphor of the same sort.)

In the case of *any* specified meaning, we may refer directly to the experienced meaning "involved" in it (to our having of the meaning). Furthermore, we may specify this experienced meaning differently and in various ways. (See the sections on "recognition," "explication," and "creative regress.") Hence, we may ask about this experienced meaning: what sort of experiencing is it? Many possible accurate answers can be specified. It will be a sort of thinking, perhaps, or a particular kind of observing, or of drawing a general or a particular or an ideal type or a causal concept. It may be a questioning, a referring, an illustrating, a supporting, an arguing, a remembering, a raising an issue about democracy, and so on. Specifications are possible on all levels of generality or specificity and in all degrees of cognitive or inexplicit specifications. Naturally, when this question (what kind of experiencing was this meaning an instance of?) is asked as part of a particular discourse, only certain kinds of specifications of experiencing are pertinent, since we are then examining a meaning as it has arisen as a transition in discourse. For example: the contrary-indication-raising ("experiencing procedure") of "but democracy is government by the people" can be seen also as an instance of the following relevant more general meanings: "problems of democracy"; "problems of democracy having to do with institutions of class"; "use of the definition of democracy in a literal sense"; "misuse of the definition of democracy in a literal sense"; "democracy as ideal or optimal, rather than empirical"; "method of ideal type definitions"; "common element of definitions of democracy as 'by the people' "; "general attempt at common element"; "attempt to get back to essential meaning assumed for democracy"; "attempt to recall desired meaning of democracy"; and so on. Any of these and other, more general meanings may play an important part in the discourse at whatever point it now is. Note that all these notions are more general than was the original statement "democracy is government by the people" and really are all new meanings, constituted by various experiencing procedures that may occur and be specified in transitions.

Now, our term "experiencing procedure" is itself an extremely general methodological category, created in this discourse. It is experienced meaning in general, considered as methodological procedure. Our creation of this category is an example of the procedure we outlined for creating methodological categories.

2. SPECIFYING EXPERIENCING AS AN INSTANCE OF ITSELF

The term "experiencing procedure" was found by asking of experienced meaning how it functions methodologically. Our answer (one of many possible answers) was to specify our experienced meaning of experienced meaning as "experiencing procedure." We noted that any experienced meaning, that is, any "having of" a meaning, is an instance of many different kinds of having, and using, and that we can term this notion of "kinds of having and using" as "experiencing procedure." Thus, any experienced meaning can be specified as an "experiencing procedure." Therefore any specified meaning can be seen to involve an "experiencing procedure."

Let us state differently what we have concluded. Let us employ the traditional term "faculty" or "operation (of a faculty)" instead of "experiencing procedure." We may speak of "operation (of a faculty)" since the experiencing usually referred to by "operation of a faculty" is the same as what we refer to by the term "experiencing procedure." Let us be explicit, however, that in our use either term refers to experienced meaning, now specified as an operation or a procedure.

What we have concluded is an (experiential) version of a traditional philosophic tenet, namely that meanings are (or involve) operations of faculties. Furthermore, one traditional fashion of defining or accounting for "meaning" is as a reflection of a faculty upon itself. (Also, as St. Thomas puts it, "the understanding turning upon itself with a full turn.") So far, we have not quite paralleled this reflexive nature of the operation of a faculty (or, as we termed it, "experiencing procedure"). Instead, we have been saying only that operations of faculties ("experiencing procedures") are uncovered ("specified") when one reflects upon a meaning. (By "reflects" we mean directly referring to the experienced meaning involved, and then specifying it as an "experiencing procedure.") We noted that in this way rather than a few methodological categories (such as "faculty" itself, and all the many other different and more or less general methodological terms) we see in this principle the possibility of creating (specifying) many, many methodological categories, and levels of categories, depending on the meaning and the point of a discourse at which the principle is applied. However, we may carry our investigation of this principle further, and reach an experiential version of the traditional reflexivity that defines meaning in terms of the turning on itself of a faculty.

Let us restate the principle. We said that "one may generalize (new) methodological categories by considering any given specified meaning as an instance of a (new) kind of methodological category of any (relevant) aspect of the meaning or its role in the discourse."

Let us call this the principle of "instance of itself" ("iofi"), recalling that we mean instance of itself qua "experiencing procedure." By "experiencing procedure" we meant an expo rienced meaning (our having of any specified meaning) qua specified as some methodological category (for example: a kind of faculty or a kind of defining, or a kind of defining democracy).

The "iofi" principle asserts that one may consider any specified meaning as an instance of *a kind of* "experiencing procedure." One may ask, "What kind of experiencing procedure do I find here?" and thus create (specify) new methodological meanings.

On the other hand, we have already shown that any meaning is really an instance of *such* an experiencing, since any meaning is general, can occur more than once, is some "respect in which" two occurrences can be said to be "like."

Hence it appears that any meaning is simultaneously *an instance* of itself (that is, an instance of a general meaning stating an aspect of it) qua "experiencing procedure" and qua meaning (aspect capable of being "like.") We must now examine this reflexive identity in detail.

3. REFLEXIVITY: EXPERIENCING AS AN "IOFI" IS MEANING

Near the start of the treatise, we formulated "meaning" in experience as a "symbolic function of experience" or "a functional relationship between experiencing and symbols." We found these two terminologies equivalent, since each "functional relationship with symbols" defines a *symbolic function of experience* (as well as of symbols) and since symbols (in the widest, most inclusive sense) are necessary if experience is to have a symbolic function.

Here is another definition of symbolic function of experience. Susanne Langer says:

No human impression [1] is only a signal from the outer world; it always is also an image in which possible impressions are formulated, that is, a *symbol* for the conception of *such* experience.[2]

Susanne Langer implies that the symbolic function of an experience is to stand for other experiences like it. We have already noted that *the respect in which* an experiencing is capable of being "like" another is basically "meaning," and conversely, that meaning is basically universality: that is, the capacity to occur more than once, and thus constitute a basis for comparison. Hence Susanne Langer's statement can be taken to mean in our terms that meaning is the capacity of experience to be (or "stand for") an experience qua *such* an experience.

1. Susanne Langer speaks of "impression," presumably impressions of the five senses. There is no reason why we should not extend her statement to experiencing in the wider sense in which we have been concerned with it.
2. Susanne K. Langer, *Feeling and Form* (New York: Charles Scribner's Sons, 1953), p. 376. Italics supplied.

To rephrase Susanne Langer: any meaning may be viewed as an instance of itself qua *such* experiencing, that is, itself qua universal. We may consider any meaning as an instance of *such* experiencing (the experiencing involved in having that meaning, that is, the experienced meaning). Let us call this manner of considering a meaning "iofi": "instance of itself."

We have noted (in all the functional relationships, and in our discussion of "creative regress") that for any given, specified meaning, we may refer also to an experienced meaning— although the relationship between them and hence the meaning of the terms ("meaning," "specified meaning," "experienced meaning involved in having it") is different in different functional relationships. Hence we have noted many different ways in which any meaning may be considered as experienced meaning. We are now adding that an experienced meaning has meaning insofar as it is an instance of itself qua *such* experiencing. That is, a meaning is a respect in which an experiencing can be *such,* general, occurring more than once, "like." In other words, an experience has meaning insofar as the experience is an instance of itself. But we said at the outset that an experience has meaning insofar as it has a "symbolic function" or enters into a "functional relationship with symbols." Are these two definitions of what constitutes meaning of an experience consistent?

In order to be *an* experience, there must be a functional relationship between experiencing and symbols, such that *an* experience is specified ("specified" has different meanings in the different functional relationships). Hence, if *an* experience is to be an instance of itself, it must be specified by some functional relationship with symbols ("symbols" in the widest sense, including things, situations, acts, and so on). Hence the two definitions of meaning of an experience imply each other.

Furthermore, the two definitions imply each other even

more directly, if we recall once more that the following three considerations come to the same thing: (a) some aspect of an experienced meaning specified in a symbolic relationship; (b) "meaning" as an aspect, in respect of which there can be "likeness" or recurrence more than once; (c) an experiencing as an instance of *such* experiencing (in some respect).

There cannot be *such* experiencing without some respect, and no respect can be created without that creation's being tantamount to a "meaning," that is, an aspect in respect of which there can be a repeatable meaning. Finally, aspects and respects are created (or specified) in symbolic relationships (such as the functional relationships outlined in this essay).

Here then we have an experiential version of the reflexive definition of "meaning" as (a faculty of) experiencing considered as an instance of itself (turning or reflecting on itself). We find, concretely and experientially, that if we consider the experienced meaning involved in the having of a specified meaning, and if we specify that experienced meaning as an "experiencing procedure," we *can specify* many and various experiencing procedures of which the given meaning is an instance. We find, then, that the meaning *is* (the respect in which there is) an experiencing qua instance of itself as *such* (in that respect).

It would be out of bounds for this study to assert that meaning in experience is constituted by (caused by) experiencing qua instance of itself in some respect. Rather, we have shown only that our characterizations of meaning imply each other in the three forms that we have put forward: respect of likeness, as aspect specified, and as experiencing qua "iofi." Instead of a causal definition of what brings about meaning, and instead of an ontological identity of these characterizations of meaning, we are offering an *experienceable* fact, that for any specified meaning an "experiencing procedure" *can be* specified as an aspect of the experienced meaning. Our conclusion is therefore an experiential version of the traditional formulation of reflexivity.

When one applies this principle (when one considers a meaning as "iofi") the usefulness of being able to experience the reflexivity becomes apparent.

At any stage of a discourse, or of an experience, or of a therapy session, one may consider a given meaning as an "iofi." One refers directly to the experienced meaning and asks, "What kind of experiencing (procedure) is this an instance of?" One may then *experience* the possibility of specifying that experienced meaning as a kind of experiencing, and thus obtain new meanings referring to new and pertinent kinds of experiencing. Above all, one is enabled to refer to experiencing now going on, regardless of how it is specified. The last sentence means that to be able to refer to and discuss the experiencing that occurs is even more important than just how it is formulated, specified. A great many important aspects of any problem become apparent when the kind of experiencing involved can be referred to, and when meanings can be made instances of the kind of experiencing they involve.

Clearly, then, we are not offering only a method to obtain new methodological categories, relevant to a specific meaning and discourse. We are also offering a method by which one may (with whatever specified meanings) refer to the experiencing that is occurring. In many problems the experiencing that existentially occurs is the vital consideration. The particular specifications of it as this or that kind, or as *of* this or that specified meaning, are often not as important. Yet the present situation in science and philosophy has so far offered no sensible way of referring to experiencing, except via reference to the specified meanings *of* which it is an experiencing. But specified meanings are only specified instances of such experiencing. For example, in psychotherapy much discussion among the schools centers on whether these or those concepts represent "depth" therapy, that is, whether complexes around parents, sexual difficulties, life style, or lack of autonomy are the deepest therapeutic issues. All these discussions ignore the experiencing that occurs in the client's consideration of these concepts. The experiencing itself is the existential occurrence of therapy. Specification of this experiencing is possible in these or those concepts. (All these schools have similar percentages of successful cases.) Yet the scientific issues center on the specifications of the experiencing, as if only concepts and no experiencing occurred. (See detailed discussion of this exemplary issue, Chapter VII.)

The preceding example emphasizes the importance of the possibility of sheer reference to the experiencing involved in having a meaning. Let us return now to the other benefit of the application of the "iofi" principle, namely the creation of new and specifically relevant methodological questions and categories, which is possible for any given meaning and discourse.

According to how it is specified (that is, formulated) an experienced meaning can be both an "experiencing procedure" and a "new and more general meaning." The latter is the respect in which the former is *such* experiencing. The former constitutes a meaning qua being instance of itself as *such* experiencing.

Hence we may rephrase any "experiencing procedure" as a general meaning, and vice versa. These general meanings, of course, refer to some methodological (that is, more general) level of discourse than the given meaning. Thus, if discourse now continues into the "iofi" of the given meaning, it proceeds on some more general, methodological level. However, these "more general, methodological" levels may still be very close, relevant, and specific to the subject matter at hand. For example, a discussion of the sort of experiencing involved in having the meaning "democracy is government by the people" at the juncture of discourse at which our example stood, could be of all levels of generality and specificity, from logical considerations of "contraries" (what sort of contrary is this, when a whole proposition is a contrary indication to a whole line of argument?) to considerations very specific to this subject, such as "so defining democracy involves both identifying and opposing government and people."

From the above examples it is clear that in thought very frequently the "ideas" that come to us relevantly and move discourse forward are specifications of the experiencing procedure involved in having the preceding meanings.

Our example was drawn from theoretical thinking, and "experiencing procedure" thus appears to be a purely logical process. Although "experiencing procedure" (the *kind* of experiencing we specify as just having been involved in an experienced meaning) certainly *can* be specified in terms relevant to logic, or to the theoretical subject at hand, it can, of course, also be specified with respect to intent, motivation, personal needs, and in fact (see Chapter IV, B, Sections 7 and 8) any relevant consideration.

We also showed that for some subject matters experiencing is itself the relevant consideration. Furthermore, in any meaningful observation of sense perception and of situations, again the meaningfulness of the observation can be specified as instances of *such* experiencing and as instances of general meanings. Since in philosophy the role of "experience" (by which is usually meant external observation) as a validating and meaning-originating source is vital, and since meaningful observation involves the broadest possible spectrum of possible respects in which experiencing could be "*such*" experiencing (that is, the broadest possible capacity for the creation of meaning), philosophy itself is concerned not only with the logical or theoretical aspects of any experiencing, but with all possible, specifiable aspects. Let us therefore phrase the "iofi" principle so that it is relevant to the role of external observation as a foundation for assertions:

Since experiencing can be specified in myriad ways and can thus be an instance of *such* experiencing in myriad ways, these myriad ways also represent the ways in which an observation can be meaningful.

Hence concept formation *from* observation can be viewed as the specification of many senses in which the experiencing (the observing) was *such* experiencing.

We may apply this principle directly to any observations or other experiencings of our own, and make universals, i.e. concepts, i.e. meanings, i.e. "respects in which it is an instance of itself," from any aspects of the experiencing we can specify. Therefore, reflection on the experienced meaning (such as "what kind of experiencing was that?" or "what kind of experiencing was that an instance of?") is a question that (through direct reference to the experiencing) can help us specify countless meanings. Since specifications of new meanings (see "metaphor") are partly determined by all the meanings relevantly present in a given moment, we are likely to arrive at some meanings relevant to the task at hand, as well as, of course, a great many possible irrelevant meanings (respects in which it is "iofi"), which we do not stop to specify because they are irrelevant.

The following example will illustrate the many possible new meanings that can be created when a given experience is considered as "iofi." However, the example suffers from the fact that it has no role in any discourse or problem or present situation. Hence all the meaning created will be irrelevant, except as illustrations of our present thinking about "iofi."

The following example also illustrates that application of the "iofi" principle must always start from a given meaning.

It might have been neater and more philosophically striking if we could have started with experiencing as a raw, meaningless something and traced how it became *such an* experiencing. This can be done only in part: the reader may attempt to do so. By attempting to do so he will take some slice, some segment, some "this" of experiencing that has not been a "this" to him prior to his so taking it—for example, these few moments up to the period "." As soon as he has done so, he has directly referred to "this," and, let us say, he continues to refer to it. (If conceived of as a "thing," it is now "back there" in time. If conceived of as a process, it is continuing and is a changing, now including all his present experience and changing.) He can easily now note "experiencing procedures": reflecting, remembering, using as an example, struggling to hold onto, focusing on a point, trying to understand, identifying a point with a moment, direct reference, introspection, complying with sudden instructions, and many other possible "experiencing procedures" that might be specified as part of his experiencing. What may be specified as procedures is multiple, as is the case with all such symbolization. Each of these procedures constitutes a meaning of the experiencing, insofar as it is a respect in which the experiencing is an instance of *such* experiencing.

We have, then, in the "iofi" principle a possible experienceable method (it is itself an experiencing procedure, if you like) by which we open up to our creation of new meaning a whole vast field of specifiable meanings in the case of any given meaning we wish. Methodology is thereby based on the experienced process of creating meaning, and must reckon with (as well as take advantage of) its relativity and multiplicity, as well as with all the characteristics of experiencing in the creation of meanings.

For example: any given set of logical processes, logical connections and implications, or logical forms of concepts, is *one* set. At any given meaning, even one involved in stating such a set, we may (by referring directly to the experienced meaning and specifying ways in which it is an instance of itself) arrive at many more new and different logical processes, relations, or concepts, as well as the ones any given set proposes. All logical rules that seem as if they controlled the formation of meanings are merely formulations of "iofi's" that could have been different. No matter what they are, we specify them in the experiencing of the meanings they appear to control (just as we showed with "likeness" or "comparing" which is philosophy's most frequent fundamental logical principle).

Any meaning is in multiple respects an instance of *an* experiencing qua *such*.

5. "IOFI" IS THE PRINCIPLE OF THE FUNCTIONAL RELATIONSHIPS

The "iofi" principle is the (or a) principle of universalizing. We have already seen that meanings are universals, that is, they are respects in which occurrences can be said to be repeatable, or to be instances. Since the "iofi" principle allows us to regress and specify, as a new meaning, some respect in which the experiencing is *such* an experiencing, it is a principle of making new meanings (new universals).

We must elucidate the relationship between "metaphor" and "iofi," since both concern newly created meaning. What is the relationship between the functional relationships (such as "metaphor") and the "iofi" principle?

The "iofi" principle is called a principle because it formulates the fundamental rule that if an experienced meaning is found to be *such an* experiencing in any respect, that respect can be universalized, that is, can be a meaning. All the functional relationships are cases in which an experienced meaning functions so that specified (symbolized) meanings are specifications of it. The "iofi" principle can be considered to be the principle of all the functional relationships.

We have already noted that the functional relationships as they are formulated and cited in this essay are only relative; that is, other formulations of functional relationships are possible, and even in our own list some could be omitted or made special cases of others. The "iofi" principle can be considered as the principle of any functional relationships (both those in this essay and other possible formulations) since it is the principle of regress to any experiencing involved in having a meaning. It is the principle of any experienced functioning of experienced meaning in the having of a specified meaning. It is thus the principle of this treatise.

The "iofi" principle was approached as a principle of creating new experiential versions of *methodological* categories, because that was the clearest way of approaching it. However, if we consider that all the functional relationships are instances of "iofi," we note immediately that only a small proportion of the applications of "iofi" are of chiefly methodological interest. Functions of experienced meaning were pointed out (in each of the functional relationships) that are vital in many kinds of situations. The "iofi" principle, although itself a methodological principle, is the principle of specifying new meaning of the experienced meaning just *involved in having* the preceding specified meaning. It asks: "What kind of experiencing was this an instance of?" ("In what respects can this experiencing be considered an instance of *such* experiencing?") The specification that answers this question *can* always be of methodological interest, but most often it is of subject-matter interest.

6. AN OPTIONAL DISTINCTION AMONG THE FUNCTIONAL RELATIONSHIPS APPLIED TO "IOFI" AND TO RELATIVITY

Looking at each functional relationship with "iofi" in mind, we find that "direct reference," "metaphor," and "circumlocution" (each in a somewhat different sense) specify a "this." They refer directly to the experiencing just then involved in having some specified meanings and they specify that experiencing as "this." They allow the symbols of the specified meanings to refer to "this." Insofar as they specify a "this" (an experiencing) they have created a meaning, since there can be *an* experiencing only if it is differentiated in some respects, i.e. in some repeatable aspects, i.e. meanings. On the other hand, these functional relationships make further multiple specifications possible, since the "iofi" principle may be applied over and over again, and since the specification of an experiencing as "this" allows one to specify (discover, create, find) in it many more further aspects, i.e. meanings.

"Recognition," "comprehension," and "relevance," on the other hand, are formulations of applications of "iofi" that focus on just the latter half of the above description: that is, they are just such "further" (also multiple) specifications of the possible meanings that can be specified of just such an already given "this."

We may, if we wish, note that in our assertions there has been involved all along a distinction between two general aspects (we are now creating two new meanings) of the "iofi" principle: creating (or specifying) a "this," and creating (or specifying) new aspects of a "this." It is really the latter that specifies meanings. The former opens up the possibility of specifying meanings. (We have seen that a metaphoric meaning is really such multiple possibilities.) Let us call these two aspects of "iofi": "entitizing" and "universalizing." Throughout this essay these two facets have arisen, but it has been impossible to relate them to each other in some one certain fashion. They involve each other in criss-crossing and mutually inclusive ways. The "iofi" principle asserts that any entity (any "this") is an instance of *such* experiencing, that is, is also an instance of universals, and vice versa, that any universal (qua experienced) is an occurrence of some experiencing to which direct reference ("this") is possible.

Since experiencing is non-numerical (until specified), aspects *of* an experiencing are themselves again *both* universals (respects in which it is *such*) *and* entities, directly referred to as ("this") experienced meanings capable of further aspects.

As we have done periodically through this treatise, we must again stop to remind ourselves that our own terms are "relative"—that is, that we *refer directly* to the functioning of experienced meanings in cognition and that this functioning could be *formulated* in terms other than our own. Our distinction of "this" and "such" (an old one in philosophy) certainly refers to something experienced, to experienced functions of experienced meanings. We have striven to communicate which experienced functions of experienced meaning the terms refer to. Other terms could refer to them, yet such other terms would create other logical implications and generate schemes other than the present one.

Relativity, itself, applies both along lines of "entitizing" and along lines of "universalizing." We have just mentioned that this distinction can be considered "relative." If we wish, for the moment, to hold this distinction constant, and apply it to relativity itself, we may note that *formulation* of "this" aspect of experiencing is relative in two respects *according* to this distinction. The experiencing involved (for example, the experiencing of which the distinction "this" and "such" is a formulation) (a) may be *entitized* differently, or again, (b) while entitized as by us, it may then be *further formulated* differently. Let us give examples of alternative possibilities of each.

(a) We may, of course, simply not make this distinction. The "iofi" principle applies to any experienced meaning (*this*) by creating respects in which it is instance of *such* experiencing. Why did we make the distinction at all? Because the ways in which the two involve each other was of importance. However, we could have entitized the distinction as between "methodological" and "subject matter." Such a distinction would have distinguished different aspects, would have "entitized" differently, yet again we could have referred to the experienced fact we wished to refer to. We could have asserted these two aspects to involve each other. (b) Then again, if the two aspects we "entitized" are held constant, we may consider their formulation as relative. Consider the following philosophical questions, which *can* all be taken as referring to the two aspects we "entitized": "essence and existence"; "generality and uniqueness"; "conception and sensation"; "comprehension and metaphor."

Of course, these issues (the issues of the relationship between the terms) *can* also be taken as referring to other aspects of experience.

We have thus shown how even the manner in which meanings are "relative" can be considered according to this distinction of the two aspects of "iofi." Naturally that would be so, not only because of characteristics 7 and 8 in Chapter IV (according to which any meaning can be applied to an experienced meaning, and aspects can be specified accordingly), but also because the "iofi" principle really is the principle of the "relativity" presented in this essay, that is, a "relativity" of multiple experiential possibilities of creation of meaning. The "iofi" principle can be viewed as the principle of this multiple experiential creativity of meaning.

There are several different "iofi's," in the sense of new methodological meanings, which we may specify from what we have been doing:

(a) "Relativity" of specified meanings applies even to different senses of "relativity" itself. Every particular way in which meanings are considered to be "relative" involves a scheme that is itself relative.

(b) Many philosophic issues can be seen to be "iofi" of the iofi principle, that is, instances of the sort of experiencing that is involved in applying the "iofi" principle. We have mentioned some issues that could be seen as instances of "iofi."

7. "IOFI," RELATIVITY, AND AN EXEMPLARY ISSUE MUTUALLY APPLIED TO EACH OTHER

Let us discuss a little further one of these issues: "generality and uniqueness." For example, in aesthetics there is frequent discussion of the fact that the work of art is somehow both *unique* and of *general* significance. A painted object is not "realistic" (if for no other reason, because it is flat), and so it isn't clear why it seems to have more general significance than a concrete instance of such an object in reality. On the other hand, it is not its flatness that gives it its uniqueness. The uniqueness presents a further problem, since it consists of deliberate artistic characteristics. A work of art may be so unique as not to "represent" anything, yet it may have general significance.

Our example was chosen from painting. In drama the case is even sharper. No one is like Hamlet. Why then does Hamlet have more general significance than one of the people we know in life?

As we said, this issue can be taken to refer to a great many different aspects and areas of experience. Let us consider it as an instance of the "iofi" principle. We would then say that the "general significance," that is, the meaning, lies in the *new* respects in which one has *such* experiencing. The more unique it is, the more *new* respects in which it is *such* experiencing. This is not saying that the work of art is like what we know. Rather it creates new respects in which some thing *can* be like something else.

In therapy the same duality of "general significance and

uniqueness" occurs. The more a client formulates his own unique feelings accurately, the more possible and easy it becomes for the counselor to understand him. He does not *merely* "entitize" (differentiate as a "this") his feelings, because entitizing also involves the creation of new respects in which something is *a* this, that is to say: *such* experiencing. Hence Wilhelm Dilthey could assert that, in principle, any human expression is understandable, no matter how unique. The more unique, the more both persons will have created new respects in which experiencing is a *such*, i.e. more meanings, i.e. more respects in which it is capable of being "like" something, i.e. the more understandable.

Let us "apply" this conclusion (about generality and uniqueness) to our discussion of relativity. "Apply" in this instance will mean letting the conclusion about uniqueness "schematize" our concept of relativity.

We noted, in our discourse on relativity, that several concepts or schemes could be taken to refer to some "same" experiencing. On the other hand, we also noted that to isolate or refer to *an* experiencing, one must already imply a scheme. Hence, on the one hand, some "same" experience may be the basis on which a group of concepts are all "relative" (that is, they all refer to, are relative to, the same experiencing). On the other hand, a "same" experiencing already depends on being specified, that is, depends on relative specification.

Now, let us apply to this point of our discourse the conclusion that the more uniquely an experienced meaning is specified, the more respects are created in which it can "mean" or be "like."

We may then conclude that any scheme (such as would entitize an experience) creates respects in which it is an instance of *such* experience, that is, it creates meanings, "respects" in which the experience can be "like" others. Hence, while schemes entitize uniquely, they *thereby* offer new possibilities of specifying "like" experiences or "same" experiences.

Relativity thus involves a "same" with respect to which there is relativity, and yet the schematizing of a sameness is also relative. It requires schematizing to entitize the "same" experience to which concepts may be relative. However, the more differently and uniquely a scheme entitizes, the more new respects can be created in which what it entitizes and other experiences can be considered as the "same" experience, to which some concepts may be relative.

It is, therefore, by referring to (and specifying) a *different, new, unique* experiencing that a scheme makes its own relativity possible, since it *thereby* specifies some respects (and makes further specification possible) in which the experience, which is so uniquely specified, can be considered the "same" as many other experiences. Of course, if one considers these respects as purely logical specified meanings, they will not fit other schemes. If, however, the "iofi" principle is applied to any scheme, then the "kinds of experiencing" involved will offer me new respects in which I, with my different scheme, may creatively specify. In that sense, the more uniquely *different* is the experiencing that another scheme specifies, the more new respects I learn in which it may be the same as (or like) the experiencing that I specify.

This conclusion also implies that different schemes and different issues may be brought together as referring to some "same" experiencing in different and relative ways. When it is said, above, that the different experiencing specified by another scheme gives me ways in which that experiencing may be like the experiencing specified by my scheme, it is evident that there is no one absolute basis in experience itself that determines which issues or schemes or concepts will be said to refer to the "same" experiencing. Instead, all creation of meaning offers new possibilities in which different concepts, schemes, and issues can be created as specifications of some new "same" "such" experiencing.

Looking back, we note that in this section we have applied and cross applied distinctions, conclusions, principles, and schemes to each other. Thus we found that our distinction of two aspects of "iofi" could be taken to be the "same" experiencing as that referred to by the issues of philosophy we listed. Then again, we found that one particular conclusion in one of these issues could be referred to the same experiencing as the two aspects of "iofi" and the relativity of concepts. *And so on!* The "iofi" principle makes it possible for every scheme, concept, meaning, to be an instance of some "same" experiencing as some other scheme, concept, or meaning, because any meaning can be an instance of respects in which this is possible.

8. REFLEXIVITY

Now, it is possible to style our "iofi" principle quite humbly or quite magnificently.

Humbly styled, it is merely one way of conceptualizing an experienced meaning: experienced meaning is multischematic. One may approach experienced meaning (characteristics 7 and 8) with any notion or scheme in mind and thus schematize it to create a new meaning. Why not, then, approach it with the notion of "experiencing procedure" (respect in which it is an instance of *such* experiencing)?

Styled magnificently, we may say "iofi" is the principle of all symbolic functions of experiencing, since they all are instances in which experiencing is specified as *such an* experiencing. It is the principle of our whole study, which, of course, seeks "experiencing procedures" of meaning, the functions of felt meaning in cognition.

What is much more than that, it is the principle of all meaning because it is the principle according to which experiencing can be seen as *such an* experiencing.

Furthermore, it is the principle of the creation of meanings about meanings, or of meanings about the relationships between meanings. This includes *both* methodology *and* any sort of new meanings insofar as newly created meanings are further respects in which the experiencing involved in having extant meanings can be instances of (newly specified) *such* experiencing.

Therefore, styled magnificently, "iofi" is the principle of all we have asserted as well as of our procedure in asserting all we have asserted. Let us apply the term "reflexivity" to this identity between what is asserted and one's procedure in asserting it.

Reflexivity is a certain attractive neatness, but it is much more than that. Of course, it is aesthetically satisfying to note that the whole also bears the forms of the parts, as for example in a painting the division of its largest areas will often be reminiscent of the shapes of some of the main objects in the painting. But this is not the main significance of our reflexivity.

The main significance of our reflexivity is that, *since we refer to experiencing directly both in assertions and in our method of reaching these assertions, naturally then, what we assert of experience must apply also to experience as we have been employing it to reach these assertions. Thus, our essay is an instance of itself qua* SUCH *experiencing.*

"Iofi" can (but need not) be seen as the principle of our essay, since it is one of many possible methodological assertions of what we have been doing. We have been creating meanings by means of directly referring to experienced meaning as we find it involved in various ways in a given meaning, and by specifying what kind of (*such*) experiencing that is.

Now, in stating the "iofi" principle itself as a general methodological meaning, we have specified what kind of experiencing is involved in all of our own procedure. (Of course, experiencing always offers multiple possibilities of specification, no matter how many meanings already schematize it. Hence, the "iofi" principle is not the only one that could specify a kind of experiencing involved in our procedure.)

"Iofi" is reflexive both (a) in that its own arising as a meaning is an instance of it (it is the kind of "experiencing procedure" we have been using in our own procedure) and (b) in that, of course, it expresses "reflexivity" as such. The term "reflexivity" refers to any case where something is an instance of itself.

Of reflexivity in general, we must say something further. Cognition depends[3] on reflexivity, as Susanne Langer stated. It depends on the capacity of experiencing to be an instance of itself qua capable of being universal.

9. THE "IOFI" PRINCIPLE AND TRADITIONAL PHILOSOPHY

Meaning is experiencing qua instance of itself. What is experiencing? I point to it in my experience. The question is like the question, "What is sense perception?" As with Aristotle's "nature," one does not *prove* its existence. Causes of experiencing, causes of sense perception or of nature are possible, but not a proof of their existence. Nor is it possible to define experiencing in a fashion that does not in some way lean on reference to it. Without such reference one does not define it, one defines causes or logical contructs. Hence, we might say that "experiencing is not a predicate." It is demonstrable, but not a demonstration; it can be conceptualized but it isn't a concept.

This is one of the most fundamental assertions made here, as obvious as it is. It accounts for the reversal of philosophic procedure in Section A of Chapter IV. It lies at the bottom of

3. (Can be seen to depend.)

our whole enterprise; it is the "iofi" principle, the functions. With it we may correct one of the most constant errors in psychology, namely the identification of a concept with the experiencing of which the concept is a conceptualization. In therapy it becomes a vital realization without which the ideational superstructure is taken for therapy instead of the experiencing, and it becomes mysterious why, as Freud said, it was easy to figure out what was wrong, but the patient could not be convinced of it, or if he could it did no good. . . .

Both the "iofi" principle and the demonstrable existence of experiencing are basic to reflexivity of cognition in general: only if some point of identity is found between experiencing as an existential occurrence on the one hand, and experienced *meaning* on the other, can meaning be accounted for in experience. Only so can experience be referred to by concepts; only so can one conceptualize experience. Of course, the experiencing we here describe can be conceptualized differently, and then reflexivity may not be the best or even a possible way of generalizing (iofi) the procedure used. Thus, we would not expect all philosophies to be reflexive even though we do expect them to refer to, conceptualize, and employ that aspect of experiencing which, in our discourse, is represented by the notion of reflexivity. In that sense reflexivity is fundamental. The fundamental aspect of experiencing to which it refers is this: experiencing qua occurrence and qua meaningful are not the same, but must at some point be identical.

This is old. Only the claim that the *experienced* identity is systematically possible is new.

For Descartes, also, any idea could be considered either as what it is about or as itself existential. Similarly, we are considering any meaning either as its specified content or as itself an experiencing. When we do the latter, we create some new meaning (of it as such an experiencing), which Spinoza called the idea of the idea. The idea of the idea (for us "of the experiencing procedure") has the first idea for its content, but is itself again an idea (a something or an experiencing). For these men the regress stops here, because an idea of the idea of the idea would again be the same as the idea of the idea. The content would be the same for the third as it was for the second. For us, however, every "iofi" point—every idea of the experiencing procedure of an idea—has non-numerical, multischematic possibilities, hence there can be many ideas of one idea—and many ideas of any one of these ideas of the idea. Given a single set of such "levels," one will reach some top level, for example, the very procedure of taking the "iofi." But choosing, perhaps, only one different possibility at some one point, will generate a different set of levels. The considerations raised up and down these levels will advance consideration of the problem and thus raise new meanings, which can again generate new levels. At any point one may choose some scheme and allow it to schematize the discussion, but one need not.

Hence, distinguished from those of Descartes and Spinoza, the present is a various and creative scheme, rather than a unitary one. The top principle might be "iofi," that is, the many possibilities in which experiencing can be general, qua experiencing procedure of having *such* a meaning. This principle thus represents endlessly various possible creativity of meaning from out of experiencing as procedure of having meaning. Rather than a logical reflexive principle of valid ideas, it is a principle representing creativity in experiencing.

CHAPTER VI

Application in Philosophy

Brief Statement

The chapter presents a method for theory. The method employs many logics and the transfer from one to another via experiencing. When we employ more than one logic or concept in relation to a given experiential meaning, it is not an arbitrary matter whether we need to reconcile logical contradictions or not. For certain purposes we need to, for others not. Also, the criteria we are employing may vary, and depending upon them we can define the rules for transition from one precise proposition to another of a different logic. At a given juncture in a discussion, we can use certain methods to establish the felt meaning with which we are concerned. Several different formulations can then be considered equivalent. Yet the next moment of discourse may raise some further question that will lead to the specification of some new aspect of the felt meaning, and in relation to this new aspect we must newly look to see whether our equivalent formulations are still equivalent. It is possible that they now are not equivalent, that they form different meanings when applied to the new aspect. Rather than leaving the two formulations "equivalent," we may then—in relation to this new aspect—work out their implications.

These and other rules are formulated.

The aim is a systematic method in which the endless possibilites of novel creation of meaning can be controlled and used without loss of the precision, logical integrity, and empirical criteria of concepts. With this method one may use every conceivable logic, theory, assumption, and theoretical model, and do so with increased power, escaping vagueness or entrapment in the confines of some one logic or concept with which one happens to have begun.

[A]
Principles of Philosophic Method as Implied by Relativity

In philosophy, problems of content and problems of method cannot be strictly divided. Assertions about method imply certain schemes about content and vice versa. Therefore, what has been said about the functional relationships will have implications for method.[1] The functional relationships are the basic ways of symbolizing experience. Hence they formulate a content that directly affects method, for methods are ultimately ways of symbolizing experience.

We have also seen that each functional relationship could be basic to all symbolization of experience. It has therefore been impossible to relate these functional relationships in

1. For example, if "comprehension" applies, the given meaning is already entitized, specified, present in experience, whereas if "metaphor" applies, it is first created in symbolization. If "circumlocution" applies, an idea really is all other meanings in discourse (for example, certain ways of drawing them in, or excluding them), whereas if "recognition" applies, each idea is a separate unity. Problems of method in philosophy can be brought down to issues between these functions. This ought to be so, since these functions represent different ways in which concepts are based on experience. If there can be variety in how concepts are based on experience, there will be methodological problems that will reflect this variety.

The fact that this is the case is another instance of the reflexivity embodied in the "iofi" principle. Our own procedure is (in many ways) an instance of itself qua general kind of procedure *and* qua general meaning of which other philosophical problems can also be seen as instances.

unique ways. Such relating is itself a schematizing and a symbolizing of experience, hence less basic than each functional relationship itself. Each one is a way of symbolizing experience, hence each one implies basic relationships between anything and anything else, hence also between the functional relationships.

Not only is this true in general, but it applies to any detailed aspect of their relationships. Each detail that might be focused on can be formulated in ways determined by one or the other functional relationship, and the further aspects to be considered in any such issue again can be formulated thus variously.[2] Therefore, the most important implications of the functional relationships for philosophic method are the primacy of the functioning of experienced meaning and the relativity of all formulations and schemes with respect to it.

Conceptualizations are relative to the variety of types of conceptualizations of experience.[3] Therefore, any conceptualization must be seen as relative within a context of many, many possible meanings that could have been conceptualized and might or might not make a difference to the particular discourse in question. Let us formulate some methodological principles of such a method; we shall discuss some methodological principles of relativity.

Of course, other principles can be specified as well. These are principles of an experiencing procedure, that is, the procedure of systematically employing direct reference to experienced meanings. Hence, many methodological principles

2. See Chapter III.

3. The relativity that the functional relationships imply for philosophic method is not a peculiarity of this formulation, but is due to the fact that conceptualization of experience is possible in multiple ways. Any other possible set of formulations of functional relationships would imply the same relativity for philosophic method. That relativity is basic to what the functions formulate, of which they are only one possible version. They represent one formulation of the relativity of conceptualization of experience, and they make the richness of this relativity available to philosophic method.

could be specified, of which this procedure is an instance. We will specify a few:

1. Countless possible meanings
2. Determinacy
3. Optional formulation
4. Open schemes
5. Evaluation of schemes
6. Relativity of *all* terms (including the most basic terms, such as "definition")
7. Functional equality
8. Logical forms

1. COUNTLESS POSSIBLE MEANINGS

Experiencing may be symbolized in countless different ways. Countless different aspects of any instance of experiencing are possible, and each can be comprehended variously. Each might be comprehended differently if some of the many other functioning meanings were different. These again are capable of different specifications and comprehensions. Therefore, at any point of any discourse countless different meanings are possible. Some of these possible meanings would in some respects be alternatives to those of the given point of discourse. Others are further possible meanings additional to that point of discourse. These further meanings again have countless alternatives themselves, as well as again offering countless possibilities for creation of further meanings.

Let us state that as the *principle of countless possible meanings* at any point of discourse or of any instance of experiencing.

2. DETERMINACY

Every symbolization and formulation has its own necessities. For each there is accuracy or inaccuracy. Each has implications. Each may select certain further aspects and relate to other things in only certain ways.

This is the case even in minimal symbolization such as

direct reference. Certain things will be true of "this" experience, other things not true. Thus, despite the countless meanings possible for each instance of experiencing, even specifying it only as "this" experiencing brings on a certain amount of determinacy. All other kinds of symbolization and formulation likewise have their determinacy. Let us call this the *principle of determinacy* of symbolization.

3. OPTIONAL FORMULATION

At any point of a discourse any of the countless possible meanings may be of value. This is possible because any of them, if formulated, will have necessary implications and select further formulation. On the other hand, any of these possible meanings may be unnecessary. One cannot formulate all the possible meanings at each point or even at any one point. Yet, whatever one does formulate *may* add something important to the discourse. Let us call this the *principle of optional formulation*.

4. OPEN SCHEMES

Every conceptual scheme could be different both as a whole and at every point within it. At every point in it countless meanings could be specified. Some of these would be in accord with the scheme and some would imply different schemes. Again, this is the case for the scheme as a whole, as well as for the schemes implied by every aspect of every point within the scheme. Every part of every conceptual scheme is open to further creation of countless meanings and each of these *may* imply something important to the discourse or subject matter. Thus, every scheme could be termed an "open scheme."

One may systematically employ any scheme as an open scheme. To do so is to be aware that one has formulated only as far as one wished to, and that one could have formulated further and differently at every point. Therefore, one may examine any point in the light of some possible alternatives and some possible further formulations. One may then choose to include these, or not. One need not be limited to what is implied by the scheme as a whole or by the scheme of some particular concept in it. One may investigate what value there would be in formulating some concept further and differently. If one then wishes to retain the results of such formulation, one may seek some formulation of them that does not contradict other aspects of the scheme, or, if that isn't possible, contradictions may raise further symbolization of aspects. We must emphasize, however, that such ventures into alternative and further formulations occur *before* possible contradictions are resolved. Even if the contradictions are not resolved, one may still retain what was discovered by the alternative formulation.

By "open" scheme is meant the fact that all possible meanings and all their contradictory implications cannot be resolved in any event. Even if everything one formulates appears to fit into one scheme, the very next specified further aspect may raise implications that do not fit it.

Similarly, if at some given point of discourse it is possible to leave some contradictions unresolved, it may become necessary at another point of discourse to resolve them. For example, suppose we are dealing with question A. Formulation X specifies certain aspects of the question, and so does formulation Y. We now answer A in terms of X and Y, leaving their relationship open. Later some point of discourse may force us to resolve that relationship. (We did this when we discussed the term "differentiate." We found that other terms such as "synthesize" were equally good. We used all these terms to state the non-numerical character of experience. We did not need, for that discourse, to resolve the contradictions between "differentiate" and "synthesize." Yet, at another juncture of our discourse we found it necessary to do so.) The immediate purposes of the given point of discourse can thus be a criterion for what must be formulated and what may be left open. If we can include what we need and leave out implications and questions that are not now pertinent, we gain immense scope at each point of discourse. Since it is impossible to formulate all possible meanings and resolve all their possible contradictory implications, we can be free to formulate, include, and deal with only what is pertinent to the given point of discourse. Thus, we gain for each point the freedom to employ any fashion of formulation that may reveal some important aspect. The employment of schemes in this fashion we term *the principle of open schemes.*

5. EVALUATION OF SCHEMES

Of what value are schemes, and how are several schemes relatively evaluated?

Schemes function to create (specify, select, symbolize) aspects of experience. Schemes may have other purposes, for example neatness, ease of memory and operation. "Purpose" itself is a term capable of many different kinds of meaning. Whatever purpose a scheme serves is related to its help in symbolizing and selecting aspects of experience. Therefore, the relative evaluation of one scheme as against another must lie in some evaluation of the aspects of experience it helps create. Are these aspects important for the purpose at hand?

When is one scheme as good as another, and when not? Again this question must be referred to the aspects of experience that are created, symbolized, specified.[4] If one can refer

4. The principle of the evaluation of schemes may be stated as the principle that all schemes, formulations, and symbolizations are empirical *questions.* Since all schemes are to be evaluated on the basis of the aspects of experiencing that they specify, a scheme may be viewed as hypo-

to and symbolize some aspect of experience equally in two schemes, then for that aspect they are equivalent. If our purpose at this junction of discourse is to formulate *that* aspect, the schemes are equivalent.

The principle of the evaluation of schemes: the value and the evaluation of schemes depend on the aspects of experience that they help symbolize. (By "aspects" of course we include aspects of aspects, and so on. Hence, one may find that a given scheme is preferable to another in formulating some aspect of some aspect of some subject, and for that point only one may wish to use that scheme.)

6. THE RELATIVITY OF ALL TERMS (including the most basic terms, whose basic nature is not thereby destroyed)

What we have so far asserted may seem to wipe out certain important distinctions of any good philosophy. Any philosophy has certain terms or principles that are basic to it and that must not be set equal to other, less basic ones. For example, Kant's categories are basic conceptions and we would

---

thetical and as awaiting our direct dealing with the aspects it specifies. If these turn out to be important and relevant, the scheme has been of value. We can then reformulate or reject the scheme, but we cannot reject the aspects of experience it referred to. If they are relevant, they will either have to be referred to by some other scheme or by this one, or by some modification of this one.

What has just been asserted is not different from Bacon's or Dewey's views, except that we have extended the concept of "empirical" to include direct reference to directly given experiencing, externally or internally observable. In both cases schemes serve to select, formulate, and schematize experience and in both cases schemes are reformulated on the basis of the experience they and other schemes select and formulate.

One may limit the term "empirical" to external observation only, thus creating a special subclass of experience with its own special attributes. Such a distinction will have its own implications. However, no matter what distinctions are drawn and what further implications result, it can be said in general that schemes can be evaluated and reformulated on the basis of the aspects of experiencing selected and symbolized by it and by all other relevant formulations.

do violence to his philosophy if our method implied that they could be no more basic than other concepts.

Let us show that *all terms in a scheme are relative*. Let us also show that such relativity does not obviate the difference, within a philosophy, between essential basic terms and other terms. Let us take the term "definition" as our example.

"Definition" traditionally is a very specific kind of delineation of a thing or concept—not just any sort of delineation. It has been that kind of delineation which embodies the basic factors that, in that system, ground propositions or inference. Of course, "definition" has therefore been different in different systems. But it has held a special place in each system.

As we casually take on and put off schemes and terms, without even fully working them out, are we not denying this vital differentiation between crucial, grounding definition and any sort of delineation of something? The answer is that we do not deny the necessities brought about by a scheme. Rather, we see a scheme's necessities within a context of relativity in respect to other schemes and their necessities. Therefore, rather than denying the fundamental nature of definitions, we assert that even the definition of "definition" is relative to other equally fundamental definitions of it.

The relativity of schemes does not obviate their internal distinctions between adequate and inadequate grounds for assertions. These schemes, together with their assertions and their distinctions of adequate and inadequate grounds, are relative to other such schemes and necessities.

The preceding principles may have made the reader quite uncomfortable. He may have felt that there is no end to relativity. All terms, all schemes, could be further differentiated and produce whole systems of terms, all of which again would be relative and each, in turn, produce whole systems of terms, which again would be relative, and so on. We have been implying that, on the one hand, one can work out implications of schemes and terms indefinitely, but that, on the other hand, one *needs to* and can work out only very little, even when the differences of terms seem obvious. The following principle governs a systematic way in which a temporary halt of formulation can be precisely defined as well as made systematically temporary.

7. FUNCTIONAL EQUALITY

When different schemes can be equated, the reason is that, at the point of discourse at which they are equated, they refer to (select, differentiate, symbolize) the same aspect of experience—which can be referred to also by "direct reference."

When different schemes are said to be "relative," it is because at the given point in a discourse neither the equality nor the difference is as yet determined. Most of the discussions in this treatise are of this third sort. Since we here are chiefly concerned with making the richness of experiencing available to discourse, we often do not have sufficient delineation of a specific discourse to enable us to declare two schemes equivalent or different. We can only say that for some points in discourses they could be equivalent, while at other points in those discourses they would further differentiate something and hence be seen to be different. This is what is meant by their being "relative."

The principle of "functional equality" has been used throughout this treatise. It has been used and explained in chapter IV, pp. 152–154.

A given point in a discourse sets up given concerns. For these concerns a great many schemes will be equivalent. For these same concerns some schemes must be seen to be different. The next stage of the discourse may show even the equated schemes to be different—as some further differentia-

tion will upset their equality. The equality can be upset because, once some different implication of the schemes or some
different aspect of the experience discussed is found, the
inner necessity of the schemes may bring about that they no
longer equally imply this new aspect.

The importance of functional equality lies in the circumstances (1) that one can use it systematically to avail oneself
of all the possibilities of many schemes and yet (2) put a
temporary stop to endless working out of all the differences
between them. One can employ many schemes at a given
point, thus being open to many implications, directions, questions, and thus (3) be protected from accepting as necessary
to the subject, many implications that really belong only to
one scheme among many.

We call it "functional equality" (as pointed out in footnote 8, p. 154) both because the function that the schemes
or terms play is the same (at a given point in discourse) and
because the sameness is provided by the function of an experienced meaning as a direct referent.

For example: the meanings "differentiate" and "synthesize"
are both specifications of one and the same experience, to
which we refer directly in our own experience (via various
descriptions, if we must communicate it). Both terms carry
along with them schemes and philosophies. Yet, if we wish to
examine just this experience of finding a new aspect "already
in" an experience, then both terms can specify that. Now,
some things would be differently specified by these two terms,
yet for our purposes the experienced meaning (our experience
of specifying a new aspect) is the same. If one were to lay the
conceptual in the preconceptual—which we do not wish to
do—one would say that just the difference between the terms
is the difference between the experiences. But this isn't so! For
our purposes it is one and the same experience, which may be
specified by either term. "For our purposes" really means

"given the meanings of the present context, that is, the total experienced meaning that functions to guide and make relevant or irrelevant all the considerations active at present." Hence, "for our purposes" again refers directly to this same felt meaning, of which the two terms are equally possible specifications!

On the other hand, it is possible that as we specify the experiences further and further we may find something that is relevant to some experienced meaning that functions in our discourse and is different for the two terms. *Then* their functional equality would be overthrown. We must be aware, therefore, that a functional equality of terms holds good only for a given relevance, for a given point in a discussion, for a given total of experiences. Since this total is unspecified except as we specify it, only our specifying can upset the functional equality. An analysis of all that such terms *can* imply in all circumstances, which is at any rate impossible, need not upset a functional equality. Of course, the terms are different in different contexts, for example, for different experienced meanings. But for this experienced meaning, at this point in its specification, they are "functionally equivalent."

However, if our purpose is to uncover new aspects of the experience at hand, we may deliberately specify the differences of functionally equivalent schemes, in order to seek differences that will reveal new and important aspects of the experience being discoursed about, or inquired into.

8. LOGICAL FORM

In our discussion of "metaphor" (Chapter III, p. 113) and of the "reversal of the philosophic order" (Chapter IV, pp. 141–144) we pointed out that a metaphor creates not only an aspect of an area of experience, but also a relation of likeness or a common organization.

We noted in characteristic 7 (Chapter IV, p. 164) that such a common organization, itself a general meaning, may be employed to schematize any experiencing. (Any meaning may be so employed, and can be viewed as a general organization in various ways.) Also, one may ask after the experiencing from which it originated. Many experiences could be found from out of which the "common organization" might have been specified. Really, when one seeks this original experience, one schematizes experiences with the organization, creating new aspects of this or that experience.

Thus, the meanings (common organizations) created assume a general and independent character. For example, certain spatial relations such as "part-whole," or "continuum," or certain emotional relations such as "impulse-result" or "impact-resistance," can be applied very generally, that is, they can be seen to arise as aspects of very many experiences.

Since we have reserved the term "metaphor" for the interaction of experienced meanings producing a new meaning, let us give the name "logical form" to this general use of meanings considered as common organizations. All concepts contain, make use of, involve, and impose on experience such "logical forms." This is another way of saying that by nature concepts are metaphoric.

The importance of this fact for us here is that from their metaphoric character or logical form come their necessities, logical implications, and the power to differentiate other experiences. For example, the syllogistic logical implications of propositions are possible only if the concepts in the propositions are viewed as "wholes" that "include" other wholes. Again, for example, if one concept (say "occurrence" on the metaphor of a "thing") is employed, some aspects of experience will be seen as exclusive of other aspects, while if another concept (say "process" on the metaphor of an electric current) is employed, experience will be seen as inclusive and interpenetrating those same aspects. We thus see that not only do some implications necessarily follow from some schemes and terms, while they don't follow from others, but the very necessity of their following is a matter of metaphoric logical forms. It is from the logical forms that logical implications follow! It is when the logical forms are imposed on (employed in symbolizing, selecting, differentiating) experience that certain differentiations in experience can be made.

All would be arbitrary if it were not for the fact that, once differentiated, an aspect of experience has its own existential, demonstrative "existence" and can therefore be directly referred to. Since one can refer directly to the aspect of experience, once differentiated, the relativity of terms and schemes does not make cognition impossible. Instead, it gives cognition a richness of tools.

The tools do seem to demand their own consistency. But when applied to experiencing this is nothing else than further differentiation, further schematizing, which symbolizes, selects, finds, creates new aspects of it.

It is now time again to remind the reader that by experiencing we do not mean only sense perception, but the total of experienced meaning, including what is otherwise called abstract thought. For example, I may be thinking about democracy. A scheme of political science that constructs the state out of parts will highlight, select, differentiate for me aspects of my experienced meaning (of democracy), which another scheme, say, of the state as an organism, might not do. Once specified, the aspect of my experienced meaning (of democracy) can be referred to directly (by direct reference) as well as by a multitude of terms that—so long as I wish only to refer to this aspect—will all be functionally equivalent.

Principle of logical form: (a) All concepts and schemes involve (or can be seen to involve) highly general metaphoric organizations or forms. (b) The necessity of the implications of concepts rests on the necessities of these forms (for example, if wholes and parts, then inclusion is necessary or impossible).

[B]
Conclusions Regarding Certain Philosophic Problems

In Chapter I, Section B, we mentioned some problems as contexts in which the problem of experienced meaning appears. These were: method in psychology, particular problems in psychology (such as "congruence" and "subception"), experience as a source of meaning, and dependence of the intellect. The first two are considered in Chapter VII. Let us deal now with the last two. These are typical of many other problems to which the problem of experienced meaning is crucial. As mentioned in the section on "iofi," many formulations of problems can be equated with respect to some one aspect of experience and some one point of discourse. Of course, any problem involves more than one aspect of experience. Hence, such a "functional equality" of formulations can always be upset when discourse requires investigation of other aspects of experience. The same will be the case with the following discussion. We shall examine formulations of problems as equated in regard to the experience of symbolizing.

Let us consider first the question of how experience can be a source of meaning. This study has presented several functional relationships in which, with the aid of symbols, experience can function meaningfully. We have answered the question regarding experience as a source of meaning by showing that felt meaning functions to make symbolized meaning possible. But, how is experience—other than felt meaning—a source of meaning? In other words, how is sense perception, external observation, or real essences (if there are such things) a source of meaning? The answer is the same: whatever is a source of meaning is so to us through the medium of felt meaning. Recall our discussion of observation as a source of meaning (Chapter II).

There are several ways of stating the personally observable fact that felt meaning is the medium of other sources of meaning. One can say that intellect is in *direct* contact (in functional relationships of mutual dependence) only with felt meaning. This terminology distinguishes purely conceptual apparatus—called intellect—from felt experiencing. Or one can say that felt meaning is a stage in cognition. This terminology includes both felt meaning and the conceptual apparatus in one process of "cognition" and thus focuses on felt meaning as an early, preconceptual stage of cognition. In either terminology it can be stated that, no matter with what intellect is in relationship, felt meaning functions also in that relationship, and the intellect depends on these functions. Thus, anything that is a source of meaning for the intellect can be looked at in terms of its effect upon the normal functional relationships in which intellect and felt meaning function. It is in this way that we have answered the question regarding perception and observation as a source of meaning.

The question might be stated more precisely once more: how is it that things, perceptions, events, come to have meaning? Leibnitz put the question well in his example of the windmill. If you were walking about in the physical machinery of the body and brain, it would be like walking around in a windmill. You would see all the wheels turning, but you would not see meaning. Meaning, although somehow related to the operations of this machine, is something that occurs on another level of abstraction from these operations. The same is the case with external observations and perceptions. How does it come that things and senses come to have meaning to us? The answer emerging from this study is that they first bring about felt experiencing and that meaning arises in symbolic interaction with felt experiencing. Meaning arises as this felt experiencing plays a role in relation to roles played by symbols. Our alternative terminology (see footnote 3, p. 97) is: meaning to us arises as experiencing obtains a symbolic function, comes to be "such" experiencing. The functional relationships are different ways in which felt experiencing comes to have a symbolic function.

The function of felt meaning is therefore a necessary medium between intellect (conceptual apparatus) and whatever else it is in relation with.

We are now in a position to consider the second problem, that of the dependence of the intellect. From this study it follows (a) that intellect is not in direct contact with perception or reality, however defined; (b) that intellect always optimally depends upon the functions of felt meaning.

In the context of these two conclusions, we may consider the problem raised by the dependence of the intellect upon cultures, periods of history, psychological needs and distortions, choice of methods and principles, or biological needs. In these cases something is said to have an unwarranted influence on the intellect, which casts doubt on its capacity to function optimally. The influence upon it puts the intellect in question. Nevertheless, only the intellect can deal with the question of this influence.

From the viewpoint of this study, these cases of influence on the intellect can be seen as cases of the *normal* optimal dependence of intellect on the functions of felt meaning. In contrast to most discussions of these problems, we do not assume that the intellect ought optimally to be in direct, untrammeled contact with its object. Therefore we do not see the influence of culture or psychological need or methods and principles as unusual. Intellect is always subject to the role of felt meaning, and thus indirectly to anything that affects felt meaning. Conversely, if these factors influence intellect, they can do so only through the medium of felt meaning. Let us see exactly how that can occur:

In examining how these facts influence intellect indirectly through an influence on the functions of felt meaning, we will be investigating these problems by putting them into the context of the functions of felt meaning. We will consider the problems in terms of functions of felt meaning. We will see that to so consider them opens an avenue of investigation into exactly how these factors can influence intellect and gives us a systematic way of dealing with the results of such influence. In examining the functions of felt meaning in cognition, we have found that it functions, for example, as "recognition" as well as in "metaphoric" creation of new meanings, as well as being a "direct referent" for many possible specified meanings and schemes. Taking these three aspects of felt meaning as examples, let us see how they form a context for the investigation of the special noticeable dependencies of the intellect.

(a) Chinese and Americans do not think in the same terms and do not seem to mean the same thing even by analogous words. This fact can be stated in terms of a difference in recognition feelings between them. Since we have further examined the many contexts in which recognition occurs, we can expect the difference between Chinese and Americans to appear in all these contexts. Now, the problem is, does this difference vitiate the optimal functioning of the intellect? Does this "cultural determinacy" amount to a poisoning of the wells? Of course not! Everyone thinks with recognition feelings. Everyone interprets observations by means of them. (See Chapters II and III for other contexts.) The difference between individuals in their recognitions does in no way detract from the optimal functioning of these recognitions in cognition. Such recognitions are not an invalid cultural determinacy of the intellect. They are one kind of symbolization, that of things, situations, and some words. As felt meaning they have the normal determinacy of the intellect on the functions (among others, recognition) of felt meaning.

(b) Metaphor is our term for the creation of new meanings from out of the experiencing of several recognitions called forth by symbols. It is clear from (a) that Chinese and Americans would not create the same new meaning even if given the same metaphor (that is, the same familiar symbols) if their recognition of them is different. On the other hand, metaphor also describes the process one would go through to create (obtain, understand) the felt meaning that the person of the other culture already has as a recognition. It is possible to communicate (that is, lead a person to create) metaphorically a felt meaning that the person has not previously had. Such a meaning can be one that, in another culture, everyone has as the recognition of such and such a symbol.

Many possible specifications and schemes can refer to and symbolize the same felt meaning. Some of the differences between the Chinese and the American will be explicable in terms of differing specifications of the same experiencing. In other words, they both have the same felt meaning (recall our discussion of the problems of that term "same") but they have specified it differently. In this case, the difference between them can be investigated and accounted for just as one would investigate and account for a difference in two philosophic formulations of some "same" experiencing. Again, their difference does not cast doubt on the optimal functioning of the intellect. We can say specifically what it does imply. Their difference implies the possibility of specifying experiencing in many more than one way. But this is the case with *all* intellectual specifications, that is, interpretations and symbolizations of experiencing. The present study has shed light on this condition of intellect in general, and has offered principles of method of procedure for it (see Chapter VI, Section A).

These apply directly to cases in which the reason of the difference in specification is a cultural difference, or a psychological one, or a methodological one.

To summarize: the dependencies of the intellect on culture, periods of history, biological or psychological needs, choices of methods and principles, are not cases of questionable intellectual processes. All these factors that influence the intellect do so through optimal, normal functions of felt meaning and can thus be examined in the light of these functions. If it is said that there is something unwarranted or prejudicial in someone's intellectual results because of one of these factors, what must be meant is that a different felt meaning or a different scheme would have produced different results. The preference of certain results over others depends on criteria to be stated. However, no poisoned wells were involved in either set of results. These cases of dependency of the intellect may indeed have unusual causes, but the dependency itself—and its results and implications—are the same as usual.

Any specific problems concerning instances of cultural or psychological or methodological dependence of the intellect can now be considered in terms of the several different functions of experienced meaning that they may involve. Every function of felt meaning describes possible indirect determinacies upon the intellect by factors other than intellect or data. Felt meaning and its specifications can indeed be affected by all these factors, and therefore the influence of these factors can be differentiated and studied in terms of these different functions.

The present study cannot consider these problems in themselves in detail. In their own formulation, each would demand its own distinctions and create its own novel aspects of what has here been said generally. Each problem would initiate a new discourse with its own requirements. No rigid application of the functional relationships as if they were categories can be envisioned. Instead, the functional relationships allow discourse to begin by referring to various (directly experienced) functions of experienced meaning, which can be considered as they are relevant to the given problem. As soon as that is done, modifications of the experiences to which the problem refers and modifications of the present general study of the function of felt meaning will immediately become necessary and possible.

CHAPTER VII *Application to*

Psychological Theory and Research

Brief   This chapter is meant to be readable independently
Statement of the earlier chapters; therefore some readers may
wish to read it first. It may provide the nonphilosophic
reader with a sense for the relevance of some of the
basic philosophic treatment.

    The distinctions made in this chapter are much less
elaborate than in the central philosophy. The implications of the philosophy are here looked at in regard to a few theoretical issues in personality theory,
as these bear on the theory and research of psychotherapy. The chapter attempts to show some of the
power of concepts about experiencing. They can, for
example, clarify several current issues. The chapter provides some foundations for personality theory. Some
research applications of these concepts are cited.

    In Section C of this chapter logical positivism and
operationalism are compared to the present method.
The *results* of the present method regarding scientific
theory and research can be stated in terms acceptable
to logical positivism and operationalism. The *process*
of arriving at these results cannot. Without the function
of experiencing (both as studied, and as used in studying) one cannot create new meanings and new logical
patterns and methods, nor can one account for their
formation. One cannot isolate significant variables of

226

observations, that is to say, one is unlikely to find and define the significant aspects of the infinite variety of possible variables of behavior. Only *after* the creation of meanings and variables do logical positivism and operationalism become relevant in the application of criteria by which already created meanings can be tested and analyzed.

The following discussion will attempt to show how the method and terms here presented apply to psychological theory and research.

In the foregoing, a method and terms referring directly to experiencing have been presented. Experiencing was found to occur in various kinds of symbolizations. It was found to have various roles in symbolic cognition that can be accounted for only by direct reference to it.

⌊A⌋
Terms That Refer to Experiencing

INTRODUCTION

Section A of this chapter will make two assertions: (a) experiencing plays a vital role in therapeutic change; (b) terms that refer to experiencing are required in the theory of psychotherapy. With such terms many current issues can be clarified.

These two assertions are interdependent. The vital role of experiencing can be stated theoretically only by means of terms that refer to it. Conversely, such terms need to be introduced into theory only if what they refer to does indeed play a central part in psychotherapy. The task of this section, therefore, is simultaneously substantive and methodological. We shall cite many observations and many current issues in which experiencing is important. Simultaneously, we shall put forward and explain some terms that can directly refer to experiencing.

In Section A, experiencing, and some terms that refer to experiencing, will be defined. Sections B and C will deal with two groups of current theoretical issues. We shall attempt to show how the use of terms referring to experiencing can help clarify each of these issues. We shall thereby be showing both that experiencing plays a vital role in therapeutic change and that terms referring to it can clarify the theory of therapy.

1. THE TASK: TO MAKE SCIENTIFIC REFERENCE TO EXPERIENCING POSSIBLE

Subjective *experiencing* is a dimension of events that everyone knows intimately. Every individual lives in his subjective experiencing and looks out at the world from it, and through it. To the extent that practical dealings with living human individuals are of concern to psychology, the class of events called subjective experiencing is an important part of its subject matter.

The recent positivistic trends toward operational definitions are now making it very difficult, in psychology, to refer at all to the everyday phenomenon of subjective experiencing. There are views (the empty organism theory) that hold that there is no such thing as subjective experiencing. Theories are supposed to consist only of either theoretical constructs, or terms that are defined by *external* observations. Neither constructs nor external observations quite succeed in replacing subjective experiencing.

Many theoretical constructs sound *as if* they referred to subjective experiencing ("experience," "anxiety," "security," "Oedipus complex," "self-concept"). However, our present scientific methodology demands that we define these either in terms of externally observed behavior or as purely theoretical constructs that are intervening variables between such externally observed behaviors. For example: "anxiety" was first used by Freud to name a certain kind of feeling (fear without a known object). It has been largely redefined as a theoretical construct, such as "the repressed is close to awareness" or "perceptions inconsistent with the self-structure."

Although theory in this way is unable to refer to subjective experiencing, scientists and others who deal with living human individuals are constantly attempting to employ the concepts and findings of psychology in relation to subjective experiencing. Therapists, case workers, teachers, group workers, TAT analysts, and psychiatrists attempt to clarify and improve their work with people by using psychological concepts. In practical use the concepts do refer to subjective experiencing, but in an implicit and confusing way. If "anxiety," for example, is defined as a theoretical construct, how do all our findings about anxiety apply to this anxious person? This anxious person, of course, is anxious in the sense that he has a certain directly felt *experiencing*. What does our psychology have to say about this experiencing? Implicitly it says a great deal, but officially and precisely it says nothing at all about experiencing.

Positivistic science, including positivistic psychology, has achieved so much that it would be highly undesirable and impractical to give up any of its advantages in order to gain this or that specific purpose. We do not wish to lose any advantages of positivism in order to refer directly to experiencing. Hence, our task is to make direct reference to experiencing possible for psychology, by means of an addition, rather than any alteration, of positivistic, behavioral, operational methodology. That is the task of this chapter.

2. OBSERVATIONS OF THE FUNCTION OF EXPERIENCING

What the term "experiencing" refers to. In order to use the term "experiencing" in theory, and in order to formulate other terms that will also refer to experiencing, we must make more precise what the term refers to. We will do so first by citing and discussing some exemplary observations. Afterward we shall deal more exactly with its definition.

Some initial sense of what the term "experiencing" refers to can be communicated by calling it "subjective experiencing." It refers to an individual's feeling of *having* experience. It is a continuous stream of feelings with some few explicit contents. It is something given in the phenomenal field of every person.

We can further clarify what the term "experiencing" refers to by contrasting it with "conceptualization." Experiencing and concepts of it can occur together, or separately. When they occur toegther, they are usually so bound in an immediate unity that we do not notice their difference. The experiencing is then the meaning-to-us of the concepts. The concepts conceptualize the experiencing. However, often we have strong feelings without "knowing what they are." In such cases we have experiencing without having a conceptualization of it. In other, equally frequent cases we have a conceptualization but very little experiencing of what the conceptualization conceptualizes. For example, a person may be talking about a feeling that he had strongly yesterday, but does not feel now.

Experiencing and conceptualization often occur together, but they are not the same thing. The fact that they are different is most noticeable when they do not occur together, that is, when we have either experiencing that we cannot conceptualize or concepts the content of which we do not now feel. For this reason, most of our examples of observations of experiencing will be instances in which conceptualization is inadequate or lacking, or in which experiencing is sometimes in evidence and sometimes not. In these examples experiencing is therefore easily noticeable *as such*. Although such instances *emphasize* that concept and experiencing are not identical, it is understood that experiencing occurs also when conceptualization of it is adequate and the distinction between the two is less noticeable.

Exemplary observation 1. It is well known that, in therapy, intellectual knowledge *about* oneself is quite different from actual experiencing and changing. Many patients and clients have accurate concepts about their problems but are far from experiencing, or feeling, or facing them and working them through. "Facing" and "working through" are imprecise common-sense terms that refer to the necessary function of experiencing in therapeutic change. The following more exact version of this example will even more clearly bring home this important role of experiencing (as against concepts) in therapeutic change.

Freud, and since Freud, therapists in general have observed that in a few hours a good diagnostician can get a cooperative patient to understand *concepts* about his conflicts. Yet it requires months and years of *experiencing* before the patient can arrive at direct reference to these conflicts in himself. Furthermore, whereas the conceptual understanding leaves him unchanged, the experiencing brings fundamental changes with it. We note how different the conceptualization is from the experiencing.

To continue our example: after two years of therapy the patient may have succeeded in directly experiencing and changing the conflicts that the diagnostician explained in the first hour. Now the patient has not only the concepts, but the experiencing as well. If he is now asked to conceptualize (explain, describe) the experiencing, he is quite likely to use some concepts very like the diagnostician's original concepts. These are likely to be even now the most accurate conceptualizations of the experiencing. However, now these concepts conceptualize his actual experiencing. At the start of therapy these same concepts, although accurate, did not do so. In this example it is clear that concepts and experiencing are different dimensions.

This example cites a universal observation of one vital role that is played by experiencing—its role in therapeutic change. To formulate this role we need terms referring directly to this experiencing. Only with such terms can we express the difference between the process that the client undergoes in the few hours with the diagnostician, and the process that he undergoes in two years of therapy. We need a theoretical formulation of this function of experiencing in therapeutic change. We also need to formulate many questions about it. We would like to know how this therapeutic role of experiencing relates to other factors; for example: what physiological changes accompany this experiencing? What therapist behaviors maximize it and what therapist behaviors discourage it? What type of conceptual operations of the client further it? What type of personality changes occur with intense experiencing and what type occur without it? And so on. But in order to formulate these questions and testable hypotheses to answer them, we need a term or terms that refer to this experiencing and its role in therapeutic change. As long as theoretical terms refer only to conceptual contents or externally observed behaviors, theory cannot formulate this role of experiencing. Therapists know and are concerned with the therapeutic role of experiencing, but there are no explicit theoretical terms for it. Naturally, therefore, many *implicit* references to experiencing at present confuse theoretical discussions. In two later sections such discussions will be cited in detail. The use of terms referring directly to experiencing can clarify such discussions. At present, let us continue to cite exemplary observations of the role of experiencing.

Exemplary observations 2–7. Let us take, as our second example of experiencing, an instance of pain. Let us say it is a toothache and the dentist gives the patient a drug to still the pain. Now, pain may be defined in physiological terms, or it may be defined by reference to the experiencing. For example, physiologically the dentist may predict that such and such will hurt. However, when he says to the patient, "I'm sorry that had to hurt," he is referring to the patient's *experiencing*.

Such a discussion, perfectly simple to a doctor or dentist, may be confused to a psychologist or a philosopher, since one may define the pain not only in terms of physiology or experiencing, but also in terms of verbal behavior. One may define the pain as the patient's behavior in saying, "Yes, that was pretty bad." However, one must assume that as far as the dentist is concerned, the statement refers to something given subjectively to the patient. Whatever one's preference about defining terms, there need be no confusion about these three *different* levels of analysis: experiencing, behavior (including verbal), physiology.

The next few observations are from psychotherapy.

3. Clients frequently speak of feeling something without knowing what it is they feel. Both client and counselor call such a feeling "this feeling" and continue to communicate about it although it isn't clear to either person just what the feeling is. Here, both persons directly refer to the client's ongoing experiencing. They do so without having a conceptualization of it. The symbols used (such as the term "this") do not conceptualize. They only point.

A similar case is one where client and counselor *do* know what the feeling is but nevertheless need to refer directly to the experiencing and not to the conceptualization. For example: "You have *known* all along that you feel this way, but you are amazed at *how strongly* you do feel that." Or the case Rogers mentions, where the client says with surprise, "I really *am* tired."[1]

Here is another similar case where direct reference to experiencing is necessary even though an accurate conceptualization is already available: a client has all along asserted something about himself, such as, "I am afraid of being rejected." After many hours of therapy he comes upon the feelings that make this so. He discovers *anew* that he is afraid of being rejected. Usually he is then somewhat troubled by the fact that the feelings are new, different, amazing, yet no better words exist for them than the old, trite "I am afraid of being rejected." The client then struggles to communicate to the counselor that now he *"really"* feels it, that it is *new*.

In these examples, it is clear that client and counselor are referring to something in the client's experience other than conceptualizations. They are talking about some aspect of the client's present *experiencing*. Sometimes conceptualizations of it also occur, sometimes not.

4. Many examples in which experiencing is noticeable as distinct from conceptualization can be found in clients' reports about their experiencing between therapy sessions. (Here again we find special cases where the client himself makes the distinction between experiencing and conceptualizations, and again, it is not the separate occurrence we wish to establish but the concrete possibility of referring to experiencing directly and as such. Instances where the distinction is made by the client simply offer the clearest example of this direct reference to experiencing.)

Clients often report being "disturbed," "unsettled," "churning," having "something going on in them" but not knowing

1. Carl R. Rogers, "The Fully Functioning Person" (University of Chicago Counseling Center paper).

what. (Other times they do know what, that is, they do conceptualize what they are experiencing. Nevertheless, they can refer to this experiencing directly. Often, as they refer to it and talk about it, the conceptualization they did have becomes insufficient as more experiencing arises.)

5. The "self-exploration" that occurs in therapy proceeds by means of the client's direct reference to his present *experiencing* (mentioned in example 3). The client refers directly to it (as "this" or as "how I feel now") and proceeds to conceptualize it and to listen to his own and the counselor's conceptualizations. Often he finds "yes, that's it!" or "no, that isn't quite it." Often he does not know how something said differs from what he feels, but he knows it differs. In all these cases it is clear that he is referring directly to his experiencing and attempting to comprehend or metaphorize it.

6. Analogous to the therapeutic role of *experiencing* (as compared with diagnostic *concepts*) is the educational role of experiencing in a classroom. Student-centered teaching principles (and internally focused theories of education generally) are based on the principle that the student's *present, ongoing experiencing* must be allowed to interact with the material to be learned. Here again the presence of relevant experiencing, as well as concepts, is required.[2]

7. Often, as the client refers directly to his own experiencing, "this feeling" (to which he refers) remains the same while he changes conceptualizations of it. By "remains the same" we mean that he is continuously referring to "this" (same)

2. We refer here to the whole educational movement away from rote learning and toward considerations of the development of motivation and of experienced significance and integration by the student of what he learns. This movement in education deals with the problem of designing the learning situation so as to allow maximal opportunity for the student to bring his *present experiencing* as richly as possible into the learning situation, so as to allow the material to interact with his present experiencing. Educational psychology therefore also needs theoretical terms that refer to present experiencing.

feeling. In another sense, "this feeling" is (often) changing as he continually refers to it with different conceptualizations. Although spatial analogies are dangerous, let us say that it is somewhat as if he held up a feeling (as if it were an object in space) and examined it from various angles. The "angles" are conceptualizations, true of it, but not identical with it, so that even after a conceptualization, "this feeling" is still here. In fact, if accurate, the conceptualization often makes "this feeling" stronger. Again, it is clear that *experiencing* as directly referred to is something different from conceptualizations.

The above observations require theoretical terms that refer to experiencing. The cited observations are examples of important and consistent kinds of occurrences in therapy. These kinds of observations can be theoretically discussed only with a term (or terms) referring to experiencing as a datum different from conceptualization. Current discussion of problems in the theory and practice of psychotherapy would be greatly clarified if these kinds of observations could be referred to by theory.

The experiencing of another person is directly observable *to him*. Many characteristics of expressions that are observable to an external observer indicate roles of present experiencing.

In order to discuss and investigate the theoretical implications of these and similar observations, we must allow a theoretical term to refer to the experiencing itself. Only with such a term can we formulate implications of these observations for a great many issues of therapy and psychology generally, some of which are cited in the later sections.

3. HOW "EXPERIENCING" CAN BE KNOWN AND DEFINED (SOME DEFINITIONS OF TERMS)

We have cited and discussed observations of experiencing, yet the fact that we can do so is in itself quite puzzling. How is it that experiencing can be known apart from conceptualization?[3] What is "conceptualization," and what sort of knowing or observing of experiencing is possible without conceptualization?

In order to answer this question, a few definitions of terms are necessary. The term "conceptualization" will be used to name a certain kind of "symbolization." The term "symbolization" will thus name a much wider class of events, of which "conceptualizations" are one specific kind.

"*Conceptualizations*" are symbolizations of the sort that (1) symbolize in terms of verbal symbols,[4] and (2) do so by representing what is symbolized. By the second qualification is meant that, in conceptualization, the concepts themselves represent, picture, reproduce, contain what is symbolized. Compare conceptualization to a different kind of symbolization, "direct reference." An example of direct reference: the client says, "this feeling is sure strong, but I don't know what it is, yet." The statement in quotation marks is, of course, also a series of symbols, but these symbols do not represent or picture what they symbolize. The counselor and the client

3. To this question the whole present treatise has been an answer. We have found that experiencing cannot be known, referred to, or talked about except as symbolized. On the other hand, we have found various *kinds* of symbolizations, among them "direct reference." We have found many characteristics of experiencing as it functions in symbolic cognition. We have shown many roles played by experiencing without which cognition of certain kinds would be impossible. We have shown that experiencing qua symbolized in one way can still be symbolized another way. Experiencing never occurs apart from symbolizations of it, but its own functions are both vital to—and different from—symbolizations. We have investigated its characteristics in these functions.

A few simple definitions are given above so that the discourse of Chapter VII may proceed. The reader is reminded that Chapter III has defined in detail what is summarized here.

4. Symbolization need not be verbal. For example, a dramatist can symbolize something on stage in terms of actions and situations. Harry S. Sullivan [*Interpersonal Theory of Psychiatry* (New York: W. W. Norton & Co., 1953)], calling all human experience "symbolic," finds that all experiences indicate (symbolize) certain things in a context of dynamisms (need satisfaction complexes).

cannot tell, from these symbols, what the feeling is—as they could, for example, tell what it was if the client had said, "I am angry." The client feels the feeling now, but tomorrow, if he doesn't then feel it, the words of the direct reference will be of no help in recalling the feeling. ("I am angry," on the other hand, would recall what the feeling was.)

"Conceptualization" is thus contrasted to what will here be called *"direct reference."* Both of these are kinds of symbolization, but the former *represents* what is symbolized while the latter only *refers* to it, as one would if one pointed at an object and said "this."

"Direct reference" can be defined as the kind of symbolization in which symbols refer to and differentiate some experiencing, but do not represent it.

In many of the observations cited above, experiencing was "directly referred" to without being "conceptualized."

Experiencing, we consider as that which may be symbolized.[5] Whether experiencing is symbolized by a conceptualization or by direct reference, in either case it is clear that experiencing is something different from the symbols that symbolize it. Conceptualization and direct reference are not the only kinds of symbolization that might be distinguished. For the moment, however, we need not mention other distinctions of kinds of symbolization. (See Chapter III.)

Experiencing is not known, observed, or referred to, except as it is "symbolized" in *some* way. However, it need not be symbolized in the sense of conceptualization. It may be symbolized by being "directly referred" to.

The terms "experiencing" and "experience" contrasted. With the aid of these definitions we may now contrast "experienc-

---

5. As noted in some of the cited observations, when experiencing is directly referred to it can still be conceptualized, and conversely, when it is conceptualized it can still be directly referred to as well. (An example of the latter was the client's saying, "I always knew I felt angry at such and such, but I had no idea how strong *that feeling* is.")

ing" with the current notion of "experience," as it occurs especially in Rogerian theory, but also in Freudian and Sullivanian theory.

We will differentiate "experiencing" from the usual usage of "experience" in two respects: (a) the term "experience" is usually a theoretical construct whereas "experiencing," in our use of it, refers to directly given phenomena. (b) The term "experience" usually means conceptual contents in some form, whereas the term "experiencing" refers to experienced or implicit *felt* meaning. Let us consider each of these two differences.

(*a*) *Construct or phenomena.* "Experiencing" refers to the directly given stream of feelings. An individual may refer to it in his own phenomenal field.

Although this definition does not seem to differ markedly from Rogers' definition of "experience," we shall see in a moment that Rogers' "experience" is a construct, whereas our term "experiencing" is defined directly by a type of observable reference (the direct reference by an individual).

(*b*) *Does the term stand for conceptual contents or does it stand for felt occurrences?* Our term "experiencing" does not refer to stimuli, things, contents,[6] or objective conditions under

6. To clarify the difference between *experiencing* and *contents* (such as concepts, perceptions, images) let us draw a distinction between a "per*ception*" and "perceiv*ing*," as well as between a "concept" and "think*ing*." Let us use the term "a perception" to name the *content* of an instance of perceiving and let us use the term "a concept" to name the content of an instance of thinking. A perception and a concept are contents, that is, *objects* of apprehension, something know*n* or notic*ed*. On the other hand, let us use the terms "perceiv*ing*" and "think*ing*" to name the experienc*ing*, the feel*ing*, or the sens*ing* that an individual goes through in the *process* of notic*ing* or know*ing* something. Perceiving and thinking are not themselves objects of our attention, except reflectively, when for some reason we observe the process we just went through. The distinction between "a perception" and "perceiving" is introduced here to call attention to the character of "a concept" and "a perception" as a content rather than a process. Perceiv*ing* is a process. "Experiencing" is also a process and can be considered to include perceiving and thinking as defined above. Subjectively felt experiencing (perceiving included) consists of trains of

which experiencing occurs, nor does it refer to perceptions or concepts. Most definitions of experience do equate experience with such contents. We have shown in the cited illustrations throughout this paper that experiencing often occurs concretely to an individual (often very intensely) without conceptual *contents*. ("I feel something very strongly but I don't know what it is.") Not only does experiencing sometimes occur without any explicitly known content, it can occur with a gradation of explicit knowledge of content. Thus, while the usual definition of "experience" refers to content, "experiencing" denotes something concretely felt and present in an individual's phenomenal field, whether conceptual content is explicitly known or not.

Rogers' definition of "experience." Since psychotherapy deals with experienc*ing,* those psychologists who are psychotherapists (Freud, Fenichel, Sullivan, Rogers)[7] refer to experienc*ing* in their general descriptive writings about therapy. They do not, however, refer to it in their explicit precise theory. Let us look at Rogers' precise theoretical definition of "experience" and then let us compare it to "experiencing."

---

feelings, a continuous stream of change. It is clear, then, that "experiencing" differs from "perceptions" as process differs from things, or as a continuous stream differs from some one object (or picture of an object) that is in some way related to one point in the stream.

Perceptions and concepts are "about" or "of" something existential. Experiencing is itself existential. By "existential" is meant something in time and space, something concrete. Experiencing is concrete. The perception (and the concept) of an object is a content, viewed as an object. The concrete process of thinking or perceiving that object is part of experiencing, and is something different from the mere concept or perception or content. The latter is like the content of a picture. Using a picture as an analogy, the representative value of the picture is analogous to the content. The oil, the canvas, and the painter's activity are analogous to experiencing. The exemplary observations here cited clarify what the term experiencing refers to, as contrasted with contents such as concepts, perceptions, or other kinds of apprehension "of" some content.

7. Although this section deals chiefly with Rogerian theory, similar problems arise for Freudian and Sullivanian theory. The proposed terms and method, therefore, are relevant to all psychological theories that deal with psychotherapy and related subjects.

Rogers defines "experience" basically through the phenomenal field of the individual:

1. Experience (noun). This term is used to include all that is going on within the envelope of the organism at any given moment. It includes events of which the individual is unaware, as well as the phenomena which are in consciousness. Thus it includes the physiological aspects of hunger, even though the individual may be so fascinated by his work or play that he is completely unaware of the hunger; it includes the impact of sights and sounds and smells on the organism, even though these are not in the focus of attention; it includes the influence of memory and past experience, as these are active in the moment, in restricting or broadening the meaning given to various stimuli. It also includes all that is present in immediate awareness or consciousness.

2. Experience (verb). To experience means simply to receive in the organism the impact of the sensory or physiological events which at the moment are transpiring. . . . Often this process term is used in the phrase "to experience in awareness" which means to symbolize in some accurate form at the conscious level the above sensory or visceral events. Since there are various degrees of completeness in symbolization, the phrase is often "to experience more fully in awareness." [8]

Rogers' term "organism" here refers to what is, *or can be,* a datum of awareness. Rogers cites examples of hunger, sights, sounds and smells, memory and past experience as included in "experience" even if unaware, since they nevertheless function in the present in the organism. However, he does not cite examples of purely physiological processes, say of blood absorption of food particles, because these could not be "experience." "Experience," for Rogers, includes only those physiological aspects which can be indices of what could, under some circumstances, be the datum of awareness. Similarly,

8. Carl R. Rogers, "A Theory of Therapy, Personality, and Interpersonal Relationships as Developed in Client-centered Framework," in S. Koch, ed., *Psychology: A Study of a Science,* Vol. 3 (New York: McGraw-Hill Book Company, 1959).

in the definition of the verb "experience," he speaks of it as "to receive in the organism the impact of the sensory or physiological events which at the moment are transpiring." Here again, "receiving in the organism" refers to what could be (but may not now be) datum of awareness rather than a purely physiological sense of "in the organism."

"Experience," then, is a momentary cross-cut (that is, it is existential in space and time)—not of what is in awareness only, nor of all that occurs physiologically, but rather of all content that is or could under some circumstances be in an individual's phenomenal field.

Despite this basically phenomenological criterion in its definition, "experience" is a "construct" without directly observable referent.

We find two dfferences between the construct "experience" and the term "experiencing":

1. "Experience" is a construct consisting of all that could be, but is not necessarily, in any sense in awareness.

"Experiencing" refers to something directly observable by the individual and observable by others indirectly in his expression of such direct observation. It is something present, although it is chiefly *felt* rather than *known*.

2. "Experience" is constituted of *contents* that are posited in the individual. These contents are the same in nature, whether they are in awareness or denied to awareness. In either case, the nature of experience is that of explicit conceptual contents. Rogers says, " 'to experience in awareness' means to symbolize in some *accurate* form." The word accurate expresses the nature of experience as contents of conceptualization. "Experience in awareness" means *explicit* contents of awareness. When denied to awareness, these *same* contents are still posited in the person, as if they were *explicit* contents of some absent conceptualization. For example, "self-*concept*"

is said to "match" or not to "match" "*experience*," thus indicating that "experience" consists of something of the same kind as "concept." The construct "experience" is thus basically identical in nature to contents of *explicit* conceptualization.

"*Experiencing*," on the other hand, is a present, felt *implicitly* meaningful datum. It is directly referred to by an individual. It is capable of many different conceptualizations, but is not itself explicit conceptual contents of such conceptualizations. To call it implicitly meaningful is to note that it can give rise to many conceptualizations, and that conceptualizations can be checked against its implicit meaning. Thus, conceptualizations of it can be accurate or inaccurate, yet the felt datum itself will still be directly present. It will still be something other than any of its conceptualized aspects. Experiencing is thus *implicitly* meaningful. It is something present, directly referred to and *felt*.

"Experiencing" is defined[9] as the felt datum of an indi-

9. The fundamental definition of "experiencing" is in terms of an individual's own direct reference to what is phenomenologically given to him as felt. However, we may add some further delineations of it:

(a) Experiencing can also be defined in terms of observable characteristics of one's "manner of experiencing," such as intensity, richness of detail, and other characteristics. (See Eugene Gendlin and Fred M. Zimring, "The Dimensions of Experiencing," *Counseling Center Discussion Paper*, Vol. I, No. 3, 1955, for many characteristics of the client's expression and behavior that indicate characteristics of *experiencing*.)

(b) Recall that we have contrasted "experiencing" with conceptualization. We pointed out that one may have conceptualizations without the relevant experiencing, and vice versa. We cited the example of a patient who grasps the concepts of his conflicts in a few hours, but requires years of *experiencing* for therapeutic change.

(c) Let us also compare "experiencing" with the common term "emotion." We said that "experiencing" is a felt datum, and this word "felt" may suggest that it must be an emotion. Often, some emotion is the most important aspect of some present "this" or experiencing. However, just as often, a client will refer to "this feeling" and when he comes to conceptualize it later it will turn out to be a complex of many meanings (such as "I know what is really at the bottom of it, it's that I feel so inferior and am afraid that I'll be caught being inferior in action and people will despise me because . . ." and so on at length). In this last-mentioned

vidual's inward direct reference in his phenomenal awareness.

Earlier we defined (and cited examples of) "direct reference."

Let us now turn to two groups of currently discussed issues in the theory of psychotherapy. We will attempt to show that each of these issues can be clarified, and theory and research concerning it can be extended, by terms referring directly to experiencing.

---

example, it is clear that the client has, for some minutes, been trying to "get at" just what the "feel" of what he is talking about is. This "feel" isn't just an emotion (in this case). It is a directly *felt* datum that *implicitly* means a great deal. Therapy is largely the process of directly referring to, "getting at," "feeling out" the feel of what the client first talks *about*. Thus, "experiencing" may be defined as the (directly referred-to) "feel" of some situation, concept, object, personal relationship, content, or the like.

(d) *Experiencing* is a changing, organic, spatiotemporal process, a continuous stream of feelings and some few explicit contents. It is the feeling process that continuously occurs in an individual's phenomenal field, no matter what may be pointed out specifically as occurring. It is capable of being referred to directly by an individual in his phenomenal field.

(e) Experiencing may be defined as just cited, or again, it may be defined by the different kinds of symbolizations of which it is capable. If there were only one kind of symbolization (for example, "conceptualization") it would be possible not to notice experiencing as such, or to identify it with conceptual content. Since experiencing can be symbolized by *"direct reference"* as well as by conceptualization, it is defined by these two kinds of symbolization as something distinguishable in both.

The term "experiencing" as here employed is not a theoretical construct. Theoretical constructs are certainly possible also. Experiencing may be represented by theoretical constructs of many kinds—for example, by some conceptual model such as a flow or an electric current. Although theoretical constructs may turn out to be quite useful, it is primarily important to enable theory to refer to experiencing as a direct datum, an observable dimension. This is made possible by the use of the term "experiencing" not as a theoretical construct of any sort, but as a term that refers to a direct datum of any individual.

The term "experiencing" refers directly to a type of empirical observation or datum, namely the ongoing feeling process to which an individual can directly refer in his phenomenal field.

The observations cited earlier show that experiencing plays an important role in therapy and other situations. Naturally, then, theoretical discussions of therapy and other situations, as well as research formulations, require terms that can explicitly refer to experiencing.

[B]
Current Issues in the Theory of Psychotherapy

1. DEGREE AND KIND OF CONCEPTUALIZATION IN THERAPY

Schools of therapy are in disagreement as to the *degree* and *kind* of conceptualization necessary for therapeutic change. The issue concerning *"degree"* refers to the insistence of some schools that "depth therapy" takes place only if a client's problem areas are fully and explicitly conceptualized. Others maintain that much change occurs on a subjective, implicit level. Many issues of technique, attitudes, and goals of therapy turn on this point.[10]

The issue as to *"kind"* of conceptualization refers to differences among schools of therapy as to which are the *basic* problem areas and, in conjunction with this issue, which are the basic terms for conceptualization necessary in therapy. For example, there are schools of therapy according to which the client achieves "depth therapy" only if he makes his expe-

10. For example, there is at present much discussion about interpretation and direction in therapy. If depth therapy occurs only when the client *explicitly* symbolizes his problem areas, the therapist's intervention will be required, both to offer explicit terms and explanations and to direct the patient toward use of them. Problems as to when this is necessary and how it ought to be done obviously requires some agreement on the amount of conceptualization needed for deep therapy. At present, schools view each other as superficial and unscientific, or as overintellectualized and autocratic.

Another example of such issues is whether or not the therapist ought to respond to the client's own internal frame of reference. Can the therapist have "faith" in the client's own capacities and ought he therefore follow the line of development the patient takes, or must he direct him to the basic problem areas and their conceptualization? Again, discussion of this issue requires first an agreement on the degree of conceptualization needed for deep therapy. In one view, a given therapeutic session might be considered hopelessly vague and superficial, while from another point of view it might be subjective, unconceptualized "working through" of basic problems. Conversely, another session might be seen by some as a great advance in insight and facing of conflicts, whereas others might consider it overintellectualized, not indicative of real therapeutic change.

rience explicit in terms of sexual conflicts, life style, interpersonal relations, or self-concept.

Consider the following hypothesis: the amount (or depth) of therapeutic change is not appreciably correlated with the degree and kind of conceptualization. This hypothesis has many times been stated in common-sense language by those who point out that many different schools of therapy have a similar proportion of successful cases. Despite the commonplace nature of this hypothesis, it cannot be stated with theoretical precision, since it implies something other than the different possible conceptualizations. It implies experiencing as distinct from degree or kind of conceptualization. This issue can be theoretically stated only if one explicitly or implicitly assumes experiencing, as well as conceptualization. In the many current discussions of this issue, that assumption has been implicit.

Not only theory, but research on this issue requires terms that refer to observations of the role of experiencing as distinct from conceptualization in therapy. One would like to measure the amount, intensity, and degree of presentness of experiencing, and other effects related to them. One would like to measure experiencing both when there are conceptualizations of it and when there are not. At present, there is only the therapist's undefined observation to determine when the client is "really experiencing" what he discusses and when it is merely conceptual.

In the following we shall cite examples of research that is possible if experiencing may be referred to. This research illustrates the possibility of referring to and measuring experiencing as such, whether it occurs with or without conceptualization. The first exemplary research to be cited attempted to measure the degree of experiencing where conceptualization did occur. The problem it investigated is yet another illustration that theoretical terms referring directly to experiencing may clarify and extend theoretical statement. That problem is the Rogerian emphasis on "present" experience. Let us first discuss this problem and then cite the research regarding it.

Problem and Research Illustrating the General Problem of

Degree and Kind of Conceptualization in Therapy

The focus on the present. Rogers and others[11] assert that therapeutic change takes place to the greatest degree when the client experiences what he deals with *in the present*.

Without a term referring to experiencing as something distinguishable from conceptualization, what does Rogers' emphasis on experience *in the present* mean? Because of the lack of precise terms, Rogers' emphasis on present experience has been widely misinterpreted[12] to mean that a client need not deal with his past experience. In such a reading of his view, Rogers' reference to the present is taken to refer to conceptual content. Rogers is misunderstood to mean that a client need only deal with the content of his present life, not with his early experience. However, Rogers means that whatever the

---

11. Fenichel and others similarly speak of a defensive kind of acceptance by the patient of therapist interpretations. This means that the patient conceptually accepts the interpretation in order to be done with the problem and thus to avoid *dealing with it in himself,* that is, in order to avoid the experiencing of it. "Thus a certain form of resistance consists in the patient's always being reasonable and refusing to have any understanding for the logic of emotions. . . ." "He may make progress in understanding the forces working within him, sense connections, and dig up new childhood recollections—and yet there is no change in his neurosis." "Or the patient may have understood what his associations and the analyst's interpretations showed him, and yet the knowledge remains entirely separated from his real life." "Or a patient may accept everything the analyst tells him merely as a matter of courtesy; but it is just this courteous attitude which protects him from reliving to the full his instinctual conflicts. . . ."—Otto Fenichel, *The Psychoanalytic Theory of Neurosis* (New York: W. W. Norton & Co., 1945), p. 28.

Both Rogers' and Fenichel's observations can be stated only by terms that refer directly to experiencing as such. Without such a term, how could one state the difference between a defensively intellectual acceptance of an interpretation and a genuine one?

12. This refers to the interpretation of Rogers that makes his view out to be that "the past is a bucket of ashes," that is, that the past need not be dealt with.

client deals with (past or present conceptual content), it is optimally dealt with only through present *experiencing*. This issue is obscured as long as theory has no terms that directly refer to experiencing. Once such a term is introduced, his view can be stated clearly: both present and past *conceptual contents* can be dealt with in therapy by a client with intense present experiencing, or they can be merely discussed in a conceptual manner.

Now, in common-sense language, both clients and therapists talk of experiencing as distinct from conceptualization. Hence research was possible on this question. In a recent research,[13] counselors were asked to rate the amount of client's "immediate experiencing" on a nine-point scale, the extremes of which were, respectively, "*express* feelings of the moment" and "talk *about* feeling past or present." Examples of client statements were given to further define the question, which at this stage of theory could not be precisely stated, namely: "Regardless of what the conceptual content may be, how much expression of present experiencing do you observe?" In order to further distinguish this scale from the question of past or present conceptual content, another scale was employed to measure "to what extent do the client's problems focus in the past (childhood or earlier years)?" As predicted, the scale measuring expression of immediate *experiencing* correlated highly with several success measures, while the scale of past or present content did not.[14]

13. This project by Gendlin, Jenney, and Shlien was part of a larger research project directed by Dr. John Shlien, at the University of Chicago Counseling Center. The project was supported by the Wieboldt Foundation. A paper concerning the rating scales, of which two are reproduced here, was read at the American Psychological Association convention, 1956, and the final results published in the *Journal of Clinical Psychology,* XVI: 2, 210–213 (April, 1960).
14. Here are the two scales:
　　5. To what extent do the problems focus in the past (childhood or earlier years)?

1	2	3	4	5	6	7	8	9

This type of research shows the possibility of measuring the counselor's observation of client's experiencing as something different from conceptualizations, in cases where conceptualization *is* occurring either with or without intense experiencing. Similarly, it is possible to investigate those rarer, but important, instances when intense experiencing occurs without conceptualization (that is to say, with only direct reference such as "this feeling," or with minimal, obviously inadequate conceptualization). Another type of research will illustrate this possibility. A "Q Sort" of thirty-two statements[15] was

---

IMMEDIACY:

6. To what extent does the client *express* his feelings, and to what extent does he rather *talk about* them? (This scale differentiates direct *expression* from *report* about one's feelings, regardless of whether the feeling is past or present.)

Examples:

"I hate you!"	"I have this feeling of hate and it's for you."
"It comes home to me *now* how scared I really was last night."	"I was scared last night."
"Gee I feel low."	"Often I feel depressed." (No indication of present feeling in either word or voice.)

1	2	3	4	5	6	7	8	9

15. 1. It was very hard to bear that we were facing each other and I didn't know what to say.
2. Something about being with the therapist was both very pleasant and very uncomfortable at the same time.
3. I felt the therapist's presence intensely, although I didn't know what to do about it.
4. I enjoyed a feeling of adventure because another person (the therapist) was ready to engage in different untried ways.
5. It turned out to be exciting not to know just what we were doing.
6. I had a certain shaky feeling because it was up to me how we proceed.
7. Something I thought we couldn't do turned out to be quite possible for us.

developed describing experiencing of the sort that is not conceptualized (for example, "I felt something intensely but I didn't know what it was"). This measure of experiencing occurring without conceptualization of it was given to clients along with other measures[16] with which it could be correlated.

---

8. It struck me that no matter what I was or said, the therapist would continue to be as he is.
9. I desired that the therapist really feel the force of what I was expressing.
10. I was wrapped up in what I was communicating to the therapist.
11. The therapist had a very special personal meaning to me today.
12. In confronting the therapist directly I had a new sense of the person I am.
13. The therapist's response somehow made what I was remembering feel as if I felt it at the moment.
14. I did (or was) something with the therapist, which I have never done (or been) with anyone before.
15. While talking to the therapist I feel stronger inside than I usually do.
16. I'd like to be in general more like I am with the therapist.
17. I came across contradictions in what I said.
18. I was various, contradictory things, but I felt very intensely.
19. I felt large and undefinable.
20. I felt able to take risks.
21. I felt certain exciting possibilities for me, though I don't know just what they are.
22. I felt as though I were steering a ship along a rocky coast.
23. I found myself feeling before I understood. My feelings were ahead of my observing mind.
24. All there was of me was my being there that moment. All the rest of me was merely different pieces.
25. I felt a certain thing (which I wish would change) more intensely than I ever have before, but it hasn't changed yet.
26. I spoke before I even knew what I was going to say.
27. As soon as I got there, the me of last time came right up in me.
28. I felt a new feeling that I really own myself.
29. I felt some feelings which I usually have little opportunity to feel.
30. I felt that I was trying to hear a part of me that I usually don't permit a hearing.
31. I felt that I came out.
32. I felt that I myself inside am a base from which I could operate.

16. TAT, Rorschach, Self & Ideal Q Sorts, Counselor & Client Ratings of Outcome and Change, Trait-Feeling Q Sort.

These beginnings of research[17] directly measuring experiencing indicate that clients and therapists observe experiencing as something distinct from conceptualization, whether it occurs with its conceptualization or alone. Theory requires terms for such experiencing. Research requires a theory with such terms, both in order to formulate better hypotheses and operational procedures and in order to formulate the significance of such observations.

Let us now turn to a second group of illustrative current issues that may be clarified by use of terms referring to experiencing: these are issues centering around the use of the term "congruence."

2. EXPERIENCE AND "CONGRUENCE"

Rogers' definition of experience has been cited in this chapter (p. 241). We noted that "experience" refers to organismic contents that can be equated with the explicit content of accurate symbolizations. Such an equation is termed "congruence."

a. "Congruence"—uses of the term. As already quoted, Rogers considers "some of the most crucial hypotheses of the theoretical system" to be those regarding discrepancies (that is, "incongruence") between experience on the one hand, and awareness, self-concept, and other variables on the other. Here are four vital Rogerian uses of the notion of "congruence":[18]

1. "Optimal psychological adjustment is synonymous with complete openness to experience" (definition 23, p. 206). "Openness to experience" means that "the concept of self would

17. See also "Galvanic Skin Response Correlates of Different Modes of Experiencing," *Journal of Clinical Psychology,* XVII: 1, 73–77 (January 1961), and C. R. Rogers, "A Tentative Scale for the Measurement of Process in Psychotherapy," *Research in Psychotherapy* (Washington, D. C.: American Psychological Association, 1959).

18. References to Rogers are from the work cited in note 8, above, pp. 184–256.

be a symbolization in awareness which would be completely congruent with his experience" (definition 22, pp. 205–206).

2. The necessary and sufficient conditions for the occurrence of therapy include "genuineness" of the counselor in the relationship with the client. This is defined as follows: "The individual is genuine in a particular respect, when his experience in this area is matched by a corresponding congruence in his awareness, and . . . in appropriate expression."

3. The process of therapy is described by Rogers in the following (among other) terms: "His (the client's) expressed feelings increasingly have reference to the *incongruity* between certain of his experiences and his concept of self" (4, p. 216). "His concept of self becomes increasingly *congruent* with his experience."

4. J. Seeman, in describing the optimal therapeutic response in client-centered therapy, also employs the term "congruent" in Rogers' sense. He says, "The counselor attempts to respond so as to be exactly *congruent* with the client's unformed emotional experience."[19]

We have cited four crucial uses of the term "congruent" in Rogerian theory. The use of this term poses problems of which Rogers is well aware. He says:

. . . most urgently needed of all is a method whereby we might give operational definition to the construct *experience* in our theory, so that discrepancies between self-concept and experience, awareness and experience, etc., might be measured. This would permit the testing of some of the most crucial hypotheses of the theoretical system.[20]

Rogers envisions the use of such a method primarily to investigate the congruence between *contents* of experience

19. J. Seeman, "Client-Centered Therapy," *Progress in Clinical Psychology*, eds. D. Brower and L. E. Abt., Vol. II (New York: Grune & Stratton, 1957).
20. Rogers, *op. cit.*, p. 67.

and conceptual contents of awareness. The problem raised by these uses of "congruence" is the lack of direct observation of "experience." (Recall that "experience" must include what is denied to awareness, as well as what is given in awareness.)

Since "congruence" is a construct (equation of aware conceptual content with *posited* conceptual content of experience), its uses just cited indicate that "adjustment," "genuineness," "process of therapy," and "therapeutic response" are also constructs. As we just saw, their precise theoretical definitions are based on "congruence with experience."

On the other hand, current discussions refer (at least implicitly) to observations and experiences of therapy. In such discussions psychologists endeavor with constructs to make statements about therapy observations and experiences. They apply to their observations constructs that have no precise definition in terms of observations.

Many vital observations of client and therapist behavior indicate experiencing, and are meaningful in terms of experiencing. Hence the discussions are a mixture of constructs without observable referents and common-sense terms referring unprecisely to experiencing.

Let us now consider this second group of problems, the four uses of the construct "congruence," to show how theoretical terms referring directly to experiencing can extend precise theoretical statement and clarify discussions.

Two deficiencies of theoretical statement will be found to cause misunderstanding throughout these discussions: (1) experiencing is identified with conceptual contents; (2) aware feeling is not precisely understood to contain implicit meaning. Use of the term "experiencing," and differentiations possible with that term, have been shown (1) to enable differentiation between experiencing and conceptual contents, and (2) to make possible the reference to aware feeling as implicitly meaningful. We shall now show how problems arising in the four uses of "congruence" can be clarified and how theoretical statement can be made possible through the correction of these two deficiencies of current theory.

1. *Congruence and optimal adjustment.* As we saw, the Rogerian definition of adjustment is complete openness to experience (that is, complete congruence between experience and awareness). Adjustment is thus defined, not socially or culturally, but in the terms of the individual. Furthermore, the optimally adjusted individual includes no internal surrogate of social values (no superego). Introjected social values are considered to cause maladjustment because they distort the individual's openness to the meanings of his own experience to him. The optimal individual, because he allows his own meanings as he finds them in his own experience, does not need socially imposed values.

This view is in sharp contrast to many views in which socially given values are basic to adjustment and form a basic part of an individual. Social controls, socially handed down meanings are seen to be vital to individual meaning and adjustment by most views in psychology (Freudian superego, for example) and social psychology (G. H. Mead, for example).

The Rogerian point of view, furthermore, is that an individual who is maximally open to his experience weighs and balances all the meanings in his experience in a *subjective process*. He need not be explicitly and conceptually aware of every possible meaning in order to take every possible meaning into account. Thus, when an optimally adjusted individual speaks and acts so as to "follow his feeling" (as this subjective process is termed) he is following a subjective resultant of all the meanings of his experience, even though he has not explicitly thought them all.

Other viewpoints emphasize the role of socially created and socially controlled meanings. Seen from these viewpoints, the

Rogerian view is a naive omission of the recent discoveries of social psychology and a dangerous, antisocial, anti-intellectual doctrine. It appears to omit the need for control of impulses and for consideration of the needs and feelings of others.

It is clear from the foregoing that a precise statement of the subjective process of implicit inclusion of meanings is needed. Rogers must assume that "feeling" *implicitly* contains social and moral meanings and values. Without a theoretical statement of implicitly meaningful experiencing, "following one's feeling" can be misunderstood as impulse-ridden and selfish. Also, without it, the unanswerable question arises as to the meaning of "congruent with experience," since it is unclear just what in awareness is congruent! Not conceptualization, since no one could exhaustively conceptualize all possible meanings of even one experience. What then? The answer must be "feeling," and this answer is indeed implied in the common-sense parts of the discussions. In the precise theoretical parts of the discussion there is no term for anything that in awareness implicitly contains meanings and values. How then can *all* relevant experience be congruently represented in "awareness and expression" (without exhaustive conceptualization)?

If precise theoretical terms can refer to experiencing (felt meaning) as aware and *implicitly* containing meaning, then Rogers' idea of adjustment can be stated. The "feeling" one optimally "follows" is in awareness and implicitly contains social, moral, and intellectual meanings. The individual *does* include the socially given meanings, yet Rogers' distinction between one's "own experience" and "introjected values" is maintained. There is a vital difference between meanings found in one's own experience (implicit in one's own feeling) that are perhaps due to society and, on the other hand, introjected concepts, conclusions, judgments also due to society that an individual has *instead* of, not implicitly in, his experiencing.[21] Successful clients in client-centered therapy most often conclude therapy with attitudes that include more of the values of society than did their attitudes at the start. They also tend to accept the needs of others to a greater extent.[22] But these social and moral attitudes are now not mere judgments that an individual feels forced to believe or obey. They have arisen from an individual's examination of the implicit meanings in his own experiencing, that is, his own feelings. To arrive at the point where an individual considers his own feelings as even worthy of such a serious examination, he usually first overthrows a great number of introjected values and judgments that prevent him from looking directly at his experiencing. When he does look directly at it, he discovers a great many attitudes and feelings that do—and a great many that do not—conform to the social values. He integrates these feelings and attitudes so as to take maximal account of all of them.[23] Thus, he is no standard copy of the social values

21. Rogers finds agreement for his view of optimal adjustment in the work of the social psychologist Schachtel who also needs a theory of experience as implicitly meaningful to the individual and also views socially given meanings as narrowing and sometimes replacing direct implicit meaning of experience. We may think of tourists in Paris who experience only what they have read in the guide book and heard others talk about. Schachtel, however, writes: "So the average traveler through life remembers chiefly what the road map or the guide book says, what he is supposed to remember because it is exactly what everybody else remembers too." He explains childhood amnesia as the lack of words in the language to express, and thus think, childhood experience. It follows from his work also that the optimally adjusted person would be open to these socially undefined and thus unconceptualized meanings of his experience.

22. C. R. Rogers and R. Dymond, *Psychotherapy and Personality Change* (Chicago: University of Chicago Press, 1954), p. 167.

23. If theory can refer to experiencing, as described above, it becomes theoretically clear that it is socially and morally safe to allow an individual to judge and act on the basis of a felt weighing of all the implicit meanings in his own experiencing. Social values are not lost thereby. Problems of social control, education, and the like would all be formulated in terms of encouraging maximal individual opportunity for sensing the implicit meanings in one's own experiencing. Social institutions that offer such

when he finishes. Nor is he oblivious to or in conflict with them. But this "taking account," both in therapy and thereafter, is a *process of feeling*. The conceptual contents of such a process might make an extremely long list, if they were exhaustively stated, but their implicit weighing in feeling can occur in a present moment.

The subjective weighing process thus does not occur in terms of explicit conceptual contents. It is a subjective feeling process that must be considered as implicitly containing all these meanings. Hence there is need for a term that theoretically states (and experientially refers to) experiencing as felt, and as implicitly meaningful. It is in awareness, but not identical with the small part that is conceptualized.

2. *Congruence and genuineness.* Let us turn now to the second cited use of the term "congruence" in Rogerian theory. One of the "necessary conditions of therapy," "genuineness," was defined as "congruence" of the counselor in the relationship with the client. Here again, Rogers does not mean by congruence complete conceptualization, and again, his term "genuineness" is misinterpreted because there is no way of theoretically stating precisely the implicit, nonconceptual awareness he does mean.

"Genuineness" is often misinterpreted as conceptual expression to the client of all kinds of irrelevant feelings of the counselor's. Of course, this is not Rogers' intention in using the term. For one thing, *complete* conceptual expression of counselor attitudes is as impossible as complete *conceptual* openness to experience. Such conceptualization would be endless. Rogers compares this impossibility to the caterpillar aware of each of his thousand legs. A genuine counselor would

---

opportunity would be differentiated from social institutions that seek imposition of judgments and values without reference to experiencing, or worse, couple such judgments and values with injunctions against sensing implicit meanings of experiencing.

have to focus all his attention on himself and his own attitudes toward the client. This obviously absurd implication is not intended. Instead, Rogers' "genuineness" and "openness to experience" imply a way of having experience that can be "congruent" without being fully conceptualized. This is just what our term "experiencing" refers to.

Hence, genuineness is consistent with a counselor's rarely giving conceptual awareness or conceptual expression to his attitudes toward the client.

If it is possible to refer to aware, felt experiencing, we can define genuineness. The counselor usually responds with some conceptualization *of the client's experience.* The question of genuineness is simply: does the counselor have the present experiencing *as well as* the conceptualizations he expresses, or only the latter? If he has experiencing as well as the conceptualization, then the counselor genuinely experiences the client.

On the other hand, the counselor's concept may describe the client, yet from the words alone we have little indication as to the counselor's actual present experiencing of the client.

The only change here made in Rogers' definition of genuineness has been that we have taken the word to refer to the presence or absence[24] of aware, felt experiencing expressed by conceptualization, whereas he takes it to be a comparison between the contents of conceptualization and the contents posited in the construct "experience."

The immediate advantage of defining genuineness (and congruence) in terms of *experiencing* is the capacity of theory to state what is observed. Genuineness, after all, is a formulation of something Rogers and others have observed to be important to therapy. The constructs "experience" and "congruence" are not observable. If the term "genuineness" formulates observations, it must refer to something that could

24. Other differentiations are possible, as well.

have been observable. (This would not obviate other kinds of definitions, that is, definitions in terms of psychological dynamics and so on.) "Experiencing," and differentiations within it, can allow us to state with some precision what, in common-sense language, is really meant by genuineness.

Genuineness, for the counselor, is rather analogous to experiencing, for the client, as mentioned in the differentiation between diagnosis and therapy. In the latter case it was noticed that in addition to the conceptual understanding of his diagnosis, the client required a long period of therapeutic *experiencing*. Similarly, genuineness requires not only counselor statements of conceptualizations of the client, but also the counselor's *experiencing* of the client.

3 *and* 4. *Process of therapy* (*becoming more congruent; therapist's responses*). We have discussed the first two uses of the notion of "congruence" by Rogers. The last two may be considered together since they both deal with the process of therapy. During therapy the client *becomes aware of incongruities* (and becomes more and more congruent) *with his experience*. The therapist endeavors to aid this process by responding so as to be "exactly congruent with the client's unformed emotional experience."

In these two uses it is clear (although not admitted into precise theory) that both client and counselor observe implicitly meaningful experience. Only with reference to this can the client become *aware of incongruities* between experience and self-concepts. Only with reference to this can the client's and counselor's conceptualizations "become increasingly" congruent. However, in present theory, concepts are said to be congruent, not with the directly referred-to experiencing observed by both persons, but with a theoretical construct that has no observable denotation. The many current theoretical discussions of optimal therapeutic responses would be immensely clarified if there were terms for directly referred-to experiencing.

We have already seen how psychotherapy (as against mere communication of concepts) involves experiencing—a long term process of change. Every hour of psychotherapy involves much experiencing. Therapists who give interpretations and diagnoses must decide at what time the patient's *experiencing* enables him to make use of an interpretation. (All agree that it is not effective to simply give conceptual interpretations at any arbitrary time.) Client-centered counselors, instead of giving interpretations, give conceptualizations of what, as far as they can observe, the client is *now* experiencing, but perhaps not making explicit. Precise theory at present allows no way of stating what the last sentence just stated. The therapist's "endeavor to be exactly congruent with the client's unformed emotional experience" can be stated only as the therapist's endeavor to state what the client "feels," which in turn is often identified with what he says or thinks.

Hence, the Rogerian therapeutic response appears to some people to be mere repetition of conceptual contents already known to the client. They wonder how the client is helped to overcome his defences, if only what he already knows is ever said. Others, who observe Rogerian therapy in action, find that Rogers has misled them, since the therapist often does seem to introduce much more information, concepts, essential conceptualizations, than Rogers' client-centered theory seems to indicate. They expected mere repetition, but find instead what they consider "direction" of the client by the therapist, that is, the introduction of new material of which the client was unaware. Theory lacks terms to state the client-centered response, which is neither mere repetition of conceptual contents, nor directive introduction of new, diagnostic concepts. Seeman states the client-centered response accurately, but his formulation cannot sufficiently clarify discussion. Theory cannot proceed until there can be a theoretically precise formulation of how a conceptualization can be "exactly congruent" with an "unformed" emotional experience. This formulation is possible if theoretical terms can refer to "unformed emotional experience" as observed by the client in his own phenomenal field, and as observed by the counselor in client behaviors.

With terms referring to felt experiencing, the client-centered therapeutic response is capable of more precise theoretical statement. The same is the case with directive, Freudian, and other therapies. The training of an analyst or psychiatrist gives him the supposedly essential vocabulary of terms, yet nearly no research exists (or can be formulated) regarding the conditions under which conceptualization is not merely intellectual, or regarding the experiential process that a patient must undergo in order to meaningfully "absorb," "use," "change himself around" the concepts of the therapist.

Thus Fiedler finds much more similarity between experienced therapists of *different* schools than between experienced and inexperienced therapists of the *same* school. Evidently, for all kinds of therapy, the vital factors are not those considered in explicit training. For these vital factors of therapy we do not even have terms as yet, except such terms as "congruent" and "congruent with unformed emotional experience" and "give the interpretation when the patient is ready for it." Theory and research concerning these questions can proceed only if the relationships between conceptualizations and *experiencing* can be delineated and investigated.

Each of the four uses of "congruence" has been shown to involve aware implicitly meaningful *experiencing*. We have shown that in each case the congruence theory really attempts to refer to a relationship between symbols and "unformed emotional experience." Theory substitutes for this observed relationship an equation, called congruence, between a construct "experience" and a conceptualization.

We have shown that absurdities in theory can be cleared away, if one restores the intended reference to observations of the role of experiencing. We have formulated some hypotheses that illustrate research application of terms referring to experiencing.

We have examined these four areas with our wider scheme of many kinds of relationships between experiencing and symbols.

3. THE ROLE OF OTHER KINDS OF SYMBOLIZATION

The four uses of congruence are only four specific areas of clinical observation, in which the term congruence is currently employed. The theory of congruence really attempts to formulate, in general, the relationship between experiencing and symbolization. In this larger task, the congruence theory implies only one kind of relationship between experiencing and symbolization, whereas the present essay found at least seven. The congruence theory attempts to reduce all kinds of relationships between experiencing and symbolization to an equation. For us, this was only one type of relationship. We termed it "comprehension" (see Chapter III). Let us therefore now show that there are areas of clinical observation in which the relationship between experiencing and symbols must be formulated in terms of functional relationships other than comprehension. We have already done so in discussing the four current uses of congruence. Nevertheless, we would like to show not only that just these four uses can be clarified and that research hypotheses can be formulated for them, but also that the relationship between experiencing and symbols can be investigated much more broadly with our terms. Using (a) direct reference and (b) metaphor, let us cite some other areas of clinical observation in which research hypotheses can be formulated concerning the relationship between experiencing and symbolization.

(a) Direct reference, although underlying all other ways in which experiencing occurs for an individual, can occur alone. For example, a client says, "This feeling, that I have now, puzzles me." This is not a conceptualization. The client refers directly to something concretely given in his field. The symbols "this feeling that puzzles me" conceptualize nothing for him. There is no possible equation of congruence, since the symbols don't attempt to state the feeling. Only the direct reference to feeling gives any meaning at all to the phrase "this feeling." Hence, congruence is inapplicable.

It is vitally important to the client that both he and the therapist refer directly to the client's feeling, whether this be conceptualized congruently or not. Recall the example of the client, who, after much use of certain concepts, has arrived at the actual experiencing that these concepts "really" meant. This client is at great pains to show the counselor that the concepts *now* refer to "this" real, strong, present experiencing. He has difficulty believing that the counselor understands, since there are no words other than the old words. The counselor's direct reference is very important to the client.

Another example of the importance to the client of the counselor's direct reference to present client experiencing is the frequent case where neither person yet knows what "this feeling" is, except perhaps that it is strong, scary, bothersome, or "gets in the way of such and such a situation." Here it is vital for therapy that both client and counselor refer directly to "this feeling." Therapy can continue if both persons so refer. Therapy, at least on a given, present problem, ceases if the client does not perceive the counselor as referring to "this feeling" in him, even if the counselor offers a conceptualization that, it may later turn out, is accurate.[25] This principle (of the necessity of counselor direct reference) lies at the base of client-centered therapeutic method. The counselor endeavors to respond in such a way that whatever he says will be considered by the client as referring to the client's present directly referred-to experiencing. If the client considers this to be the aim of the therapist, and if the client takes the therapist's response to refer to his experiencing, and if the therapist's response is such that the client can refer it directly to his present experiencing, only then does the question of accuracy arise. The client then finds that the counselor's response symbolizes his experiencing accurately, or that it does not. If not, he may correct the counselor or try again to communicate the unformed experience. But direct reference by the counselor to the client's experiencing is first. The counselor can always respond in some way, no matter how inaccurately. If the client

25. For example: the client may just have expressed his fear of a certain situation. The counselor may respond with an accurate (congruent) conceptualization of the fear. Let us assume that the fear really is—and that the client will soon discover that it really is—his fear of being rejected in that situation. The counselor may respond: "You are afraid that if you go into this situation you will be rejected." Such a (by assumption, accurate) response by the counselor does not necessarily aid the client at arriving at this symbolization of his own experience. It is likely to aid him only if he considers the counselor's response as referring directly to the feeling he himself now refers to. Let us say that he does not so consider the counselor's response. He may feel instead that the counselor is trying to explain the feeling, or push him into the situation, or does not appreciate how scared he is, or isn't willing to deal with his being scared for one reason or another (perhaps the counselor seems to the client to be afraid of fear). In these ways of considering the response the client does not consider the therapist to be referring to the client's feeling. He will then probably not be aided in symbolizing his own fear. He will probably answer, "Yes, yes, I know, but I'm still scared."

It is not enough that the conceptual content of the counselor's response be congruent with the conceptual content *posited* in the client's *construct* experience. Rather, this accurate conceptualization will aid the client only if he refers it directly to the "unformed emotional experience," that is, his own experiencing. If, for one of many possible reasons, the client does not so refer the counselor's response, he is left with only the concepts of that response.

takes the counselor's response as referring to this aspect of his experiencing, the matter is brought into the therapeutic situation. It may not be accurately symbolized, but it has not been dropped, ignored, or allowed to remain totally unspecified. Both client's and counselor's direct reference are vital. The client may not yet have specified the experience as a "this."[26] Whether he has done so or not, direct reference to it as a "this" has important, observable therapeutic effects.

Thus, "direct reference" both by client and by counselor is a kind of symbolization vital to therapy. Congruence does not primarily apply to this kind of symbolization. Hypotheses as to therapeutic change can be formulated for just this one kind of symbolization. One could employ the Osgood meaning scales or some other instrument that measures change in particular problem areas, and one could compare cases in which clients and/or counselors did and did not employ direct reference.

We can formulate hypotheses, such as: "If the client does not consider the counselor's response to refer directly to his own directly referred-to experiencing, then conceptual accuracy by the counselor is not likely to be therapeutically effective."

With "direct reference," then, we can formulate observations of a kind of symbolization other than that which "congruence" implies.

(b) Another kind of symbolization different from that which "congruence" implies has in this treatise been called "metaphor." It was defined as the case where a symbolic vehicle and a (partly) new experience are created simultaneously.[27]

Our distinctions of kinds of symbolization are based on differentiations capable of being made in an individual's ex-

26. That is, whether he has directly referred to it already himself, or not.
27. For example, a person reading a poem nearly always has novel experiencing as well as novel symbolization.

periencing. Theories have long attempted to reduce all relationships between experience and symbols to one of these
kinds. If experience is a construct, this reduction is possible.
Examples from actual experiencing can then be cited to illustrate the basic notion of symbolization chosen by the
theory. Thus, Rogers illustrates his theory by illustrations we
would call "comprehension," while Shlien[28] illustrates his
theory with instances of metaphor. The Rogerian theory assumes that all meanings are already in experience and need
only be conceptualized, while Shlien's theory denies an unconscious because it assumes that both experience and meaning are created in the act of symbolization. But we can refer
to experiencing of all these sorts, if terms may refer to experiencing. How then can we investigate the whole broad field of
relationship between experiencing and symbolization? Let us
pose our question differently: since we have shown that all
these kinds of relationships sometimes apply, let us ask: when
does each apply?

We have shown that, on purely theoretical grounds, each
can be made to apply to all instances of experiencing. Thus
our question has no one theoretical answer. However, we may
turn it into an empirical question, if we set up empirical criteria for the aspects of experiencing that each kind of symbolization emphasizes.

For direct reference [in (a) above] the aspect of experiencing we specified was the role of the individual's own direct
reference, attention, feeling, and working with his immediately
given felt data. We showed that there are operational indices
of this kind of occurrence and that we can formulate important
hypotheses regarding its role in therapy, education, and other
areas.

28. John M. Shlien, "Some Notes on the Concept of 'Repression' and
the Concept of the 'Self,'" *Counseling Center Discussion Papers*, Vol. II,
No. 30 (1956).

Metaphor emphasizes that experiencing itself changes in the act of symbolizing it. In practice, it is an important question why a client's or a student's expressing, stating, symbolizing what he does feel, sometimes changes it.

Theoretically we may argue that symbolization always changes experiencing, but why not set up empirical criteria for such change? Such a criterion might be change on personality tests, physiological change, change in feeling on an Osgood scale, or change in manner of statement of a personal problem. Once we agree with respect to what criterion "change" in experiencing is being asserted, we may ask, "Is this an instance of metaphor?"—that is, did experiencing change in the defined way when its symbolization occurred?

Note that this important question cannot be formulated if one theoretically assumes that all meanings are already in experience. On the other hand, one need not argue that they are in no sense already there. With terms that refer directly to experiencing, and criteria of "change," one can formulate hypotheses regarding change in experiencing when symbolization of it occurs.

We have been attempting to show that the whole field of relationships between experiencing and symbols can be fruitfully formulated and investigated by use of our terms.

We have been illustrating that the proposed terms and method may help clarify and extend theory and may advance research.

Experiencing (certain functions of it) is a process that brings about therapeutic change. Therapists, on the basis of clinical observation, assume that a therapy hour full of intense experiencing is a "good hour." Terms referring directly to experiencing, which may be used to make differentiations in experiencing, can then be related to other kinds of observations, so that operational research can test hypotheses thus formulated.

We shall then be able to test specific hypotheses of how experiencing brings about therapeutic change.

Of course, such hypotheses can *then* be reformulated as correlations between externally observable behaviors (related to experiencing) and psychologically defined observations. Theoretical terms referring to the process of experiencing can *then* be considered to refer merely to the behavioral observations. Now, however, to bring that stage of research about, we need terms that refer to, and can differentiate, experiencing itself, and can formulate hypotheses about the role of experiencing in therapeutic change and in many other contexts.

[C]
Relationship Between the Proposed Method and Logical Positivism and Operationalism in Psychology

The method proposed in this essay augments, but does not alter, the current methods of positivistic science. It is true that one of the prime tenets of positivistic and operational science is that terms must either refer to external observations (externally observable consequences of operations) or be theoretical constructs that relate terms that do so refer. Terms that refer directly to experiencing, as proposed in this section, thus seem excluded from positivistic scientific method. However, terms defined by direct reference to experiencing need not obviate other terms defined by external observations. Of course, even if the same word be used, terms defined in these different ways must, and easily can, be carefully distinguished. If this is done, we can show that the proposed method of using terms referring directly to experiencing has two important roles that augment current positivistic methods: (1) at a stage prior to the stage of an investigation at which the positivistic method begins, and (2) at a stage after the stage of conclusions of the positivistic method.

1. PRIOR TO THE FIRST POSITIVISTIC STAGE OF AN INVESTIGATION

As we have shown in a number of instances, current theory cannot refer to an individual's directly referred-to experiencing. Its terms either refer to externally observable behavior, or they are theoretical constructs without observable referents at all. However, most of the practical and live meaning of theory in the field of psychology (psychotherapy, anthropology, and other related fields) lies in the personal experience of the psychologist. Hence, he employs that personal experience both to give implicit meaning to his terms and to help him formulate meaningful hypotheses. Insofar as he does this, he is at present not considered a scientist. In other words, his heuristic operations (to state, generalize, and hypothesize about his experience) are, at present, a private, unsystematic, unscientific, intuitive affair. However, psychologists must engage in this process of referring to and specifying their experiences in order to arrive at meaningful hypotheses. They also talk to each other in this manner in a common-sense phenomenological language. For the current scientific methods, then, this process occurs, but is prior to science.

The present treatise proposes to make this necessary part of the scientific process systematic and intersubjective. A method is proposed to define the references of terms to experiencing. Of course, terms that so refer must be carefully distinguished from terms (perhaps the same words, but different terms since different in meaning) that are defined operationally or by external observation, or as constructs.

If differently defined terms are carefully distinguished, no type of term need exclude another type. Theoretical statements could be very much extended and implicit references to experiencing could be clarified and made precise. Hypotheses could first be stated in terms referring to experiencing. Carefully defined terms that refer to experiencing can then make redefinition into externally observable terms much easier.

Differentiations that at first are possible only in experiencing can then be investigated through such observable redefinition. The reverse order is rarely the case: rarely do differentiations in behavior or other external observation lead to just those differentiations which a direct specification of experiencing reveals. Differentiations first found in external observations are often important, of course. But they are not likely to be just the observable marks of some differentiation important in experiencing. Therefore a psychologist often starts with differentiations referring directly to experiencing—or to verbal behaviors indicative of differentiations in someone's experiencing—and seeks to redefine these in externally observable terms. On the other hand, once the differentiations are made and redefined, then it is possible to assert, from a certain philosophic viewpoint, that the experienced differentiations "really mean" the externally observable ones.[29] Therefore, the current positivistic method can remain intact and can even

29. As here proposed, some theoretical terms would refer directly to experiencing throughout, not only before and after operational statement. However, from the viewpoint of operationalism, such terms can be considered as necessary only before and after operational definitions. The reason is that terms referring to experiencing would be related to terms denoting external observations of effects and relationships. Thus, if a theoretical term x refers to experiencing of a certain kind, and x is eventually found to be correlated with observable effects a, b, c, and it is found that a, b, c are correlated with an important factor, D, then theory will be able to state *both* that the aspect of experiencing x is correlated to factor D and that observable effects a, b, c are correlated with D. Only then can one assert from an operationalist viewpoint that everything can, after all, be stated in terms of a, b, c, and D. Theory would continue to be able to state their relationship to x as well, though at that stage employing the term x might be necessary only for further hypotheses and for practical application by individuals in the field.

be employed to analyze discoveries made by differentiations directly in experiencing, retranslated into operational language. Such analysis, however, is applicable only after the discoveries have been made and translated into operational terms.

We conclude, then, that the proposed method and terms would leave positivistic operational methods intact, but would provide the possibility of formulating theory and hypotheses referring to experiencing. Systematic and intersubjective definition would be given to meanings that at present are private, intuitive, and cannot be easily communicated.

2. AT THE STAGE AFTER OPERATIONAL CONCLUSIONS

At present, research conclusions and theoretical conclusions are stated only in terms of operationally defined terms or constructs relating such terms. Hence, the actual significance of findings to people practicing in the field, that is, the kind of experiencing and the kind of attitudes, situations, expressions, and feelings had in practical situations, remain untouched by theory. Hence research findings and theoretical statements cannot easily be applied to practice. Application, like hypotheses generation, is at present a private, intuitive, unscientific, personal realm. Communication is at a minimum in this realm. Despite our growing science, the application of this science to practice remains unscientific.

The proposed method and terms enable one to *re*translate operational conclusions into terms referring directly to experiencing. Such a retranslation would take nothing away from the operational conclusions as such and would contradict no postulates as to the metaphysical or epistemological primacy of operational terms. A retranslation into terms referring to experience would allow the application of scientific findings in terms of attitudes, feelings, experiencings of many sorts.

Differentiations in experiencing, once defined, could be employed in theory to state conclusions not only operationally but also experientially. At present, the reference to experiencing is nearly everywhere implicitly assumed. The proposed method aims to make this implicit reference explicit, systematic, defined, and communicable.

Since theoretical research conclusions are also again generative of further hypotheses, our first and second roles of the proposed method merge. If conclusions can be retranslated into terms referring directly to experiencing, this in itself also provides theory with the capacity to formulate explicit and communicable further hypotheses.

The realm of private experiencing may perhaps always exceed what may be stated communicably. However, it is possible to give theory the capacity to state much of this realm with increasing precision. At least, theory will be enabled to state as much of it as is now implicitly referred to but not communicated in the theories of therapy and other kinds of practice.

3. NEW FORMS AND PRINCIPLES OF INQUIRY

Reference to experiencing is needed not only in the generation of hypotheses but also for new logical forms and principles of inquiry. Dewey, Carnap, and others are in agreement that postulates and principles of science themselves develop in the course of science, and their validity lies in their fruitfulness in use. We have shown that the proposed method is capable of discovering a great many new and different logical forms and postulates at any point in a discourse (see Chapters V and VI). The discovery or invention of novel postulates, principles, and methods cannot be accounted for by principles of choice such as fruitfulness. The current views leave discovery and invention to chance, intuition, private experience;

that is, they leave it outside the realm of science and inter-subjective communication.

The two views mentioned differ somewhat in this regard. Carnap and other logical positivists leave novelty of scientific methods and principles entirely outside the scope of their concerns. They deal only with choice between finished products offered. Dewey and the pragmatists, on the other hand, are concerned with novelty of methods and principles, and show how they arise in the evolution of science as a social endeavor. However, Dewey's view implies a decided determinacy of novel methods and principles by current methods and principles. Quite intentionally, Dewey sees polarization in science, that is to say, a process of snowballing by which successful current methods determine that further developments will be more like what has been found to be successful. There is little question that indeed this happens in science, and thus, that Dewey's assertion is based on observation of science.

However, is such polarization desirable? For example: if we tend to be more successful currently with technological solutions to problems, does this mean that it is desirable to determine further developments in the same direction? If radios have not met the present human needs for companionship or meaning in life, is it desirable that the next development be TV?[30] Recall that such a next development is determined by the methods and principles of science that have been found to be most successful. If curative medicine initially made more progress than preventive medicine, is it desirable that science tends now to approach problems more and more exclusively by curative, rather than preventive, methods? If positivistic, operational science generally has been extremely successful, is it desirable that new tasks and the creation of new methods

---

30. Thus, for example, scientific methods in all fields will be profoundly influenced by the annual 40 billion dollars we spend on certain kinds of research as against other kinds on which we spend little.

of science be approached exclusively in an operational manner?

Once the question is posed in this way, the answer appears to be that indeed what has been found to be successful in the past has a good chance of succeeding in the future, but this should not exclude new methods and principles. The proposed method is both a case of such new methods and itself a method for obtaining such new methods, principles, and logical forms. In the analysis of symbolization from experiencing, as here presented, the process of creation of logical forms is examined. This does not replace Dewey's or Carnap's treatment of choice among logical forms and principles, but it does offer something not given by them, namely systematic *creation* of logical forms and principles.

Novel logical forms and principles are thus in exactly the same situation with respect to operational and positivistic methods as are novel differentiations made in experiencing. Both may be represented operationally, *once created*. Both may be tested as to validity (or fruitful use) as is currently done. However, neither the creation of novel differentiations nor the creation of novel logical forms is dealt with by current pragmatism and positivism except after the creation. The proposed method and terms deal with the creation itself. As a method, the proposed one makes systematic creation of novel differentiations and logical forms possible. As a philosophic analysis, its scope is extended to include not only the choice between, but the creation of, logical forms and principles as symbolizations of experiencing.

Appendix to Chapter I

The following appendix will cite certain parts of the works of four contemporary philosophers. Our purpose is to point out exactly what, in these philosophies, can contribute to the task of the present work. Therefore, I consider here only those bits of the thought of these men that are relevant.

The proper place of this appendix is between Chapters I and II; that is to say, it comes just after we have defined the problem and before we embark on its treatment.

As far as these authors have gone, they help us in starting our task. For example, a great deal of traditional and contemporary discussion assumes that thought always involves *words or images*. Since the view seems to ignore common observation it is difficult to disprove. Therefore, it is of great value to us to cite Husserl, who notes the fact that thought most frequently occurs without explicit words and without auditory or visual images.

Similarly, although we offer in Chapter II much of descriptive evidence for the implicit *meaningfulness* of feeling, it is so widely overlooked that we appreciate being able to cite mention of it by Sartre. Even more, we value citing Merleau-Ponty, who recognizes that there are necessary (albeit undefined) *roles* that feeling plays in our uses of meaning.

We are further aided by Richards, whose discussion shows the need for the task of this book. Also, he describes the need for some method by which the direct use of both cognition and feeling could be made possible *in the inquiry itself* so that inquiry would not be falsified from the start by the imposition of cognitive presuppositions upon feeling.

These and other contributions (cited below) are preparatory to our task; they help define it and they are some steps toward it that have been taken. Chapters II–VI, then, can be thought of as beginning where this appendix ends.

Husserl

Husserl contributes to an investigation of experienced meaning in several respects.

1. PHENOMENOLOGICAL METHOD

The phenomenological vantage point of his whole method demonstrates that what is given to awareness may be directly referred to. Husserl does not restrict himself to the data of direct reference. Many of his concepts are principles that are based on evidence of phenomenological data but far exceed it. For example, his concept of "intention" (or "act") is not a datum of awareness; rather, it is a principle presupposed by such data. The scheme of epistemology that Husserl devises through the employment of such principles does not concern us here. However, he does establish a method involving direct reference to data of awareness. He considers cognition at least partly from the vantage point of experiencing. The data of awareness of the human knower as he experiences cognition can be directly referred to.

2. THE EXPERIENCE OF MEANING CAN BE DISTINGUISHED AND HAS A DISTINCT FUNCTION IN COGNITION

Husserl does not explicitly state that the datum given in awareness when meaning is had is a *felt* experiencing. He calls it a meaning-giving experience (*sinnverleihendes Erlebnis*) and defines it as a separate act. He differentiates this datum and its functions from images, symbols, and perceptions. It is then not quite clear just what this experience is, and Husserl describes it only to the extent of making a separate place for it. Let us look at Husserl's discussion step by step.

Aber ein wahrhaft sinnloses Sprechen wäre überhaupt kein Sprechen, es stände gleich dem Gerassel einer Maschiene. Dergleichen kommt allenfalls vor beim gedankenlosen Hersagen eingelernter Verse. . . .[1]

Husserl points out the experienced difference between meaningful and meaningless signs. He focuses on the fact that meaningfulness is not a property of a sign qua physical, but is experienced. Meaning is created by an "act" or an "intention" (all acts are intentional in Husserl's explicit definition of the term). The act itself is a principle of epistemology, presupposed in the difference between meaningful and meaningless experiences that are otherwise alike, for example meaningful and meaningless sounds:

wenn wir uns den Unterschied zwischen einem bloßen Lautgebild und demselben Lautgebild als verstandenem Namen klar machen . . . haben wir . . . die Existenz eines Vorstellung*saktes* direkt konstatiert.—II-I, 508.

Some experience or act must account for the difference between meaningful and meaningless symbols. Meaning depends on a distinct act. The distinct function of this act is shown just by the difference in our experience of meaningful and meaningless symbols.

3. THE EXPERIENCE OF MEANING IS DISTINGUISHED FROM IMAGES AND FROM PERCEPTIONS

Meaning depends on an act that is distinct from images. Imagery and representations may "fill up" a meaning, but

1. Edmund Husserl, *Logische Untersuchungen* Vol. II (Halle A.D.S.: Max Neimeyer, 1922), pt. I, p. 67.

meaning can be thought with or without such filling up. When imagery or some other kind of representation fills up or "illustrates" a meaning, it is after all the same meaning that it was already prior to the filling up. Hence meaning does not depend on the images or representations.

Husserl further points out that meaningful speech and thought can occur without perception.

Liegt die Bedeutung nicht in der Anschauung, so wird das anschauungslose Sprechen darum kein gedankenloses sein müssen. Entfällt die Anschauung, so bleibt am Ausdruck . . . eben ein Akt derselben Art hängen, wie derjenige, der . . . die Erkentniss ihres Gegenstandes vermittlet. So ist der Akt, in dem sich das Bedeuten vollzieht, im einen und anderen Falle vorhanden.— II-I, 67.

Meaning is independent of perceptions:

Auf Grund dieser selben Wahrnehmung könnte ja die Aussage noch ganz anders lauten und dabei einen ganz anderen Sinn entfalten.—II-II, 14.

. . . der Name mein Tintenfass "legt sich" gleichsam dem wahrgenommenen Gegenstande "auf" gehört sozusagen fühlbar zu ihm.—II-II, 24.

. . . Empfindungen . . . sinnlich vereinheitlicht . . . und durchgeistigt von einem gewissen, ihnen objektiven Sinn verleihenden Aktcharacter der "Auffassung." Dieser Aktcharacter macht es, dasz uns ein Gegenstand . . . erscheint. Also nicht Wort und Titenfass, sondern die beschriebenen Akterlebnisse, in denen sie erscheinen . . . treten in Beziehung.—II-II, 24–25.

Selbstverständlich kann man nach dieser Darlegung wie die Erfüllung auch das Erkennen—was ja nur ein anderes Wort ist— als einen indentifizierenden Akt bezeichnen.—II-II, 35.

. . . Verständniss—oder Bedeutungscharacter, der schon im anschauungslosen Ausdruck als sinnverleihendes Erlebnis dient . . .—II-I, 77.

Not only does meaning not depend on the given perception (many meanings can be based on one and the same perception and many perceptions could lead to one and the same meaning) but the act that creates meaning is presupposed in the presentation of an object. When we *recognize* an object, two acts interrelate: that act which creates the object and that which—in the meaningful use of the word—creates the meaning that itself intends an object. Hence recognition of a perception is a congruence (*Deckung*) or "identification" between these two distinct acts.

Regardless of whether we are aware of the identification as such, we are aware of the unity that presupposes this identification:

Identifizierende Deckung sei erlebt, mag auch die bewusste Intention auf Identität, das beziehende Identifizieren unterblieben sein.—II-II, 36.

4. MEANING IS EXPERIENCED AS DISTINCT FROM SYMBOLIC THOUGHT

Having distinguished the act and experience of meaning from imagery and from perception, we now turn to Husserl's discussion of symbols and his distinction between meaning and symbolic thought:

. . . das symbolische Denken (ist) ein Denken nur . . . um des neuen "intentionalen" oder Aktcharacters willen, der das Unterscheidene des bedeutsamen Zeichens ausmacht, gegenüber dem "blossen" Zeichen, das ist dem Wortlaut. . . .—II-I, 68.
Indessen meint doch auch der symbolisch fungierende Ausdruck etwas und nichts anderes als der anschaulich geklärte. —II-I, 71.
. . . das Wesen des Ausdrückens . . . liegt . . . in der Bedeutungsintention . . . und nicht in den . . . Verbildlichungen, die sich ihr erfüllend zugesellen mögen.—II-I, 98.

Before "filling" by imagery, a meaning is thought purely by the aid of symbols. It is not the symbols, we note, that inform the symbols with meaning. That is a separate "act."

When images fill and explicate this meaning, it is still the same meaning.

We shall ask just in what sense the meaning is thought, or had, or experienced at the point when the imaginative filling has not taken place. Husserl's logical differentiation between meaning on the one hand, and symbol, image, perception on the other, is quite a contribution to our task, as it differentiates our subject matter clearly from these. But what then is the experience of meaning, so differentiated? How can it function? Husserl answers both questions by means of his theory of "acts" and the interrelation of acts. Here we will not follow him, although we will not contradict him either.

1. A method involving direct reference to data of awareness is possible.

2. Our experience of meaning has (or points to) a distinct function in cognition.

3. Experience of meaning is distinguished from images and perceptions, and can occur without them.

4. Experience of meaning is distinguished from symbolic thought and can occur without verbal symbols.

Sartre

Sartre's basic term is "a consciousness." For him *a* "consciousness" is distinguished from another consciousness by the way in which it presents an object to itself. Hence there is a distinguishable "imaginative conciousness."[2] "To perceive, conceive, imagine: these are the three types of consciousness by which the same object can be given to us." (p. 9)

Thought is characterized by the following:

2. Jean-Paul Sartre, *The Psychology of Imagination* (New York: Philosophical Library, 1948), p. 8.

I am at the center of my idea, I seize it in its entirety at one glance. This does not mean, of course, that my idea does not need to complete itself by an infinite progression. But I can think of the concrete essences in a single act of consciousness; I do not have to re-establish the appearance, I have no apprenticeship to serve. Such is, no doubt, the clearest difference between a thought and a perception. (p. 10)

We note that thinking has been differentiated from perception. On the other hand, we note that Sartre disagrees with Husserl who wrote that a single meaning was made up of many *Bedeutungsmomente* each constituted by an act. Since both base themselves on the supposedly certain evidence of the immediately given, doubt is cast on both the notion of "act" and that of "consciousness" (in this case *Bedeutungsakt* and "conceiving consciousness" or idea).
For Sartre,

an image . . . reveals at a single stroke what it is. (p. 12) It delivers . . . the object . . . in a lump. No risk, no anticipation: only certainty. My perception can deceive me, but not my image.

Here again, a different condition is asserted of imagery than that Husserl asserted. No gradual "filling up" of meaning here. On the other hand, there is, for Sartre, a gradation of distance of an image from a perception:

The farther removed that the material of the imaginative consciousness is from the material of perception, the more that it becomes penetrated with knowledge, the more does its resemblance to the objective picture become attenuated. A new phenomenon appears: that of equivalence. The intuitive material is chosen for its equivalent relationships to the material of the object. The movement is hypostatized as the equivalent of the form, and the luminosity as the equivalent of the color. What this means is that knowledge plays an increasingly more important role as it replaces intuition on the very soil of intuition. (p. 74)

Sartre, then, like Husserl, takes note of the fact that we sometimes think with clear full images, sometimes with nearly no imagery, and sometimes even without any imagery at all.

Here Sartre outlines the problem of the present essay: What is the experience of meaning apart from an image? How shall we describe the function of our inarticulate experience, not of an explicated set of symbols? Sartre has two things to say at this juncture:

Knowledge . . . must undergo a debasement (when) . . . it becomes intuitive in the flow of pantomime; it flows in the movements. A new phenomenon appears: the symbolic movement, which, by its very nature as movement, belongs to intuition, and, by its meaning, belongs to pure thought. (p. 74)

Let us look at "symbolic movement" and at "debased knowledge" further.

"We have already seen that in the image consciousness we apprehend an object as an 'analogue' of another object." "It would now seem that all we need do is to describe this analogical content just as we described the material contents of the consciousness of the portrait. . . . But here we meet with the greatest difficulty." (p. 76) "We are confronted with another synthetic consciousness which has nothing in common with the first. We cannot therefore hope to get at this content by introspection."

Sartre has previously described imagery that, akin to perception, was similar to the object—for example, a portrait. Now he has turned to imagery the content of which is only analogous to the object, not itself similar to it. Hence he is confronted with the choice of either describing the perceptual content itself (say dots), or of dealing with that of which it is an analogue. The first would be trivial, but of the latter he says:

We know that in the mental images there is a psychic factor which functions as analogue, but when we wish to ascertain more clearly the nature and components of this factor we are reduced to conjectures.

The section that follows is entitled by Sartre: "The probable."

Sartre has led right up to the point where the subject matter of the present essay would enter, but then he proceeds to a purely logical analysis of the analogous function of images. He no longer finds experiential, phenomenologically describable contents of awareness. We do. We find felt meaning functioning just at this point where a meaning is had but where the images function only as analogous symbolic helps, not as real images. Once felt meaning is noted we find also that felt meaning functions at all times, but that in such junctures as here it is vital for a logical analysis. This is shown further by Sartre's assertion that "the knowledge can exist in the free state (apart from an image), that is, constitute a consciousness only to itself." It isn't clear just what an adequate description of the experience of such "free-state" knowledge is, but it is clear that Sartre notes that knowledge can be independent of images altogether.

Sartre's discussion of "debased knowledge" delimits our subject matter: "Husserl was the victim of the illusion of immanence" (p. 83) because to speak of imagery "filling in" a meaning is to assert presence of images "in" something. Sartre prefers: "the image . . . is itself a conciousness." Consequently he questions whether "knowledge in passing from the free state . . . undergoes no other change than a filling in. Is it not rather the object of a radical change? Psychologists . . . have discovered in their subjects some strange conditions, namely, that alongside the pure knowledge . . . there appear some strange states which, although containing no representative elements whatsoever, are nevertheless reported by the subject

as images. 'I had an undetermined image of an "opening." ' "
(pp. 83–84) Of this Sartre says ". . . [It is] still knowledge,
but knowledge that is debased."

Sartre discusses reading, where also meanings are thought
and experienced, but imagery as such does not occur. Yet
Sartre notes that "the reader is in the presence of a world."
(p. 90)

Therefore everything that exceeds, includes, orients, and localizes
the naked meaning of the phrase I am reading is the object of a
knowledge. But this knowledge is not a pure "meaning." It is not
as meaning that I think "office," "third floor," "building," "sub-
urb of Paris." I think of them in terms of things.

No doubt but that the knowledge is always an empty consciousness of an order, a rule. But at times the knowledge . . . envisions
the object first and the order only insofar as it is constitutive of
the object. But what are we to understand here by Object? (p. 92)

He concludes that ". . . in reading we have a hybrid consciousness, half-meaningful and half-imaginative." We note
that in his discussion both of reading and of "debased knowledge" Sartre has delineated our subject matter and cited some
of its important functions. His analysis of it, although he
explicitly allows himself conjecture, is quite minimal. Rather,
the debased knowledge occurs in the context of his logical
analysis of the functions of images. Hence we find nothing
with which we must disagree. Even his terminology of "consciousness" is merely one preference, as against other possible
ones, of what to assign to the grammatical functions of nouns.
For Sartre each distinguishable functioning apprehension is
a consciousness. However, to say that reading is a "hybrid"
consciousness shows the need for direct description of just
how, in a case like reading, meaning is experienced.

Feeling, Sartre asserts, is *of* something. "In a word, feelings
have special intentionalities, they represent one way—among
others—of self-*transcendence*." (p. 98)

However, Sartre is chiefly thinking of emotions: "love," "hatred," "fear," "indignation." Hence it appears to him, as to most traditional philosophers, that feeling, so conceived, is a "special" kind of intentionality, not related to anything that functions to grasp meaning, even in such purely felt instances as "debased knowledge." He notes, however, that feeling is capable of a much finer and more representative intention than merely the sense in which love is of someone:

Citing as an example the feeling of loving someone's delicate hands, Sartre says:

I assume therefore that in the absence of a certain person it is the feeling which was inspired in me by her beautiful hand that reappears. Let us suppose, for the sake of greater clarity, that the feeling is pure of all knowledge. This is obviously an unusual case, but one which we have the right to imagine.

This feeling is not a pure subjective content, it does not escape the law of all consciousness: it transcends itself, analysis reveals in it a primary content which animates intentions of a very special type; in short, it is an affective consciousness *of* those hands. Only this consciousness does not posit the hands it envisions, *as hands,* that is as a synthesis of representations. Knowledge and sensible representations are lacking (by hypothesis). The consciousness is rather of something fine, graceful, pure, with a nuance of strictly individual fineness and purity. What is unique for me in those hands—and which cannot express itself in a knowledge, even imaginative—namely, the tint of the skin at the finger tips, the shape of the fingernails, the small wrinkles around the phalanx, all this does, no doubt, *appear* to me. But these details do not present themselves in their representative aspect. I become aware of them as an undifferentiated mass which defies all description. And this affective mass has a character which lacks clear and complete knowledge: the mass is *present.* What this means is, that the feeling is present so that the affective structure of the objects builds itself up together with a determined affective consciousness. A feeling is thus not an empty consciousness: it is already a possession. Those hands present themselves to me under their affective form. (pp. 100–101)

Here then, Sartre gives us a description of feeling as intending or meaning. However, Sartre remains with an absolute disjunction of the two types of consciousness. No representative aspect is implied for him in the feeling. Hence it must "defy all description." We may conclude, however, that such a state can function in a description or articulation in symbols or in representative form; we may still use Sartre's terms if we wish. Perhaps the only bar to our use of his terms might be that they focus on the differences (here the difference between a felt and a representative aspect) to the exclusion of the functional relationships between them. However, this need not be the emphasis taken. Sartre's is a good description of the experience of felt meaning. That he is here concerned with what sort of separate consciousness it is in his "conjectural" scheme of logical and objective analysis, does not detract from it for us. And in his terms there is no reason to disagree and to assert representative aspects to feeling. Sartre, instead, notes the function of felt meaning as "analogue."

So we discover two analogical materials for an imaginative consciousness: the kinaesthetic impression . . . and the affective object. But these two materials serve the same purpose. The affective substitute is transcendent but not external, it shows the object in its fullest and inexpressible nature. (p. 117)

So, in the consciousness which is clearly imaginary there is a zone of semi-darkness where almost imperceptible states, empty imaginative cognitions which are almost images, and symbolic apprehensions of movement appear and disappear rapidly. Let one of these cognitions fix itself for a moment on one of these movements, and the imaginative consciousness is born. (p. 119)

Merleau-Ponty

Merleau-Ponty, in his discussions of language, notes what the present essay calls the function of felt meaning:

On découvrait donc derrière le mot une attitude, une fonction de la parole qui le conditionnent.[3] (*PP* 204)

C'est alors que pourront survenir les pensées sur le discours ou sur le texte, auparavant le discours etait improvisé et le texte comprise sans une seule pensée, le sens était présent partout, mais nulle part posé pour lui-même.

. . . la présence prochaine des mots que je sais: ils sont derrière moi, comme les objets derrière mon dos . . .

. . . mais je n'ai aucune "image verbale." S'ils persistent en moi, c'est plutôt comme l'Imago freudienne qui est beaucoup moins la représentation d'une perception ancienne qu'une essence émotionnelle très précise et très générale. (*PP* 210)

For Merleau-Ponty this "emotional essence" constitutes our experience of the meanings of words, rather than images or pure thoughts. It is a property of the body, analogous to gestures and one's sense of one's physical surroundings.

Je m'engage avec mon corps parmi les choses . . . cette vie dans les choses n'a rien de commun avec la construction des objets scientifiques. De la même manière, je ne comprends pas les gestes d'autrui par un acte d'interpretation intellectuelle . . .

. . . je me joins à lui dans une sorte de reconnaissance aveugle qui précède la définition et l'élaboration intellectuelle du sens. (*PP* 216)

C'est donc que la parole ou les mots portent une première couche de signification qui leur est adhérente et qui donne la pensée comme style, comme valeur affective. (*PP* 212)

Some vital functions, which Merleau-Ponty notes that such *sens emotionnel* or *valeur affective* performs, are:

(1) They show that language, rather than being arbitrary symbols, is a way of being in—and "singing"—the world. Hence, owing to felt meaning, linguistic expression is a direct way of articulating experience in the world:

3. Merleau-Ponty, *Phénoménologie de la perception* (Paris: Gallimard, 1945). Page references to be indicated here by *PP*.

Si nous ne considérons que le sens conceptuel et terminal des mots, il est vrai que la forme verbale—. . . semble arbitraire. Il n'en serait plus ainsi si nous faisions entrer en compte le sens émotionnel du mot. . . . (*PP* 218)

(2) Merleau-Ponty views those words, the meaning of which is already common and set, over which a person may dispose, as "sediments" of past successful expressions. The actual nature of language is revealed rather in acts of expressing than in results of past acts. We note, therefore, that Merleau-Ponty's analysis of language, by discriminating felt meaning, enables him to note its function in expressing and articulating experience especially in the case of *novel* ideas and expressions.

Par exemple, certaines formes d'expression entrant en décadence par le seul fait qu'elles ont été employées et ont perdu leur "expressivité," on monrera comment les lacunes ou les zones de faiblesse ainsi créées suscitent, de la part des sujets parlants qui veulent communiquer, une reprise des débris linguistiques laissés par le système en voie de régression et leur utilisation selon un nouveau principe. C'est ainsi que se conçoit dans la langue un nouveau moyen d'expression et qu'une logique obstinée traverse les effets d'usure et la volubilité même de la langue.[4] (*PL* 94–95)

De même que l'intention significative qui a mis en mouvement la parole d'autrui n'est pas une pensée explicite, mais un certain manque que cherche à se combler, de même la reprise par moi de cette intention n'est pas une opération de ma pensée, mais une modulation synchronique de ma propre existence, une transformation de mon être. (*PP* 214)

Exprimer, pour le sujet parlant, c'est prendre conscience; il n'exprime pas seulement pour les autres, il exprime pour savoir lui-même ce qu'il vise. (*PL* 99)

I. A. Richards

I. A. Richards goes much further in our direction than did Vico, when he considers metaphor:

4. Merleau-Ponty, "Sur la phénoménologie du langage," *Problèmes actuels de la phénoménologie,* Édités par H. L. Van Breda (Paris: Desclée De Brouwer & Cie., 1952). Page references to be indicated here by *PL*.

It is worth remarking with regard to Chinese-English translation that the great traditional metaphors of Western thought play so large a part in shaping our conceptions that a study of any metaphors which have played a comparable part in Chinese thought suggests itself as possibly a key move. Examples in the Western tradition would be: the metaphor of conception used in the previous sentence. . . .[5] (p. 33)

The remedy is, perhaps, through a deeper, more systematic study of metaphor. (p. 34)

Richards asserts and constantly illustrates a reflexive self-consciousness of the use of words and concepts in the very process of using them to examine whatever he examines—usually, in fact, the very use of words. This is best shown by one of his special quote or "shriek marks," namely "? . . . ?" which, when placed around a word, is intended "to show that how the word or phrase is to be comprehended, is the question." (p. 3) He seeks a "comprehensive view of comprehending." (p. 18) He says of comprehending, that:

Whatever it compares is compared in a respect or respects. These respects are the instruments of the exploration. And it is with them as with the instruments of investigation in physics, but more so: the properties of the instruments enter into the account of the investigation. . . . Indeed, this mutual subjection or control seems to be the 'αρχή for a doctrine of comprehension—that upon which all else depends. (p. 19)

Meanings may, if we so wish, be compared in an indefinitely great number of respects or in as few as will serve some purpose. The purpose decides which respects are relevant. (p. 21)

Richards notes a reflexivity due to the fact that the meaning and use of concepts, respects of comparison, and distinctions are all themselves dependent on the use of such "respects," and so on.

Richards thus calls attention to a reflexivity inherent in all

5. I. A. Richards, *Speculative Instruments* (Chicago: The University of Chicago Press, 1955).

discourse: whatever conceptions are employed, whatever distinctions are made, these employments are themselves relative to their own creation and to the presuppositions implied in it. Richards points out that this can be inexplicit:

The comprehending of an utterance is guided by any number of partially similar situations in which partially similar utterances have occurred. More exactly, the comprehending is a function of the comparison field from which it derives. Let the units of which comparison fields consist be *utterances-within-situations*—the utterance and its situation being partners in the network of transactions with other utterances in other situations which lend significance to the utterance. (p. 23)

The past utterances-within-situations need not have been consciously remarked or wittingly analyzed; still less need they be explicitly remembered when the comprehending occurs. (p. 24)

The problem posed by Richards' discussion is to analyze comprehension but to do it comprehensively, that is, with attention to the terms, concepts, respects in which comprehension is occurring as it analyzes itself. Looking at these tools of comprehension at work (in such an analysis of comprehension) is likely to tell us more about comprehension than if we were to pay attention only to the results of the use of these tools. Richards' "shriek marks" therefore are this method in action. With the marks a concept in use calls attention to its use, whereas as it stands on the page normally it is simply employed to mean what it does about the subject matter.

Since the possible respects in which a meaning (in use) could be analyzed are endlessly numerous, Richards says that the purpose must guide the choice of respects in which it will be necessary to analyze it.

Richards notes that this vast multiplicity of respects functions as inexplicit and situationally experienced bases of interpreting. One understands or interprets a communication not only on the basis of explicit concepts but rather on the basis of an immense number of "in-situation utterances" experienced in the past.

Because he is concerned with this multiplicity at the root of conceptions, and because he sees this complexity as experienced rather than explicit, Richards points to a method of analysis that would employ emotive or affective meaning.

We have already noted that he proposes an analysis of metaphor. He proposes further "the study of metaphor through metaphor" as "a central and governing part of the study of language." (p. 41)

In answer to "Black's admirably discerning and penetrating phrase" that Richards has changed his views "at the cost of an intrusive and pervasive dissolution of structure," Richards says: "And we seem to be still in as much need as ever of a clarification of the relations between the cognitive and the affective functions of symbolism." (p. 40)

What sort of clarification? Perhaps that which a play or an essay might offer?

I am asking whether any *prose* theory designed on traditional lines and current lines can be or provide a suitable instrument. And by stressing *prose* so I have implied (by means which would elude a strictly logical analysis) that *poetic* theory might supply what is lacking. It would not be a prose account of poetry so much as a poetic account of prose—or rather of the mixed mode whose troubles make us write about them here. (p. 41)

We note, then, that the reflexive attention to the use of concepts as one employs them to study them, also applies to the use of emotive or metaphorical meaning. One must study their use by using them. Only these themselves can shed light on themselves:

This peculiar self-knowledge by a phrase of its own functions in the exercising of them—so my phrases and those I read . . . tell me—is their only guide; they are lost without it. Only a knowledge of what they are doing will tell them how to do it.

Language works emotively, of course, in other ways than through metaphor. (p. 48)

Richards' questions about metaphor define the sort of problem he poses (and it is the problem posed in the present essay):

The problems which do concern us all practically as well as theoretically are, I suggest, those of metaphor. Eminent among them are these: What sorts or orders of? truth? are appropriate to (or possible to) whatever may be ?said? only through metaphor? When and how is what is ?said? through metaphor the same as what said without it? Is it ?said? in the same sense, or has ʷsaidʷ here taken a metaphoric step? Can we distinguish between *functional* metaphors (those needed in presenting—or promoting— certain meanings) and *ornamental* metaphors? If so, how? Are those senses (or motions) of ?true? which are appropriate to utterances using functional metaphors derived themselves by metaphor from other utterances? Or are they independent?

Thus sparely stated these questions may not seem to extend a very inviting field of study, or one of great practical immediate importance. And yet consider how much of men's most serious and sustained thought and feeling has been focused by religion and what place these problems . . . have had, or should have had, there.

Richards goes on to mention many other instances where these problems are important in areas vital to men.

He concludes about "the two sorts of meaning" (emotive and referential), that an instrument for their study is needed: "This instrument must be able to mediate, it must have a foot in each boat and yet be run away with by neither. And yet again, it must leave both functions free. . . ." (p. 49) We may conclude from Richards that:

1. There is need for a method that *employs* metaphor and

other functions of emotive and poetic meaning *to study* the functions of emotive meaning.

2. There is a vast multiplicity of possible respects in which conceptions imply meanings and schemes, and therefore none of these can be the arche of a system of emotive meaning. Rather the purpose, which here is the reflexive self-analysis of these modes of meaning, must act as the arche of the inquiry.

3. Much of what must be said about emotive meaning is itself emotive and not easily made explicit in the usual fashion. Another way of allowing this sort of meaning to enter an inquiry into itself must be found.

4. The inquiry must not prejudice either the emotive or the cognitive uses of language and their principles, but must "leave both functions free."

5. A method such as Richards asks for, has not yet been devised. These questions call for this book.

Index